TESSA BOFFIN has been staging scenes, with the consent of others, for as long as she cares to remember. Her missionary quest to promote cultural activism and sexual diversity has taken her into the realms of part-time teaching and collaborative projects. Her last exhibition and book, *Ecstatic Antibodies: Resisting the AIDS Mythology*, was co-ordinated with Sunil Gupta. The exhibition toured Britain, where it faced censorship, and North America.

JEAN FRASER is a freelance photographer living in London. She curated *Same Difference* (Camerawork, 1986) with Sunil Gupta and has organised photographic workshops for lesbian and gay young people. Her own work has appeared in *Ten.8* and has been exhibited in conventional galleries and in lesbian and gay exhibitions opposing Section 28. She is a regular contributor to the gay and lesbian press.

STOLEN GLANCES

LESBIANS TAKE PHOTOGRAPHS

EDITED BY
TESSA BOFFIN
AND
JEAN FRASER

Pandora
An Imprint of HarperCollinsPublishers

Pandora Press
An Imprint of GraftonBooks
A Division of HarperCollins*Publishers*
77-85 Fulham Palace Road
Hammersmith, London W6 8JB

Published by Pandora Press 1991

10 9 8 7 6 5 4 3 2 1

See page 8 for copyright lines

The Authors assert the moral right to
be identified as the authors of this work

**Published with financial assistance from
the Arts Council of Great Britain**

British Library Cataloguing in Publication Data
Stolen glances: lesbians take photographs.
  1. Lesbianism
  I. Fraser, Jean   II. Boffin, Tessa
  306.7663

  ISBN 0-04-440707-6

Typeset by Harper Phototypesetters Limited,
Northampton, England
Printed in Great Britain by Butler & Tanner Ltd,
Frome, Somerset

CONTENTS

ACKNOWLEDGEMENTS

Throughout the editing of this book, we have had much support and encouragement. Many people have helped with research and ideas. In particular we would like to thank the following: Inge Blackman, Deborah Bright, Sunil Gupta, Nina Levitt and Simon Watney for help with initial contacts, and Simon for constant updates on relevant literature; for their constructive suggestions and feedback: Mitch Cleary, Annabel Faraday, Roz Kaveney, Roberta McGrath, Rita O'Brien, Sue O'Sullivan, Gillian Rogerson, Linda Semple, Anna Marie Smith, Elizabeth Wilson and, especially, Mandy Merck, Cherry Smyth and Valerie Mason John.

In addition we would like to thank the Arts Council of Great Britain for its financial endorsement both of this book and the exhibition which accompanies it, and The Cambridge Darkroom and Stills Gallery, Edinburgh, for touring the show.

We are especially grateful to Philippa Brewster and Ginny Iliff of Pandora Press for their commitment to this project, their patience and their extension of deadlines. For their love, support and endurance our thanks to Jane Harmer, Mel Bingham and, especially, Rita O'Brien.

And finally, to all the contributors without whom this book would not have been possible . . . thank you.

Tessa Boffin
Jean Fraser

INTRODUCTION

In the summer of 1988, while sitting in a car on the Walworth Road in London, we conceived the idea for this book about lesbian representation by lesbian photographers and writers. Lesbians and gay men in the UK were fresh from the struggle against Section 28 of the Local Government Act,[1] disappointed that we had not succeeded in preventing it from being passed into law, yet exhilarated by the increased sense of lesbian and gay community that those struggles had engendered. We were aware of the irony that, despite its attempts to repress us, Section 28 had given us more visibility in the mainstream media than ever before. We wanted our work to be visible too. We had seen exciting photographic work by lesbians both here and in North America, and we knew there must be more, but this work existed in isolated contexts; we wanted to make it accessible to a wider audience of lesbians and the 'independent' photography sector. We also knew that there were many parallels between the USA and the UK in relation to right-wing promotion of traditional family values, repression of diversity and a growing climate of censorship. Section 28 legislates against 'the promotion of homosexuality', we felt that promotion was precisely what was needed. To the embryonic idea of a book, we added an exhibition.

Our imagination was caught by the inventiveness of lesbian photographers who had 'stolen' and inverted the meanings of mainstream, heterosexual imagery. We therefore set out to produce a book which addressed the representation of lesbianism and lesbian identities in this way. Lesbianism exists in a complex relation to many other identities; concerns of sexuality intersect with those of race, class and the body, and our contributors discuss these issues. When we set out to select contributions, rather than attempting to naturalise a 'lesbian aesthetic', we looked for work which concentrated on constructed, staged or self-consciously manipulated imagery which might mirror the socially constructed nature of sexuality. We have not included much documentary work as the realism of documentary has often been used ideologically to reinforce notions of naturalness. We do not want this book to claim a natural status for lesbianism but rather to celebrate that there is no natural sexuality at all.

SEXUAL DIFFERENCE

Theories of sexual difference which emerged in the early 1980s attempted to counter notions of biological determination which go hand in glove with documentary realism. These ideas gained currency both within theoretical journals and gallery selection criteria. We are, however, concerned that sexual difference theory has almost entirely failed to consider same sex desire, and seems to have concentrated solely on heterosexual difference. A landmark exhibition, *Difference: On Representation and Sexuality*, organised by Kate Linker and Jane Weinstock in 1984, sadly falls straight into this trap. Kate Linker opened her foreword to the catalogue with this promising summary of the origins of sexual difference theory and objectives of the show:

> Over the past ten years, a significant body of work has explored a complex terrain triangulated by the terms sexuality, meaning, and language . . . attention has focused on sexuality as a cultural construction, opposing a perspective based on a natural or biological 'truth'. This exhibition charts this territory in the visual arts . . . its thesis – the continuous production of sexual difference – offers possibilities for change, for it suggests that this need not entail reproduction, but rather revision of our conventional categories of opposition.[2]

The word 'reproduction' assumed a focal position in the catalogue, both in its relation to representation and to sexuality. If sexuality and representation are mutually constituted, then it cannot be possible to discuss them as two discrete entities, one existing before the other. Representations do not merely reflect sexuality but play an active role in its production. Sexuality is always mediated and it is through representations that our bodies, and our fantasies, come to be sexually organised.

This stance on sexuality and representation would seem, at first sight, ideally suited to challenge the heterosexual regime produced and reproduced by representations. However, lesbian and gay photographers and writers, on both sides of the Atlantic, were acutely disappointed by the show. William Olander, curator at the New Museum of Contemporary Art in New York City where the show first appeared, referred to it as a 'stunning failure' with regard to homosexuality.[3] A virtual counter-exhibition entitled *Same Difference* curated by Jean Fraser and Sunil Gupta was held at Camerawork Gallery, London in July 1986, while the American photographic journal *Exposure* carried an article also titled 'Same Difference' by Martha Gever and Nathalie Magnan stating that the *Difference* show had 'framed' representation to reproduce only heterosexual ideology and imagery. This article represented the start of a fight-back in which lesbian and gay cultural producers began to highlight the inadequacies of sexual difference theory, and we reprint it here.

The video component of the *Difference* exhibition, which was not seen in London, did attempt to engage with homosexuality by screening Stuart Marshall's *A Journey of the Plague Year* and Chantal Akerman's *Je, Tu, Il, Elle*.[4] However, this programming could only allow male gayness to be discussed in the show's catalogue in relation to AIDS, while lesbianism was referenced solely in terms of Akerman's chameleon-like heroine. 'She has no reality,' comments Jane Weinstock, and, as William Olander points out, this is an unintentionally apt commentary on the organisers' view of homosexuality. There is also the example of Yve Lomax, whose images appeared in the exhibition unaccompanied by her parallel text critiquing the heterosexual bias of difference theory. This had to be rescued several years later by Emmanuel Cooper's *The Sexual Perspective: Homosexuality and Art in the Last 100 Years in the West*, the 'Deconstructing "Difference"' issue of *Screen* and Griselda Pollock in *Vision and Difference: Femininity, Feminism and Histories of Art*.[5]

Subsequent exhibitions in the UK and North America which have dealt with sexuality and representation have attempted to depose the heterosexual imperative of sexual difference theory with varying degrees of success. The Photographers' Gallery exhibition *The Body Politic* (1987) imag(in)ed, in the words of its curator Alex Noble, a 'heterogeneity of vision' informed by a multiplicity of theories, in order to 'transcend' the barriers of 'race, gender and national cultures.'[6] This well-intentioned pluralism was flawed by its own liberal and contradictory claim, but at least the work of five lesbian and gay photographers was included in the show, and in terms of numbers this was a step forward.

A further exhibition, this time in the USA, *Sexual Difference: Both Sides of the Camera* (1987-8) seemed optimistic, seeking to offer a diversity of analyses relating to the construction of sexual difference, but its curator, Abigail Solomon-Godeau, herself expressed reservations:

> The greatest risk in such an enterprise – a risk that lies in taking masculinity and femininity as the alpha and omega of sexual difference – is the occlusion or repression of homosexuality; at very least in the presumption of a heterosexual spectator . . . the denial of this other difference entails its own repressive politics. Whilst there is work included in the exhibition that may have presumed a gay male gender . . . this does not exempt me from the implications of an analysis that is based on a masculine/feminine opposition, and as such, does not theoretically address what could be termed a difference within a difference.[7]

Gay men are acknowledged this time, as are the limitations of sexual difference theory, but there is still only one gay photographer in the entire show, Baron Von Gloeden,[8] a nineteenth-century homosexual, included in an exhibition devoted to the work of twentieth-century straights. And lesbians are not even granted a footnote in this scenario!

POSITIVE TACTICS

Within galleries, funding bodies, community darkrooms and educational institutions complaints have been voiced by lesbians and gay men about this under-representation. Equal opportunities policies have been adopted in an attempt to redress this power imbalance, not only in relation to sexual orientation, but also in relation to race, disability, class and age. However, on their own such policies do not necessarily benefit a lesbian and gay politics of resistance as they fail to engage with the ideological structures which are the cause of discrimination. While we obviously would not want to dispense with strategies which encourage the entry of lesbian and gay students into education, and the publishing, funding or exhibition of the work of marginalised practitioners, increasing the number of lesbian and gay photographers is in itself insufficient. Placing the camera in the hands of a lesbian or gay man is no automatic guarantee that the image produced will be intrinsically progressive or 'positive'.

'Positive image' strategies initially gained currency within the feminist and Black communities in the late seventies and early eighties where a need was felt to replace 'negative', stereotypical representations with 'positive' ones. These campaigns, when later adopted by the lesbian and gay communities, attempted to replace one myth with another – a simultaneous normalisation and idealisation, which presupposed some essence or common identity, in place of a radical recognition of multiple differences, both social and psychic. There was an implicit assumption that negative meanings can be inverted by a simple act of will and read as positive.

The political potential of positive images has until recently been limited as their creators have ignored how subjectivity is produced or meaning constructed. The role of the spectator's unconscious in actively producing meaning has been disavowed because representations have tended to be seen solely as reflections of reality. This has also ignored the shifting nature of meaning, which, in photography, is affected far more by visual codes and conventions (lighting, camera angles, body language of the subject and so on), by contextualisation (in galleries, magazines or the press) and by the class, race, gender and sexual identity of the spectator, than by the intentions of the photographer.

However, in the present climate of AIDS hysteria and increased homophobia, a new generation of cultural activists have found positive images effective as one strategic form of intervention within public spaces. For example, the Gran Fury collective (an offshoot of ACT-UP, the AIDS Coalition To Unleash Power, in New York City) have used both billboards and city transport to confront public prejudice and ignorance about HIV and AIDS. Imaginative forms of direct action, such as the lesbian abseilers' invasion of the House of Lords during the Section 28 debates, are constructing what Simon Watney terms 'an effective political theatre of images' which can challenge mainstream media representation of our struggles. [9]

Jan Zita Grover points out in her chapter how:

> . . . subcultural positive images propose a complex 'forgetting' of present realities – a resistance to, say, the painful realities of war, powerlessness or poverty – and 'remembering' of possible alternatives: peace, security and affluence. Thus it is naïve – or very cynical – to dismiss positive images as merely sentimental or old-fashioned. To do so is to treat them as if they proposed no arguments, embodied no aspirations, reflected no ongoing struggles.

A case in point is the AIDS epidemic and Deborah Bright examines how the very diverse work of lesbian photographers 'from positive

KISSING DOESN'T KILL: GREED AND INDIFFERENCE DO.

This advertisement by the New York-based collective Gran Fury appeared on public buses in New York and San Francisco, 1989.

Buckingham Palace, 8 March 1988. Action against Clause 28.
Photograph by Sara Furse.

images to targetted pro-active propaganda'
forms part of a wider spectrum of
photographic and political resistance to
dominant AIDS mythology and
misinformation.

DEFINING LESBIAN PHOTOGRAPHY
There is no easy way to define a lesbian
photograph. It is unclear whether its status
depends on the photographer, the subject
matter depicted, the audience of the
photograph or the context in which it appears.
And it is open to discussion whether an image
has to satisfy all of these categories or only one
of them. For instance, although biographical
research on the lives of lesbian photographers
of the past can effectively reveal previously
suppressed personal details, such material is
both rare and potentially reductive. It just isn't

possible to transpose to our predecessors late
twentieth-century definitions of what it means
to be a lesbian.

Contemporary image-makers, theoreticians
and curators who do not want to conflate the
sexuality of the photographer on one side of
the lens with its representation on the other,
have therefore to distinguish clearly between
at least four different kinds of work produced
by lesbians.

First, there are photographs, usually
documentary, which frequently appear in
family albums or in the lesbian or gay press.
Then there are images in mainstream,
predominantly heterosexual, photographic
galleries and journals whose lesbian producers
still cling to a modernist commitment to a
purity of visual image, which transcends
sexuality, language, culture and politics. A

third body of work is defined in relation to a lesbian essence, its producers maintaining that it emits a 'lesbian aura', aesthetic or sensibility. This, we feel, presents problems in that a lesbian sensibility seeks to privilege a particular use of photography as essentially lesbian, instead of seeing photography as a medium with subversive potential for everyone.

Fourthly, there are those photographers who deal overtly with lesbian issues; in the main they do not assume that their sexuality could ever in itself be the defining factor for their work or that content, or the style they deploy, could ever be essentially lesbian. What they do share is an interest in subversive strategies of representation, and a scepticism about the reflective nature of the photograph. It is mainly work in this fourth category that we have sought to include here; we believe this work holds the greatest potential for a progressive, and transgressive, lesbian and gay photographic practice. A politics of resistance can never be solely the product of lesbian experience, or of a 'lesbian aesthetic', since clearly no such unity or cohesiveness exists.

The post-modernist interest in reworking available material has afforded lesbian photogaphers an opportunity to use strategies of appropriation as an assault on homophobia, and as an assertion of our rights to a social and sexual existence. As Deborah Bright points out in relation to feminist struggles, in her 'Dream Girls', 'politicised appropriations of given signifying systems . . . [are] a useful and sophisticated weapon against our invisibility . . .'

Much of the work in this book examines how lesbian identities are forged and enriched through the appropriation of images from mainstream and marginalised discourses. Sue Golding, for example, writes about the identity of a lesbian hermaphrodite, a James Dean look-alike, whose composite image is copied again and again from icons in the public domain. Deborah Bright's photographic series

inserts a lesbian presence into Hollywood movie stills in order to examine how this transforms a conventional heterosexual narrative, and creates deviant readings. Similarly, Lynette Molnar and Linda Thornburg montage into various advertising and journalistic images a photograph of women embracing. The strip cartoon format is used by Kaucyila Brooke to examine through her heroine Badgirl, how lesbian stories intersect with mainstream popular culture.

Other photographers, such as Della Grace, Morgan Gwenwald and Jill Posener, appropriate the visual codes of pornography precisely in order to hijack heterosexual sites and customs. Their work also invades public space and challenges legal and moral assumptions that same-sex desire should only be enacted by 'consenting adults in private'.[10] Jude Johnston, on the other hand, inscribes lesbianism into a public space by the superimposition of text onto the photograph of an everyday street scene, juxtaposed with a private embrace. Cindy Patton compares the 'real', and documented, space of gay male desire – the pornographic cinema where cruising can take place – with the more imaginary and under-represented space of lesbian desire, and calls for a 'safe house' for lesbians which will enable these desires and images to be enacted.

The majority of photographic work in this book consists of manipulated imagery. Some photographers stage scenarios: Alice Austen, Tessa Boffin, Kaucyila Brooke, Jacqui Duckworth, Jean Fraser, Della Grace, Morgan Gwenwald, Mumtaz Karimjee, Rosy Martin, Ingrid Pollard, Jill Posener, Hinda Schuman. Others add text at the post-production stage (Jude Johnston, Connie Samaras) or use solarization (Tee Corinne), positive/negative reversal (Nina Levitt) and photo-montage (Deborah Bright, Lynette Molnar) to undermine the 'naturalness' of the straight image.

VISIBILITY AND THE BODY

Most lesbians and gay men have acknowledged the significance of visibility in relation to their sexuality, whilst accepting visibility can sometimes be a privilege not equally available across all cultures or social positions. Joan E. Biren (JEB), an American lesbian feminist photographer, wrote in 1983:

> Without a visual identity, we have no community, no support network, no movement. Making ourselves visible is a political act. Making ourselves visible is a continual process. [11]

Visibility, however, has largely been understood in terms of the representation of the body. Yet sexual orientation is not a physical phenomenon. There are no equivalents to the biological markers of sex. There are, though, ways of being seen to be lesbian; dressing in a particular style, wearing badges, earrings, T-shirts, for instance, signalling with one's body language or haircut, frequenting certain clubs and so on, bespeak lesbianism in a way which one's mute body cannot. As Elizabeth Wilson discusses in her chapter about deviant style, signs of lesbian self-adornment are *cultural* forms developed to show what the body alone cannot utter; they are a way of making visible the invisible, one's sexuality or desires. Mikki Ferrill's photo-series illustrates this signalling very clearly in terms of contemporary lesbian fashion, while in her chapter 'Developing Identities', Sonja Ruehl looks back to studio portraiture and informal snapshots of affluent or well-known lesbians of the 1920s and 1930s to draw a parallel between the way both photographic practices and sexological theory at that time were more comfortable representing the sexual identity of the single lesbian, rather than the lesbian couple. This is significant given sexologists' conception of lesbianism as a congenital condition rather than a social or sexual identity.

MEDICAL 'TRUTHS'

The pursuit of visibility has always been an obsession both for lesbians and gay men who are trying to establish a positive sense of identity, and for those institutions such as the police and the medical profession who have used photographs to establish documentary evidence of criminal or pathological characteristics. The latter part of the nineteenth century saw a move from conceptualising homosexuality in terms of certain *acts* which could be committed by anyone to a new definition of 'the homosexual' as a *sexual identity*, a category open to investigation, surveillance and control. The writings of sexologists such as Krafft-Ebbing and Havelock Ellis established the 'medical model' of homosexuality, and the eye of authority was now focused through the medium of photography on the 'homosexual body'. As *The Lancet* commented in 1859:

> Photography is so essentially the art of Truth – that it would seem to be the essential means of reproducing all forms and structures which science seeks for delineation. [12]

Homosexuals and other 'deviant' types were classified according to a range of physiological elements: cranial and cerebral characteristics, anomalies of the face and body – the visual signs of 'sickness'. During this decade of the AIDS crisis, photojournalism has colluded with the medical profession to give these definitions a new and dangerous currency, so that every photograph of a person with AIDS is read as signifying the equation: homosexuality = disease = death. As Mandy Merck also points out in this book:

Spurred by the discourses surrounding AIDS, a new generation of taxonomists reconstruct an old anatomy of desire, discovering in every weakened body the predestined consequences of perversion.

Michael Ruse tells us of a hilarious piece of research which was published in 1968 and sought to establish the 'lesbian body' in a manner reminiscent of the late nineteenth century approach to sexual types. Based on a survey of 123 lesbians and a similar number of controls, it confidently asserted that 'the three measurements which significantly distinguish lesbians from controls are weight, waist and bust. Lesbians are heavier, with bigger busts and waists. Ruse quotes more recent research on a group of forty-two lesbians which qualified these findings. This research found that 'lesbians are taller rather than shorter, although if anything the evidence was that lesbians tend to be more "solid" than heterosexuals . . .'[13]

And as Sue Golding points out in relation to female hermaphrodites, 'Woe be it to any woman so possessed of these fine attributes.'

Nevertheless, for the French philosopher and historian Michel Foucault, this power to

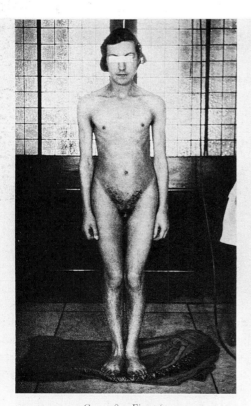

CASE 38. Fig. 16.
(Female) with Bilateral undescent of Testes. Psychological Female.

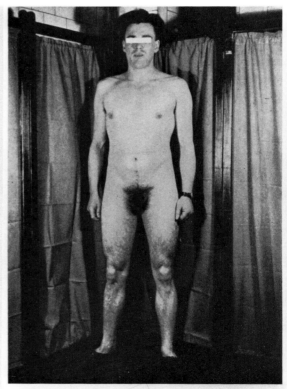

CASE 41. Fig. 19.
(Female) with Bilateral undescent of Testes. Psychological Male.

Gesture and body language are used here to reinforce the psychological 'truth' of these physical hermaphrodites. From L.R. Broster et al., eds, The Adrenal Cortex and Intersexuality *(Chapman and Hall, 1938).*

define is not just repressive but forms the basis of a 'reverse discourse' of group identity whereby homosexuals can demand acceptance using the very same categories which have been employed medically to disqualify us. However, such discourses are unfortunately open to incorporation or annihilation; yet despite this they are a critical element of resistance in the construction of marginalised identities. [14]

For example, in Germany in the 1920s Magnus Hirschfield assembled his photographic archive at the Institute of Sexual Science in a similar manner to other sexologists. However, while those sexologists used their photographic records to establish their subjects' status as deviant people whose bodies exhibited signs of degeneracy, Hirschfield inverted this equation. His photographic records were collected to assert the visibility – and thus the *viability* – of a social group, which Hirschfield termed an intermediate or third sex. Sadly, he overestimated the stable significance of such representations and their potential to challenge the existing social order. This, combined with Hirschfield's prominence as an untiring campaigner on behalf of civil rights for gay men and lesbians, women and illegitimate children, made the Institute's collection of photographic materials on anatomy and sexuality a target for the Nazis.

Some of this book's participants are engaged in what appears to be a more promising reverse discourse of the body. There has been a move away from the biological body in order to flesh out fantasies: a shift of emphasis from the corporeal sexual body to imag(in)ing how the body of desire could otherwise appear. After all, as Roland Barthes poetically states, we are dealing with more than one body:

> We have several of them; the body of
> anatomists and physiologists, the one
> science sees or discusses . . . But we also
> have the body of bliss consisting solely of
> erotic relations, utterly distinct from the
> first body. [15]

Anonymous, Zwei sich liebkosende Frauen, die eine in ketten gefesselt, about 1930. Amsterdam Historical Museum.

Nina Levitt's *Conspiracy of Silence*, for example, deals with the problem of representing lesbian desire using similar visual strategies to British feminist Mary Kelly's widely-exhibited *Interim* series. [16] Both these women refer to the sexual body of the woman, be it lesbian or straight, through its physical absence; desire is displaced onto fetishised undergarments, which in Levitt's work appear as ghostly superimpositions over the covers of pulp novels from the late 1950s and early 1960s. Tee Corinne does photograph women's bodies but protects the identity of her lesbian subjects through technical obscuring of their anatomy, using solarization, multiple exposures and the use of images printed in negative. Corinne also makes a point of portraying fat women, older women and women with disabilities, as subjects in her photographs, in order to challenge the dominant visual regime of beauty. Jacqui Duckworth meets a different kind of challenge: in an attempt to escape the limitations of positive images of disability, Duckworth draws upon the rhetoric of surrealism to explore a growing sense of physical dislocation.

Ingrid Pollard's work refers to feminist debates around visual fragmentation of the body. Her use of the codes of fragmentation emphasises the denial of the whole subject, one whose identity cannot be reduced to the level of the body alone. This conception of the Black subject's identity – and indeed all identities – as being fractured and multiple is reinforced structurally by a fragmented narrative. Pollard both draws upon American discourses of modernism which often represent Black subjects as genital body parts (Mapplethorpe, for example), and disrupts them through the depiction of androgynous details such as shoulders and backs. Simultaneously, there is the ironic deployment of the sexual mythologies of colonial fantasies: the Black dyke as castrator or garland bearer.

Mumtaz Karimjee's photographic series *In Search of an Image* engages with colonial myths of the Orient and her own struggle to establish a cultural identity in the West within the shadow of these myths. To critique western forms of classification which embody sexual deviance in the extraordinary physical attributes of the exotic, oriental lesbian, Karimjee reconstructs a lush harem environment within which she has placed her own swathed body.

HYSTERICAL MORALS

This book is emerging into a climate characterised by increasing homophobia, racism and censorship, and fierce promotion by the moral Right of 'family' values. In Britain these have been embodied by the passing into law of Section 28 of the Local Government Act. The first part of this Section prohibits local authorities from funding any activities (exhibitions, workshops, meetings or the production and distribution of leaflets and so on) which could be deemed to 'promote homosexuality'. The second bans the teaching in state-funded schools of the acceptability of lesbian and gay relationships, defining them as 'pretended family relationships'.

Anna Marie Smith points out in her chapter on the implications of Section 28 for lesbian representation, that lesbianism, unlike gayness, is not seen as a sexual threat but as a fundamental undermining of the traditional heterosexual family. Consequently, she argues for the promotion of images of lesbian motherhood on the one hand, and on the other for alternative imagery which contradicts the New Right conception of lesbianism as asexual and therefore harmless.

Cathy Cade explores the different ways lesbians construct themselves through their family albums – the albums which were made for them when they were children and the albums they create for themselves and their own children. The 'unconscious' myth of the happy [heterosexual] family is exploded by Rosy Martin through the practice of phototherapy, which makes visible the absences and oppressions hidden within the traditional family album. On a more affirmative note, Jackie Kay, through the juxtaposition of family album photographs and her own poetry, examines the complexity of identity as it is mapped across race, nation, sexuality and parenting. Hinda Schuman's photo-diary documents through wry, staged scenarios, letters and journal entries, her emergence as a lesbian – 'I've gone from a married woman to a sexual minority in one embrace' – and her consequent rejection by her best friend.

In the USA similarly intentioned legislation to Section 28 has been introduced by the virulent right-wing homophobe, Jesse Helms. Whilst it does not directly target the status of lesbian and gay families, this legislation has resulted in an unprecedented defunding programme by the National Endowment for the Arts for cultural production with explicit lesbian or gay homoerotic content.

These repressive initiatives have had enormous implications for lesbian and gay representation. Section 28's intention has been to create a climate of fear and self-censorship; local authority-funded exhibition spaces (the main venues for the exhibition of lesbian and gay work) are less willing to take risks for fear of prosecution, and the pressure is on lesbian and gay photographers and artists to play safe to ensure that their work does not become invisible.

To date, no test case has been brought under Section 28, for the Section has functioned as a pre-emptive measure; some exhibitions have received no bookings or have been cancelled at the eleventh hour. Both of us have been involved with exhibitions which have been affected in this way. *Someone To Talk To: Young Lesbians and Gay Men at School*, produced before the Section passed into law in Spring 1988, had an enthusiastic take-up by secondary schools around the country. The exhibition resulted from a photographic workshop for lesbian and gay young people organised by Jean Fraser, and co-tutored with Sunil Gupta. Its bookings fell off dramatically as soon as the Section came into effect.[17]

A more recent example is the cancellation of *Ecstatic Antibodies: Resisting the AIDS Mythology*, a group exhibition curated by Tessa Boffin and Sunil Gupta, which was due to be shown in October 1989 at Viewpoint Gallery in Salford.[18] This venue is directly funded by the City Council whose officers invoked the spectre of Section 28 to justify censoring homoerotic work which they construed to be pornographic and unsuitable for a 'family gallery'. Funded by the Arts Council of Great Britain, *Ecstatic Antibodies* has had their

unequivocal support.

In the USA, the attack initially focussed on the photography of Robert Mapplethorpe and *Piss Christ* – a photograph by Andres Serrano showing a crucific submerged in four gallons of his own urine. Carole Vance has pointed out how negative symbols have figured prominently in fundamentalist campaigns as forms of mass mobilisation, symbols which are consciously chosen because it is clearly difficult to defend them.[19] What is new is that the Right has shifted its focus from popular to 'high' culture; previous moral panics have centred on targets such as pornography (the Meese Commission) and rock music. The success of these new moral panics can be seen in the apathy of most of the arts community and the self-censorship of, for instance, the Corcoran Gallery in Washington DC in cancelling Mapplethorpe's retrospective, *The Perfect Moment*.

But where pre-emptive self-censorship has proved ineffective, cases are being brought. Cincinnati gallery owner Dennis Barrie was recently acquitted under the First Amendment for violating local obscenity laws by exhibiting Mapplethorpe's work. While his case demonstrates the advantages, not available to us in the UK, of a constitutional defence, no one is fooling themselves that this might represent the dawn of a more permissive climate. Stringent restrictions preventing the National Endowment for the Arts funding work which may be considered obscene – and obscenity is here defined as homoerotica, sado-masochism and the sex act in general – have just been endorsed for a further five-year stretch. Nowadays, American galleries have to sign a pledge guaranteeing compliance with these conditions in order to qualify for funding. And there are further restrictions. Grants are made by instalment while work is monitored for moral purity; repayments are to be sought from artists and galleries convicted of obscenity, while no grants at all may be made to anyone so convicted during the previous three years.

And if state regulation and surveillance in both the USA and the UK were not enough, there is no shortage of moral attitude from within sections of the Women's Movement and the lesbian community. *Quim*, a UK-produced magazine of lesbian erotica, and the 1990 American *On Our Backs* calendar were censored from feminist and lesbian and gay bookshops in the UK, one of which had only recently fought a major Customs and Excise seizure of its stock. At the Lesbian Summer School in London in 1989, revolutionary feminists attempted to halt a screening of the American film, *She Must Be Seeing Things*, by trying to overturn the projector.[20]

In the USA in 1984, the Feminists Against Censorship Taskforce (FACT) formed following the introduction by Catherine MacKinnon and Andrea Dworkin of the Minneapolis Ordinance, which permitted women to take civil action against anyone producing or distributing pornography on the grounds that they had been harmed by its images of their sexuality. In Britain, Feminists Against Censorship (FAC) formed in 1989 in reaction to the attempts by Dworkin-inspired groups such as the Campaign Against Pornography and the Campaign against Pornography and Censorship, to establish a feminist orthodoxy in favour of anti-pornography legislation. As Feminists Against Censorship observe:

> Suddenly the feminist movement that once fought for freedom and sexual self-determination is advocating giving power over our lives to the judges and the police; suddenly what it says about our freedom and our sexual desires sounds like the ravings of the Right. Suddenly feminism is about censorship rather than about opening possibilities.[21]

The collusion of anti-pornography feminists with right-wing organisations has serious implications for lesbians and gay men, whose own images are likely to be the first casualties of any new censorship legislation. Carole Vance has pointed out how minority communities need affirmative images of themselves within the public arena:

> People deprived of images become demoralised and isolated, and they become increasingly vulnerable to attacks on their private expressions of nonconformity, which are inevitable once sources of public solidarity and resistance have been eliminated.[22]

This underlines the crucial importance of a diversity of representation for the lesbian and gay communities. Rather than seeing this book as the quintessential handbook of lesbian photography, we hope it will be a useful contribution to the on-going struggle to keep our selves and our images visible to the outside world and to each other. We hope that it will engage with contemporary debates on the politics of representation and that it will motivate further image production in gallery exhibitions, books and public spaces.

Tessa Boffin and Jean Fraser
November 1990

NOTES
[1] For further discussion of Section 28 of the Local Government Act, see below in this introduction and Anna Marie Smith's essay in this book: 'Which One's the Pretender? Section 28 and Lesbian Representation'.

[2] Kate Linker, Foreword in *Difference: On Representation and Sexuality* (New York: New Museum of Contemporary Art, 1984), p. 5.

[3] William Olander, *HOMO VIDEO: Where We Are Now* (New York: New Museum of Contemporary Art, 1986), p. 1.

[4] *A Journey of the Plague Year*, 1984, dir. Stuart Marshall, GB, 24 mins, colour; *Je, Tu, Il, Elle*, 1974, dir. Chantal Akerman, France, 85 mins, black and white.

[5] Emmanuel Cooper, *The Sexual Perspective:*

Homosexuality and Art in the Last 100 Years in the West (London and New York: HarperCollins, 1986); 'Deconstructing "Difference" in *Screen*', vol. 28, no. 1, Winter 1987; and Griselda Pollock, *Vision and Difference: Feminity, Feminism and Histories of Art* (London and New York: Routledge, 1988).

6 *Ten.8*, no. 25, the 'Body Politic' issue, 1987, p. 3.

7 Abigail Solomon-Godeau, Foreword in *Sexual Difference: Both Sides of the Camera* (New York: Columbia University, 1988).

8 See Cindy Patton's footnote on Baron Von Gloeden.

9 Simon Watney, Introduction in *Taking Liberties: AIDS and Cultural Politics*, eds, Erica Carter and Simon Watney (London: Serpents Tail, 1989), p. 51.

10 See Jeffrey Weeks's discussion of *The Wolfenden Report on Homosexual Offences and Prostitution* (1957) in *Sex, Politics and Society: The Regulation of Sexuality since 1800* (London: Longman, 1981), pp. 239–44.

11 Joan E. Biren, 'Lesbian Photography – Seeing Through Our Own Eyes' in *Studies in Visual Communication*, vol. 9, no. 2, Spring 1983, p. 81.

12 *The Lancet*, 22 January 1859, vol. 1, p. 89, quoted by John Tagg in 'Power and Photography' in *Screen Education*, no. 36, 1980, p. 41.

13 Michael Ruse, *Homosexuality* (Oxford: Basil Blackwell, 1988), pp. 12–13, cited by Simon Watney in 'The Homosexual Body: Resources and a Note on Theory' in *Public* 3, Carnal Knowledge, 1990 p. 45.

14 Michel Foucault, *The History of Sexuality: An Introduction* (London: Penguin, 1984), p. 101.

15 Roland Barthes, *The Pleasure of the Text* (New York: Hill and Wang, 1975), p. 16.

16 Mary Kelly, *Interim*, Fruitmarket Gallery, Kettles Yard Gallery & Riverside Studios, 1986, and *New Formations*, vol. II, Summer 1987.

17 Jean Fraser interview with Mel Burns and Ritu Kurana in *Ten.8*, no. 32, 1989. *Someone To Talk To* is available from Camerawork, 121 Roman Road, London E2, UK.

18 Tessa Boffin and Sunil Gupta eds, *Ecstatic Antibodies: Resisting the AIDS Mythology* (London: Rivers Oram Press, 1990). The exhibition is available for hire from Impressions Gallery, 17 Colliergate, York, UK.

19 Carole S. Vance, 'The War on Culture' in *Art in America*, vol. 77, no. 9, September 1989.

20 *She Must Be Seeing Things,* 1987, dir. Sheila McLaughlin. See interview with Sheila McLaughlin by Alison Butler in *Screen*, vol. 28, no. 4, Autumn 1987.

21 *Ask Yourself: Do You Really Want More Censorship?* Feminists Against Censorship pamphlet 1989. See also Gillian Rodgerson and Linda Semple, 'Who Watches the Watchwomen?' in *Feminist Review* no. 36, Autumn 1990.

22 Carole Vance, op. cit.

'TRANSFORMING THE SUIT.'

A CENTURY OF LESBIAN SELF-PORTRAITS

Mandy Merck

'But what about those old photographs?' asks Esther Newton in a pioneering essay. 'Was the mannish lesbian a myth created by "the [male] pornographic mind" or by male sexologists intent on labelling nineteenth-century feminists as deviant? Maybe the old photographs portray a few misguided souls – or perhaps those "premovement" women thought men's ties were pretty and practical?'

Newton describes what 'you see' in these photographs: a female figure 'with legs solidly planted, wearing a top hat and a man's jacket, staring defiantly out of the frame, her hair slicked back or clipped over the ears'.[1] The ontology of the photograph, its relation to a 'real' referent, is her first piece of evidence in an historical account of the 'new social/sexual category "lesbian"' (p.10). So unproblematic is this ontology – the photograph as visible proof of the subject's existence – that it needn't be put to the test. No actual photograph is illustrated or even cited by Newton. Instead, photography's power, what Barthes described as 'the power of authentication',[2] is harnessed

to a less evidential medium, the novel.

The novel in question is Radclyffe Hall's *The Well of Loneliness* (1928), and as Newton's essay demonstrates, it is *about* visibility. Indeed, it can be seen as the textual culmination of an entire socio-medical tradition which sought to 'embody' sexual deviance. Hall's lesbian heroine is born a 'narrow-hipped, wide-shouldered' baby, whose infant features include an incipiently cleft chin.[3] Throughout the novel she is subjected to the frequent, invariably productive, scrutiny of others as well as herself:

> 'Doesn't Miss Stephen look exactly like a boy? I believe she must be a boy with them shoulders, and them funny gawky legs she's got on her!' (p.16)

> That night she stared at herself in the glass; and even as she did so she hated her body with its muscular shoulders, its small compact breasts and its slender flanks of an athlete. (p.187)

People looked at Stephen curiously; her height, her clothes, the scar on her face, had immediately riveted their attention. (p.352)

In the massively influential first volume of his *History of Sexuality*, Foucault attributes the invention of this homosexual body – and that of the homosexual soul, or psyche – to the taxonomical impulses of the nineteenth century.[4] Among its categories were those pertaining to the origins of the orientation – 'innate' and 'acquired'. From Leopold Casper's development of this distinction at mid-century flowed a vast literature, in which the reader of *The Well* will recognise three names: Karl Heinrich Ulrichs, the German lawyer and writer who proposed a theory of homosexual development in the embryo brain; Richard von Krafft-Ebing, the Austrian psychiatrist whose vast *Psychopathia Sexualis* numbered '238 histories and 437 pages by the 12th edition of 1903';[5] and Havelock Ellis, the English social reformer whose study *Sexual Inversion* argued for legal tolerance on behalf of an incurable minority. All three espoused (in different ways) a theory of congenital homosexuality, or 'inversion', with associated cross-gender characteristics. And all three names figure in the novel: Ulrichs as the author of the mysterious text poured over by young Stephen's father; Krafft-Ebing as the source for her own later discoveries; and Ellis as the contributor of the novel's foreword.

It is with the last that Hall's work is most associated, not least because his arguments combined biological determinism with moral exculpation, attributing to female inverts a degree of moral sensitivity in direct proportion to their homosexual predisposition. From his six case histories of female homosexuality, Ellis fashioned a 'portrait' of the female invert neatly synthesised by Hall's biographer, Michael Baker: 'a nervy, artistic type, boyish in manners and looks, deep-voiced, capable of whistling, and prone to deeply felt attachments'.[6] It is an

image which, as Newton revealingly argues, Hall and many of her contemporaries 'embraced' – a term which suggests the eroticised introjection of an external ideal. Such a process is readily equated with 'identification' or 'self-recognition', but its dynamism, the required transposition from outside to in, belies any simple idea of a reflection or pre-existing equivalence. As both Newton and Baker observe, Hall's life was in many ways different from that of her martyred heroine (the author being both less aristocratic and more successful with women). If Stephen Gordon is an effort at lesbian self-portraiture, she serves to remind us just how constructed such portraits are.

This brings us back to photography, and Hall's efforts to construct her own image (efforts which extended to having the luxuriant curls of her childhood portrait obliterated in conformity with Ellis's theory of congenital gender reversal).[7] Hall was never reluctant to involve herself in the marketing of her books, and she furnished *The Well*'s American publisher, Blanche Knopf, with photographs for its launch there. Among her stipulations to Knopf are directions to avoid a publicity photograph used by her previous publisher, a silhouetted image which, she wrote, resembled a 'middle-aged gent who is given to imbibing, or worse still a stout old lady masquerading' (p.208). Some images of the mythic mannish lesbian were clearly more acceptable than others, even to the legendary progenitor of that figure.

The recurrence of the 'mannish' figure in lesbian self-portraits has elicited a variety of explanations. Newton herself moves between simple verisimilitude – 'Many lesbians *are* masculine' – and the cultural masculinisation of sexual desire between women. Teresa de Lauretis raises in reply the question of visibility. Lesbian representation, she observes, is 'still unwittingly caught in the paradox of socio-sexual (in)difference . . . (homo)sexuality being in the last instance what can not be seen'. [8] But if what she terms (after Newton) 'male body drag' does confer visibility, it does not confer meaning. We are still left with Newton's opening question: What *about* such photographs?

Consider, for example, case number 160 of the twelfth edition of *Psychopathia Sexualis*, 'Mrs von T'. Krafft-Ebing reports that this patient had been brought to him by her husband 'because after a banquet she had fallen upon the neck of a lady guest, covered her profusely with kisses and caressed her like a lover, thus causing a scandal'. [9] Her case history records sufficient evidence of both homosexual practice and masculine identification to elicit the diagnosis of 'Homosexuality in Transition to Viraginity', one of Krafft-Ebing's sub-categories of congenital inversion:

> Her love for sport, smoking and drinking, her preference for clothes cut in the fashion of men, her lack of skill in and liking for female occupations, her love for the study of obtuse and philosophical subjects, her gait and carriage, severe features, deep voice, robust skeleton, powerful muscles and absence of adipose layers have the stamp of masculine character. (p.278)

Mrs von T offers the first portrait for our consideration. Among her affairs with women the case history notes a liaison with a dressmaker's model 'with whom she had herself photographed in man's attire, visited, in the same costume, with her places of amusement and was finally arrested on one of those occasions. She escaped with a warning and gave up male attire out-of-doors' (p.277).

Had Krafft-Ebing commissioned that photograph, it would have admirably illustrated one function of the newly-invented medium, the visualisation of socio-sexual deviance as an image of the body, whose every feature – from carriage to clothing – is biologically ordained and medically legible. [10] But this portrait was ordered by its subject, which calls to mind another function of the nineteenth-century photograph.

In his account of the parallel rise of the photographic portrait and the middle classes, John Tagg characterises the medium as 'a sign whose purpose is both the *description* of an individual and the *inscription* of a social identity'. [11] The latter function, Tagg argues, is performed both by the photograph's replacement of the earlier portrait media by which the rising classes claimed their social place – the painted miniature, the silhouette and the engraving – and by its role as a commodity in itself, an object whose very purchase conferred a certain status upon the purchaser. From its invention, then, photography registered an ontological split, between a claim to record the sitter's 'nature' and a promise to advance his (the gender is deliberate) rank. Somewhere along this faultline, Krafft-Ebing's patient posed 'in man's attire' with her woman lover, an image which might well have confirmed a diagnosis of 'congenital inversion', but which also, of course, represented the social mobility traditionally afforded the 'passing' woman.

During the period which saw Krafft-Ebing compile his case histories and Ellis embark on *Studies in the Psychology of Sex*, another woman pictured herself 'in man's attire'. In 1891-2, Alice Austen, an American of independent means who photographed the domestic life around her Staten Island home, undertook a number of self-portraits which still survive. Among them is *Julia Martin, Julia Bredt and Self Dressed up as Men 4.40 pm, Thursday October 15th, 1891*. Unlike the masquerade of Mrs von T, this photograph has been read as an attempt to parody the male prerogative rather than lay claim to it. The broad poses and highly typified dress-styles (capped respectively by the deerstalker, boater and top hat), the 'ridiculously phallic umbrella', the sheer amusement suggested by Austen's smiling stance (one which reveals, as Susan Butler notes, both a feminine bosom and the fringe beneath her hat) – all have been adduced to suggest high jinks rather than hysteria:

> For if these women steal the attributes of masculinity, as the central axis of the umbrella leaves no doubt, they hardly do it in a spirit of aspiration. Their theft and their playacting serve rather to reveal patriarchal postures precisely as such: a series of assumed poses. [12]

By making representation – the patriarchal pose – its subject, Austen's photograph seems to resist the continuity of image and identity assumed by the medical gaze. The suited bodies cannot be read symptomatically, as forensic evidence of some transgressive identification, nor as actual disguises. In short, these women look neither butch nor male, particularly in the context of the other two Austen photographs from the 1987 exhibition *Staging the Self. Self-Portrait, Full Length with Fan Monday September 9th, 1892* discloses the photographer in evening dress, her hair formally coiffed, neck bared, arms gloved. She is seated on a high-backed chair whose wooden carvings repeat the insistent patterning of her lace-collared dress and the

greenery in the background – palm fronds, leaves and a curtain of ivy. Her flounced skirt rests on a carpet whose pattern multiplies the motif. Upon it lies a casually splayed bouquet.

Susan Butler notes that the loosely-clad figure of the previous photograph is now tightly corseted in the style of the time. This, and the photographer's hyperdetailed *mise-en-scene*, in which virtually every organic form is doubled by its artificial equivalent (the fan splayed like the flowers, the jardinière and its pedestal decorated in ceramic vegetation, the lace trim filigreed like the ivy) might suggest another masquerade, one which leads Butler to register 'a reverse Pygmalion effect . . . of woman become sculpture'.

Ironically, this statuesquely 'feminine' portrait may accomplish the phallic imposture parodied in the previous photograph. As Freud reminds us of another scene of multiplied

Self-Portrait, Full Length with Fan Monday September 9th, 1892. Photograph by Alice Austen (Staten Island Historical Society).

Julia Martin, Julia Bredt and Self Dressed Up as Men 4.40 pm, Thursday October 15th, 1891. Photograph by Alice Austen (Staten Island Historical Society).

symbols and bodies turned to stone, the threat of castration can be warded off by the stiffening of the flesh. And art has often assigned this consoling erection to the original source of the horror, the figure of the woman.[12] If this interpretation holds for Austen's *Self-Portrait . . . with Fan*, it reminds us of one of the many paradoxes in the relation of visibility to sexuality: the artistically perfected 'feminine' figure may be more phallic than any woman in male attire.

It is questionable whether one would even hazard these speculations about Austen's work without the 'evidence' provided by her third photograph in *Staging the Self*. In this surprisingly surreal image, two masked women face each other in identical poses, identically clad in white petticoats which reveal their bare arms and stockinged calves. Both hold cigarettes which almost touch, in this evocation of the female figure and her mirror image in the intimacy of the boudoir. The symmetry of the pose and the artifice of its staging are emphasised by the theatrical curtains which border the pair, and apparently enclose the alcove in which they stand. The photograph's title – *Trude and I Masked, Short Skirts 11pm, August 6th 1891* – records the lateness

Trude and I Masked, Short Skirts 11pm, August 6th, 1891. Photograph by Alice Austen. (Staten Island Historical Society).

of the hour, while a description which accompanies the glass negative identifies the setting as the bedrom of Gertrude Tate, 'the woman with whom [Austen] was to share her life and work for over forty years'.[14]

The time, the place, the partial undress of these women and their gaze at each other offers an irresistibly erotic reading. This photograph, Butler notes, 'speaks of desire'. But whose desire? And for whom? The very doubling that implies a sexual pairing also denies it in a repetition too exact to suggest an encounter rather than a reflection. Two women, two cigarettes, two curtains, with that endlessly repeated floral pattern – the signs of intimacy proliferate indifferently, to suggest desire without identity. These figures, after all, are *masked*. If this anonymity is required by the transgressive circumstances (signalled by the cigarettes and the short skirts as well as the pose), then it presents a problem for self-portraiture. Homosexual desire may be representable, but not the homosexual 'self'. Or again, if the doubling works to represent the homoerotic as fundamentally narcissistic – the desire for the same – identity collapses in a crisis of liminality. Which is self and which is other?

'Or perhaps the question is rather, is there a "true" Alice,' Susan Butler concludes in response to this bewildering trio of self-portraits; 'one that could be singled out from the multiple selves or aspects Alice Austen confronts us with?'

We are now a century on from these photographs, a century which has made the deconstruction of the 'true' self one of its central critical projects. But the problems which confronted the representation of homosexuality then still remain. Jean-François Chevrier may consign 'the idea that some reflection of a psychological truth may be recognised in a person's bodily form' to a dark age of Positivism, but in the case of homosexuality the notion of a visible psychology displayed on the body pesists.[15]

Spurred by the discourses surrounding AIDS, a new generation of taxonomists reconstruct an old anatomy of desire, discovering in every weakened body the predestined consequences of perversion. Meanwhile, we negotiate the contradictions of 'identity politics' in an era which privileges subjective experience even as it declares the crisis of the subject.[16] The recent efforts of the British photographer Rosy Martin to take on both imperatives furnishes us with a final sequence of self-portraits.

Martin's work on lesbian representation emerged from a project of 'phototherapy' developed with Jo Spence. In a joint essay they distinguish the practice from traditional portraiture, 'typified by the notion that people can be represented by showing aspects of their "character" . . . In the course of this work, we have amply demonstrated to ourselves that there is no single self but many fragmented selves, each vying for conscious expression, many never acknowledged'.[17]

To represent this fragmented identity, and its challenge to the historical iconography of lesbianism, Martin returns us to the 1890s and Ellis's characterisation of the female invert: 'a disdain for the petty feminine artifices of the toilette' . . . 'masculine straight-forwardness' . . . 'a decided taste and toleration for cigars' . . . 'nothing of that sexual shyness and engaging air of weakness and dependence which are an invitation to men'.[18] These phrases accompany a five-panel 1986 project entitled *Extract from Transforming the Suit*. Martin is the model in all the photographs, which can be read from left to right, from long shot to medium close-up, from phallic (the admonishing finger and brandished cigar) to vaginal (the lily), from domineering to withdrawn.

This spectrum of psychic identities anticipates a prominent new current in the theorisation of lesbianism, to judge not only from the 'Perverse Politics' issue of the British journal *Feminist Review*, but also recent philosophical studies like Judith Butler's *Gender Trouble*. While the latter poses the homosexual as the postmodern Proteus, whose 'sexual nonidentity' exposes 'the illusion of an abiding gendered self',[19] the contributors to the former issue queue up to formulate a definition of lesbianism 'based on a mobility of desire, an oscillation of identifications'.[20]

> Today's lesbian 'self' is a thoroughly urban creature who interprets fashion as something to be worn and discarded. Nothing is sacred for very long. Constantly changing, she dabbles in fashion, constructing one self after another, expressing her desires in a continual process of experimentation.[21]

It isn't inappropriate to characterise this model Ms in the rhetoric of the fashion spread,

Transforming the Suit – What Do Lesbians Look Like? Rosy Martin, Sitter/Director; Jo Spence, Photographer/Therapist.

since she seems subject to a process of idealisation not wholly unlike that which led Hall's readers to 'embrace' Stephen Gordon. So self-conscious a celebration of evanescent selfhood brings to mind Laura Marcus's reservations about the recent vogue in psychoanalytic autobiography: 'the autobiographical self can remain intact while gesturing towards and remaining in authority over structures which could disrupt this position.'[22]

A similar reluctance to de-centre the subject is detectable, I would argue, in *Transforming the Suit*. 'Many fragmented selves' may be on display, but they are not ordered arbitrarily. Both the title and the traditional direction of reading draw us away from the severely tailored figure of Ellis's description, while a similar pull is exerted by the successive reframings, which build to the alluring intimacy of the close-up. But the coy femme at the extreme right is as stylised as the bossy butch opposite, and the sense of exaggeration sends us back to the median figure, whose centrality, scale and apparently uninflected pose mark it as the apex of the series. This symbolic mid-point coincides with a direct gaze (emphasised by the spectacles), unfussy hairstyle, softly-tailored suit . . . and the flower, now worn as a boutonnière: a combination of gender signifiers to be sure, but organised into a single, intact (and historically recognisable) 'identity'.

The paradoxical project of *Transforming the Suit* – the simultaneous assertion and deconstruction of identity – provoked these thoughts on the lesbian self-portrait. Indeed, all the images here could be exhibited under Martin's title. My concern in tracing such transformations across a century of photographic practice is not to document a succession of lesbian identities so much as to register that paradox, and the problems it presents to photography's promise to record identity. If these photographs 'show' us anything, it may only be this: that the lesbian self-portrait is as persistent as it is impossible.

NOTES

1 Esther Newton, 'The Mythic Mannish Lesbian: Radclyffe Hall and the New Woman' in *The Lesbian Issue: Essays from SIGNS,* ed. Estelle B. Freedman, Barbara C. Gelpi, Susan L. Johnson, Kathleen M. Weston (Chicago: University of Chicago Press, 1985), p.8. Additional page citations will be given in the text, unless otherwise indicated.

2 Roland Barthes, *Camera Lucida* (London: Jonathan Cape, 1981), pp.88-9.

3 Radclyffe Hall, *The Well of Loneliness* (London: Virago, 1982), p.9. Additional page citations will be given in the text.

4 Michel Foucault, *The History of Sexuality, Volume 1: An Introduction* (London: Penguin, 1984).

5 Jeffrey Weeks, *Sexuality and its Discontents: Meanings, Myths & Modern Sexualities* (London: Routledge, 1985), pp.67-8.

6 Michael Baker, *Our Three Selves: A Life of Radclyffe Hall* (London: Hamish Hamilton, 1985), p.218. Additional page citations will be given in the text.

7 This retouching was more easily accomplished in *The Well*'s description of a Millais portrait of the child Stephen and her mother, revealing 'that indefinable quality in Stephen that made her look wrong in the clothes she was wearing' (p.23).

8 Teresa de Lauretis, 'Sexual Indifference and Lesbian Representation' in *Theatre Journal*, vol. 40, no. 2, May 1988, p.177.

9 Richard von Krafft-Ebing, *Psychopathia Sexualis* (London: Mayflower-Dell, 1967), p.276. Additional page citations will be given in the text.

10 See Roberta McGrath, 'Medical Police' in *Ten.8*, no. 14, pp.13-18.

11 John Tagg, *The Burden of Representation: Essays on Photographies and Histories* (London: Macmillan, 1988), p.37 (my italics).

12 Susan Butler, 'So How Do I Look? Women Before and Behind the Camera' in *Staging the Self: Self-Portrait Photography 1840s-1980s* (London: National Portrait Gallery, 1987), pp.52-3.

13 Sigmund Freud, 'Medusa's Head' (1922) in *Sexuality and the Psychology of Love* (New York: Collier Books, 1978).

14 Emmanuel Cooper, *The Sexual Perspective* (London and New York: HarperCollins, 1986), pp.88-9.

15 Contrast Jean-Francois Chevrier, 'The Image of the

Other' in *Staging the Self* with Simon Watney, 'The Homosexual Body: Resources and a Note on Theory' in *Public*, no. 3, 1990, pp.44-59; and Stuart Marshall, 'Picturing Deviancy' in *Ecstatic Antibodies: Resisting the AIDS Mythology*, ed. Tessa Boffin and Sunil Gupta (London: Rivers Oram Press, 1990), pp.19-36.

16 See Diana Fuss, *Essentially Speaking: Feminism, Nature & Difference* (London and New York: Routledge, 1990), pp.97-112.

17 Rosy Martin and Jo Spence, 'Phototherapy: New Portraits for Old' in *Putting Myself in the Picture*, Jo Spence (London: Camden Press, 1986), p.172.

18 Havelock Ellis, *Studies in the Psychology of Sex, Volume II: Sexual Inversion* (Philadelphia: F. A. Davis Company, 1924), pp.250. (My reference for this photo-text is *Ten.8*, 'Body Politics' issue no. 25, pp.46-7.)

19 Judith Butler, *Gender Trouble: Feminism and the Subversion of Identity* (London and New York: Routledge, 1990), pp.101, 140.

20 Diane Hamer, 'Significant Others: Lesbianism and Psychoanalytic Theory' in *Feminist Review*, no. 34, Spring 1990, p.149.

21 Inge Blackman and Kathryn Perry, 'Skirting the Issue: Lesbian Fashion for the 1990s' in *Feminist Review*, no. 34, Spring 1990, p.77.

22 Laura Marcus, '"Enough About You, Let's Talk About Me": Recent Autobiographical Writing' in *New Formations*, no. 1, Spring 1987, p.92.

IN SEARCH OF AN IMAGE

Mumtaz Karimjee

'In Search Of An Image' is the beginning of an
exploration of the racism, sexism and
homophobia of the white dominant society in
which I live and the sexism and homophobia of
the society into which I was born. I pick my
way between the two, sifting through and
reshaping the ground I walk upon, building the
foundations of a self-defined identity.

The Moslem Harem is a great school for this 'Lesbian (which I call Atossan) love'; these tribades [1] are mostly known by peculiarities of form and features, hairy cheeks and upper lips, gruff voices, hircine [2] odour and the large projecting clitoris with erectile powers.
Burton, *Thousand Nights*, vol. ii, p. 234, as quoted by Raṇa Kabbani in *Europe's Myths of Orient* (Pandora Press, 1988), p. 53.

. . . indignant at Miss Cumming (who was half Indian) for having made such an accusation in the first place:

The judges suggested that Miss Cumming, having been raised in the lascivious East, had no idea of the horror such an accusation would stir in Britain. Lord Meadowbank explained . . . that he had been to India, and he would venture to guess that Miss Cumming had developed her curiosity about sexual matters from her lewd Indian nurses, who were, in contrast to British women, entirely capable of obscene chatter on such subjects.

Lord Boyle, on the other hand, did not believe tribadism impossible among savages, but certainly improbable in civilised Britain.
Raṇa Kabbani, *Europe's Myths of Orient* (Pandora Press, 1988), p. 53.

The Eastern Disease?

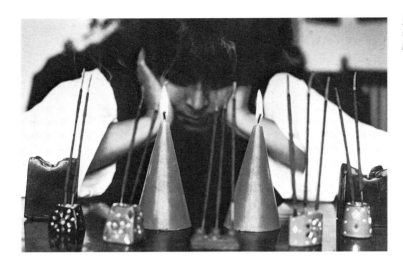

Burdened with carrying the weight of the honour of the patriachal society and injured in the name of protecting that honour.

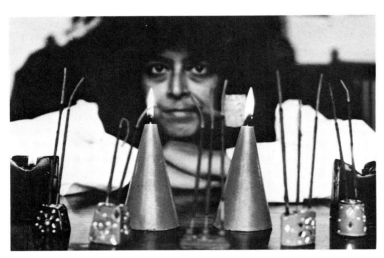

So, don't give me your tenets and your laws. Don't give me your lukewarm gods. What I want is an accounting with all three cultures – white, Moslem,[3] *Indian. I want the freedom to carve and chisel my own face, to staunch the bleeding with ashes, to fashion my own gods out of my entrails. And if going home is denied me then I will have to stand and claim my space, making a new culture – una cultura mestiza – with my own lumber, my own bricks and mortar and my own feminist architecture.*

Gloria Anzaldua, *Borderlands/La Frontera*
(Spinsters/Aunt Lute, 1987), p. 22.

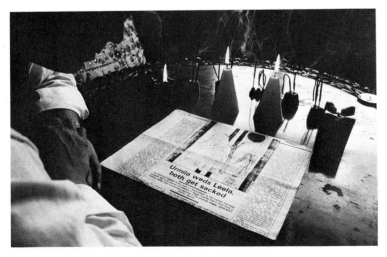

The Western Disease?

NOTES
[1] 'A woman who practises unnatural vice with other women' (*The Shorter Oxford Dictionary*).

[2] 'Of, belonging to, or resembling a goat; having a goatish smell' (*The Shorter Oxford Dictionary*).

[3] In putting together this piece of work, I have changed 'Mexican' for 'Moslem' – *Mumtaz Karimjee*.

DEVELOPING IDENTITIES

Sonja Ruehl

The 1920s and 1930s saw the clear formation of a lesbian identity and an increase in public awareness of lesbianism, or sexual 'inversion'. The scandal and moral panic surrounding Radclyffe Hall's novel, *The Well of Loneliness*, and its subsequent trial for obscenity in 1928, constituted one famous occasion for such increased awareness.

It is interesting to speculate on the place of photography in sharpening the definition of a lesbian identity around this time. Full consideration of this needs to take into account the distribution of photographic images in the public domain – for instance, which images appeared in the popular press, the socialite press or in literary publications at the time.

This chapter will not attempt such a full consideration, but will instead be limited to looking at certain photographic images of lesbians produced during those two decades, and asking in what way they convey a sense of 'a lesbian identity'. The photographs chosen perhaps inevitably take as subjects women who were affluent or well known, or both. They cannot be taken as representative of the majority of lesbians of the time, whose lives and images are in the main unrecorded, inaccessible or lost. We are the poorer for the lack of information about the unknown lesbian. But it may be argued that photographs of the well-off or well known, sometimes photographed by photographers who were famous as well, were more significant in shaping a public understanding of 'a lesbian identity'.

I will look at a very few, selected photographs as images or representations in themselves. These photographs are chosen to illustrate two simple ideas: firstly, that it is chiefly in portrait photographs of single individuals that elements of a lesbian identity are most apparent; secondly, that it is in formal, studio portraits that a lesbian identity comes into play, rather than in informal snapshots.

The first point is related to the sexological theories current at the time. These included ideas of lesbianism as an inborn 'inversion' of sexual feeling, or even of lesbians as a kind of intersex or 'third sex'. Such ideas, of course, place the origin of lesbian feelings entirely within the physical constitution of a single individual woman. Lesbianism was thus seen by sexologists to be the expression of an essential inner nature. And at least one sexologist – Havelock Ellis – believed that this inner nature had physical correlates. He was never quite sure what they were but had in mind physical features like the distribution of body hair or the width of shoulders. The 'statement' of lesbianism as a sexual identity is curiously an *individual* statement at that time, rather than something involving sexual and social relationships.

Lesbianism, then, would be just the sort of thing to be 'revealed' in a portrait; an artistic project which is meant to open up a window on an individual's inner self. If lesbianism is seen as a congenital condition, not a sexual-social relationship, then a single individual can quite well exhibit a lesbian identity in isolation. According to this view, the individual woman is almost 'an example' of lesbianism. In fact, sexological theory at that time had much more difficulty with the idea of a lesbian *relationship* or a lesbian *couple* since it viewed only one partner as a 'true' lesbian – the identity of the *partner* of such a congenital 'invert' was never satisfactorily defined. It is interesting that portrait photography should correspondingly find lesbian identity easier to cope with in a single individual, even though the subject or subjects of the photograph might be women who themselves rejected the current state of theory as over-simplified.

The second, simple organising idea behind this chapter is that of the greater importance of lesbian identity in formal photographs than in 'snapshot' photographs taken by friends and acquaintances. This is at first a surprising idea. If photographs are thought to give clues about the 'real life' of their subjects, then it may be supposed that casual, unposed shots taken in relaxed circumstances on the beach, in the garden, in natural light and so on, would give a richer and more intimate slice of life than a formal picture would do. If the life were a lesbian one, then a snapshot might be thought to give the viewer a bigger helping of 'lesbian identity' than a studio portrait.

This seems not to be the case, which in turn suggests that the process of forming sexual identities, recognisable in the public domain, is one of conscious composition, not just a reflection of what goes on in private life. Casual shots of lesbians, lovers and friends could often be photographs of just about anyone. It is rather in careful, formal photographic compositions that a lesbian identity is delicately but deliberately conveyed.

In many ways, the obvious place to start would seem to be with photographs of Radclyffe Hall herself. Her lesbian identity was after all the cause of her notoriety, if not her fame. Photographs of Hall and her lover appeared widely in the popular press. In these, Hall is pictured as the uncompromising 'invert' she believed herself to be. However, these photographs are already well known and accessible elsewhere and that is the main reason I have chosen to concentrate on images other than hers.

The first is a photograph of Janet Flanner, the American journalist who lived from 1925 among the expatriate Paris community which included many famous figures, among them Gertrude Stein and Alice B. Toklas. Janet Flanner was herself well known for her features on French life which regularly appeared in the *New Yorker*. Her pieces reflected the part-bohemian, part-socialite world she moved in in Paris. She is now also known for a volume of letters originally written to her Italian woman lover.[1]

The photograph of Janet Flanner was taken by Berenice Abbott and shows her in men's formal dress, wearing a top hat with two masks bound around it. Dated somewhere between

Janet Flanner by Berenice Abbott, 1926–9 (courtesy of Berenice Abbott/Commerce Graphics Ltd, Inc).

1926 and 1929, the photograph was it seems occasioned by a costume party – a fashionable kind of event frequently held in her Parisian circles.[2] Cross-dressing is of course an aspect of many fancy-dress costumes but even so, the image of Janet Flanner in her men's clothes must have had a certain resonance. Michael de Lisio also made a sculpture of her in this costume.

The photograph shows Janet Flanner in a classic 'portrait' pose, leaning on one hand which is positioned to reveal a ring on her little finger. She is wearing a dark jacket and white shirt with cuff-links, which are all distinctly masculine, as well as the top hat. There are some 'feminine' touches to the portrait too – wearing a brooch or fancy tie-pin at the neck, the subject is slightly less than full-face to camera, which allows a curl of hair to frame her face on one side. All the same, the overall costume is undoubtedly a masculine one.

As Katrina Rolley has pointed out, in the 1920s dressing in masculine clothes could well signify 'the modern woman' and not necessarily 'the lesbian woman'.[3] Women adopted men's clothing as a sign of emancipation generally, not always of sexual identity specifically. Nevertheless, a lesbian identity is strongly hinted here. What is intriguing in the portrait is the pair of masks, one dark and one light, to which the viewer's gaze is immediately drawn, presenting the viewer with an enigma to contemplate – what do they signify?

In one way, the masks do emphasise Janet Flanner's own features – the shape of the eyes in the masks echoes her own rather soulful ones. Yet the masks also deflect attention away from the sitter's face – a peculiar ploy in a portrait and one which suggests that the masks are there as a clue to her character.

Masks convey ambiguity – the dark and the light, the masculine and feminine, perhaps sexual ambiguity too. These masks *could* be suggestive of the revelation of truth – the face behind the mask revealed, the truth uncovered. This idea would coexist quite nicely with a theory of inversion which preached the 'truth' of an individual's nature as revealed in her or his sexuality, a powerful idea of the time.

There are, though, other possibilities. Masks also connote theatricality, play, a world of alternatives, a gap between representation and reality. In this photograph, the masks are *not* in fact a disguise that has been discarded – they are firmly part of the picture, they are presented *along with* the face of the sitter. They are part of the set-up of the sitter's presentation. They seem to show a self-conscious playing with self-presentation on the part of the sitter, which includes a lesbian sexual identity. Overall, the portrait does then convey a lesbian identity, but one which is more complex than that of a sexual identity as 'inner truth revealed'.

Incidentally, this corresponds with what is known about the views on sexual identity of Janet Flanner and her circle. This circle was somewhat bohemian and avant-garde and was disapproved of by Radclyffe Hall, aspiring as she did to a life approximating that of the 'country gent'. On their part, the Paris set found Hall naïve and her view of sexuality over-simplified. They were by no means uncritical adherents of views such as Havelock Ellis's on 'congenital inversion'. Janet Flanner herself, recalling the scandal of the *Well of Loneliness* trial in later life, writes that the book excited 'very little admiration as a literary or psychological study . . . This rather innocent and confused book was the first of the Sapphic interpretations in modern life.'[4]

Radclyffe Hall saw a lesbian or 'inverted' identity as the *solution* to a puzzle – that of a 'masculine' individual in a female body, essentially. Janet Flanner's portrait conveys a lesbian identity that is not so straightforward but, rather, complex and ambiguous. Yet incongruity of gender and hence the sexual identity of the sitter does seem to be the portrait's major point.

It is interesting to turn from portraits of single individuals to look at the way *pairs* of women were represented in photographs in the 1920s and 1930s. Psychological theory had trouble in relating lesbian relationships to the theory of sexual inversion – what kind of creature was the 'true invert's' lover supposed to be? If 'feminine', to balance the invert's 'masculine' sexuality, why did the lover choose a woman as a lover? Or else, if 'masculine' herself to some degree, how did sexual attraction operate, when sexological theory still saw it as an attraction of masculine and feminine opposites even in the case of lesbians? This problem was reflected in the self-presentation of Radclyffe Hall and her lover, both adherents to the current psychological theory, in that they sometimes appeared in a masculine/feminine polarity, at other times as *both* defiantly uncompromising 'inverts'.[5]

It is interesting, though, to look at photographs where self-presentation is perhaps less consciously thought out and in which the

Gertrude Stein and Alice B. Toklas by Cecil Beaton, mid-1930s (courtesy of Sotheby's, London).

photographer's decisions are more important – again, in a formal studio setting. The first photograph is of Gertrude Stein and Alice B. Toklas, taken by Cecil Beaton in the mid-1930s.

The portrait does show a deliberate balancing of the two figures of Alice and Gertrude but, very unusually, their 'couple' relationship is indicated by their standing opposite one another, gazing at each other. This places the two figures in a juxtaposition which is very *un*like the conventional portrait of a couple, entwined to suggest a single entity, together gazing out towards the viewer. This unusual composition of figures conveys a sense of *equal* partnership, perhaps unexpectedly, given Gertrude's fame as an author. It also conveys a sense of independence along with relationship. Alice's rather bird-like hat gives to her height and breadth to counterbalance Gertrude's bulk. While Gertrude's stance, hands folded in front of her, conveys a clear feeling of self-confidence and composure,

Alice too stands squarely in an uncluttered posture, hands by her side.

Even though the relationship of the two figures is in many ways equal, there is also a subtle sense of 'equal but opposite' about the picture. Gertrude stands with a pool of her own shadow at her feet, which adds to the feeling of her being very firmly rooted. Her androgynous garb with its long skirt and uninterrupted line has a hint of priestly garments. Alice, on the other hand, appears as a literally more 'shadowy' figure. Her own shadow surrounds her entirely and her face falls into the shadow of her hat, like a veil. The shaped jacket and shorter skirt give a somewhat more 'feminine' silhouette, as does the greater formality of her dress. She is wearing hat and gloves while Gertrude is not. Her figure appears on the left and Gertrude's on the right. The opposition of the figures, conveyed through these subtle nuances, certainly could be read as a masculine/ feminine one, though that is not the only possible reading. That of famous author and admiring friend would be another.

What *is* clear is that this is a portrait photograph of a pair of women each absorbed in and focused on the other. The relationship between the two is central to the portrait. This is not a family portrait of a pair of sisters arm-in-arm, or a seated mother with her daughter standing behind her, faces to camera to reveal family resemblances. This is a portrait of two women whose composition falls outside the conventions of such portraits. It is really this question over the relationship of the two figures that raises the question of a lesbian identity for them, rather than anything in particular about either figure taken alone. Neither figure is looking out to the camera, neither is 'presenting' itself as an example of innate 'inversion' to be collected or studied individually. Furthermore, whereas the Janet Flanner portrait conveys a lesbian identity by working within the conventions of portrait photography, the sense of a lesbian *relationship* is

conveyed by working outside them. This also makes the sense of lesbian identity stronger in the individual portrait photograph than in the photograph of a lesbian couple.

The portrait of Alice and Gertrude, then, is one in which their 'lesbian identity' is one of the elements, but only one. This is supported by its similarity to other portraits which are *not* portraits of a lesbian couple, but which find a similar solution to the problem of how to photograph a pair of women who are related to each other but not by blood or marriage – by friendship in this next example. This is a portrait of two women from the same Parisian milieu, though the photograph was probably taken in the early 1920s in New York. It is a photograph by Man Ray of Djuna Barnes and her friend and neighbour, Mina Loy.

Here again, the two figures are looking not out towards the camera but at each other. Mina Loy, placed to the left of Djuna Barnes, is enveloped in her own shadow, though it does not cover her face. There are more 'masculine' elements to Djuna Barnes's appearance, even though both women are wearing rather undefined clothes, and hats. Djuna Barnes is dressed in darker clothing with an upturned collar; she is looking slightly downwards at Mina Loy. Loy's lighter clothing and hat is more 'feminine' and she is wearing a drop

Mina Loy and Djuna Barnes by Man Ray, early 1920s © ADAGP, Paris and DACS, London 1991.

earring; her lips are slightly open. There are slight, and ambiguous, elements of masculine/feminine juxtaposition here too. The figures are in close physical proximity, though, and indeed look as if they are probably touching. There are several points of similarity with the Toklas/Stein portrait, yet the Man Ray is not a portrait of a famous lesbian couple, but rather of a pair of friends of whom only one, Djuna Barnes, was even intermittently lesbian. Mina Loy seems to have been the accepted 'token heterosexual' at many gatherings of the Paris group.[6] The similarity of the Toklas/Stein portrait and the Barnes/Loy one probably derives from the photographers' common problem of how to photograph two women in relation to each other, outside the conventions of family portraiture. The line between friendship and sexual relationship is correspondingly blurred.

In fact, it so happens that Man Ray mentions this very photograph in his autobiographical *Self-Portrait*.[7] The two women were among his very first sitters when he began commercial portrait photography, it seems. His comment is that one day there appeared at his studio 'two handsome young women writers, Mina Loy and Djuna Barnes, one in light tan clothes of her own design, the other all in black with a veil. They were stunning subjects; I photographed them together and the contrast made a fine picture.' The photographer's clear pleasure lies in the contrast of colour and style, not sexual identity. Indeed, their 'identity' to him appears to present no contrast at all – both are 'young', 'handsome', 'stunning' and 'writers'.

The blurring of friendship and sexual relationship is even more true with informal photography, and the example chosen here is a photograph of two women from the same Paris group, though taken somewhat later, which seems to be a casual snapshot taken on a balcony, probably during a holiday in Nice. It gives a glimpse of the daily lives of two lesbian women of the time, but it is very hard to distill a sense of 'lesbian identity' from the snapshot.

It is of, again, Djuna Barnes, this time with Natalie Barney, sometime between 1928 and 1930. Barney was also a prominent feature of the expatriate American world, together with a succession of her women lovers. But although Djuna Barnes was near the end of a very stormy lesbian relationship at the time of the photograph, these two were not lovers.

In the photograph, there is close physical contact between the two figures – Djuna Barnes rests an arm on Natalie Barney's leg, and she has a hand on each of Barnes's shoulders. However, the whole arrangement looks more as if it is designed to stop Natalie Barney falling off her perch on the balcony than anything else. There is a lack of tension about the relationship of the figures which makes it seem an almost accidental arrangement. The sense that the photo gives to

Djuna Barnes and Natalie Barney, 1928-30 (courtesy of George Wilkes).

me, therefore, is that it is of a pair of women who are friends – even 'chums' – and who could be just about anybody.

The two women are casually relaxed and smiling, in a sunny setting; Natalie Barney literally has her hair down. Djuna Barnes is wearing a noticeably stylish, feminine dress, plus discreet jewellery, and her friend is in an undefined sort of kaftan. But there seems to be no deliberate juxtaposition of figures or opposing styles in the photo in terms of clothing or posture, and the casualness of the pair is perhaps most emphasised because of the divergence of their direction of gaze. Djuna Barnes is looking over the balcony at the scenery while Natalie Barney is laughing towards the camera. They are neither a couple facing the world together, nor are they looking at each other. Despite their physical closeness and despite the fact that both were well-known lesbians in avant-garde Paris at the time, this snapshot does not seem to me to have a 'lesbian identity' as one of its elements. It could be a snapshot of more or less any two women on holiday.

It would be much too grandiose to try to draw 'conclusions' from such a limited look at a small range of illustrations taken from a time period spanning a decade at least. But it is worth pausing to think where this discussion leaves us.

First, it suggests that the strength of 'lesbian identity' conveyed in these photographs seems to be clearest where the fit with conventions of mainstream portraiture is closest – in individual portraiture, where the convention of giving clues to a character's supposed inner nature was already very well established. As it happened, this fitted well with contemporary theories of lesbian sexuality, which saw it as a sort of inborn inner nature.

The sense of 'lesbian identity' is much more ambiguous and mixed up with other elements, however, in portraits of lesbian couples. They fall outside the mainstream conventions of family portraits and those of engaged or of married couples. To convey a sense of *sexual* relationship between two women at that time perhaps required an unorthodox solution in terms of portraiture. However, this meant that the photograph would not draw added strength of meaning from an adherence to established forms. Further, it would not strike such a clear chord of correspondence with sexological theory in the 1920s and 1930s, which was much more confused about lesbian relationships than about lesbian individuals.

These conclusions are specific to time and place, of course – to a particular period of recent history with its photographic conventions, its ways of circulating photographic images, its rules about press censorship, its sexual mores and morality, the prevailing state of sexological theory at that time, and so on. My conclusion about the strength of lesbian identity conveyed by *individual* portraits, rather than portraits of couples, I argue, holds at a time when there was no 'mainstream' convention of explicitly sexual photographs of lesbian pairs. The presence of another woman in a photograph would not, at that time, connote a *sexual* relationship.

Contemporary writers do now reach a very different conclusion about contemporary lesbian images – images produced at a time when a 'mainstream' convention for pornographic lesbian images does exist, and the presence of two women together in a portrait, even if it is not an explicitly 'sexual' portrait, is liable to be given a sexual interpretation by the viewer.

Thus Jan Zita Grover, writing in 1988, considers that in producing portraits of a couple of women together, the photographer has included 'the most conventional marker of lesbianism – another woman who reminds the viewer of the lesbian's sexual choice'.[8] In Grover's view this is because lesbians are identifiable 'in mainstream imagery' solely through their sexual activity with one another. She is writing of a contemporary world in which a great variety of sexological theories compete, in which sexual connotations almost saturate the social world, a world in which explicitly sexual lesbian photographs can be considered a 'mainstream', if pornographic, convention.

She is also writing of a social world in which 'lesbian institutions' and networks actually exist, in which lesbian photographers can strive to produce lesbian images and self-definitions for a primarily lesbian audience. She considers that in this lesbian subcultural context, portraits of women alone, both formal and informal, can 'propose lesbianism as a social identity rather than an exclusively sexual one' by the ascription of names, ages, occupations or other 'public' elements of identity, if this is what the lesbian photographer wants to achieve – and she argues that many do. The sexual content of the lesbian identity, she argues, then depends only on the general context in which the photograph appears, 'a book or slide show on lesbian people/identities distributed through primarily lesbian institutions'. That is, a lesbian sexual identity can, in this context, be separated from anything inherent in the image itself, if the photograph is of a woman alone, but not if it is a photograph of a couple.

All of this adds up to a very different world from that of the 1920s and 1930s, when lesbianism was only just emerging as a sexual identity discussed in the public domain at all.

Though Jan Grover's and my own specific conclusions are very different this is more a case of *autre temps, autres moeurs* than any particular theoretical divergence of opinion. What shows through strongly in each case, whether in the 1920s or the 1980s, is the need to recognise the importance of mainstream photographic conventions in shaping the development of lesbian identities defined through the lens.

NOTES
[1] Janet Flanner, *Letters to a Friend,* ed. Natalia Danesi Murray (London and New York: Pandora Press, 1988).

[2] See Janet Flanner, *Paris Was Yesterday,* ed. Irving Drutman (New York: Viking, 1972). The information is noted on the jacket illustration.

[3] Katrina Rolley, 'Cutting a Dash: The Dressing of Radclyffe Hall and Una Troubridge' in *Feminist Review*, no. 35, Summer 1990.

[4] Janet Flanner, *Paris Was Yesterday*, p.48.

[5] Katrina Rolley, op. cit.

[6] Gillian Hanscombe and Virginia L. Smyers, *Writing For Their Lives: The Modernist Women 1910–1940* (London: Women's Press, 1960).

[7] Man Ray, *Self-Portrait* (London: 2nd ed., Bloomsbury, 1988), p.86.

[8] Jan Zita Grover, 'Dykes in Context' in *Ten.8*, no. 30, 1988.

THE KNIGHT'S MOVE

Tessa Boffin

SOMEWHERE IN A CEMETERY
DOWN A DARK PATHWAY
UNDERNEATH A STONE ANGEL
I STUMBLE ACROSS YOUR PHOTOGRAPHS.
WHERE IS MY KNIGHT
MY KNAVE
MY ANGEL
MY CASANOVA
MY LADY-IN-WAITING?
I COULD HARDLY FIND YOU
IN MY HISTORY BOOKS
BUT NOW IN THIS SCENE
YOU ALL COME TOGETHER.

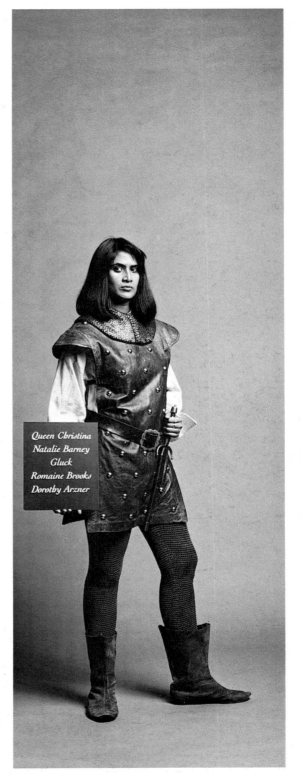

Queen Christina
Natalie Barney
Gluck
Romaine Brooks
Dorothy Arzner

. . . it is worth remembering that all discourse is 'placed', and the heart has its reasons.

Stuart Hall, 'Cultural Identity and Diaspora' in *Identity: Community, Culture, Difference*.[1]

My starting point for *The Knight's Move* was the intense frustration I feel when people prioritise reality – everyday experience, 'real' sex and so on – over and above fantasies. Staged 'scenes' and photo-tableaux are all seen as second best since they are always self-consciously (and even unconsciously) constructed and played out. Photography, with its supposedly intimate connection with reality, is inevitably viewed as a documentation of the 'Real', never (heaven forbid) as a fantasy. I wanted to throw this equation into question by looking at how our identities as dykes are constructed through historical role models, both in fact *and* in fantasy.

As John Preston has recently urged:

We need to resurrect and honour the concept of role models which was so important to the early gay movement . . .[2]

Yet we need to acknowledge that the stakes are remarkably high because of the relative paucity of lesbian imagery. There are so few representations and so many unfulfilled desires. The burdens imposed by this scarcity of representations can, however, be overcome if we go beyond our impoverished archives to create new icons. One way we can move forward is by embracing our idealised fantasy figures, by placing ourselves into the great heterosexual narratives of courtly and romantic love: by making *The Knight's Move* – a lateral or sideways leap.[3]

In writing about Caribbean and Black British cinemas, Stuart Hall proposes that there are at least two different ways of thinking about cultural identity. The two positions he discusses could also be read, quite productively in this instance, across lesbian identity and representation. The first position, he argues, defines cultural identity in terms of a shared, collective culture which can be uncovered, excavated, brought to light and expressed through representations. The second position entails quite a different form of cultural practice:

not the rediscovery but the *production* of identity. Not an identity grounded in the archaeology, but in the *re-telling* of the past.[4]

It is this second position which recognises the ruptures and discontinuities underlying the supposed unity of our communities' actual history. It recognises the injustices of race and class, as well as the sheer diversity of lesbian desires and sexual practices.

We should not, for a moment, underestimate or neglect the importance of the act of imaginative discovery embodied by the first position. This discovery of hidden images and histories restores to us an imaginary fullness or plentitude which we can set against the broken kaleidoscope of our past:

They are resources of resistance and identity, with which to confront the fragmented and pathological ways in which that experience has been reconstructed within the dominant regimes of cinematic and visual representation[5] . . .

However, we must not be content solely with delving into the past in order to find consoling elements to counteract the harm and under-representation, or mis-representation, we have suffered as a marginalised community. We cannot just innocently rediscover a lesbian Golden Age because our readings of history are always a history of the present, shaped by our positions in the present. We also have to re-invent; we have to produce ourselves through representations in the present, here and now. These images may draw upon our past histories, or they may transgressively take from others; but they will certainly shape our future and play with our desires.

For subcultures such as lesbians' that are consistently unrepresented then, the notion of roles models is both essential, and simultaneously restrictive. Essential in that it is necessary for representations of our communities to be both visible to us, and acknowledged by the 'general public', of which we are also a part. Restrictive in that we as a marginalised group have so few historical lesbian images upon which to model our psychic or social selves.

If we persist in prioritising reality – actual historical role models at the expense of fantasy figures – we leave our sense of selves and our imagery wanting, and certain questions unasked. For example, who mobilises our desires and fantasies, given that they cut across the fragile boundaries of sexual identity and gender; and which archetypes do our desires attach themselves to? Are these dramatis personae the same as the real life historical role models? Somewhere within this tension, this gap between reality and fantasy, we model ourselves on old tattered photographs and hazy daydreams.

NOTES

[1] Stuart Hall, 'Cultural Identity and Diaspora' in *Identity: Community, Culture, Difference*, ed. Jonathan Rutherford (London: Lawrence and Wishart, 1990), p. 223.

[2] John Preston, 'Gay Men and Sex in the Eighties' in *Mandate*, vol. 14, no. 4, April 1988, p. 87, cited in Simon Watney, 'The Homosexual Body: Resources and a Note on Theory' in *Public* 3, Carnal Knowledge (Canada, 1990), p. 53.

[3] In a game of chess the knight can move to the side as part of a forward advance.

[4] Stuart Hall, op. cit., p. 236.

[5] ibid., p. 225.

CREDITS

The photographs in the first cemetery scene are of famous and not-so-famous lesbians from the past: Sylvia Beach and Janet Flanner by Berenice Abbott; two of Alice Austen's self-portraits; and Gertrude Stein by Cecil Beaton. Similarly, the names on the boards in the studio shots are of prominent lesbian figures from history.

ACKNOWLEDGEMENTS

I would like to thank the following individuals and institutions who helped realise this project: firstly, the models – Mel Bingham (the Knight), Rishma Janmohamed (the Knave), Katy (the Angel), Vida Russell (Casanova) and Sophie Moorcock (the Lady-in-Waiting); secondly, Malcolm Venville for his technical assistance, and thirdly, the Polytechnic of Central London for access to their facilities. Finally there are a number of friends who offered suggestions at various stages, so thank you one and all to Mel Bingham, Jean Fraser, Sue Golding, Della Grace, Elaine Kramer, Anna Marie Smith, Simon Watney and Malcolm Venville.

MAKING AN APPEARANCE

Elizabeth Wilson

Feminist debates concerning sexuality have placed representation firmly centre-stage. These debates have included the role of pornography, advertising, photography and other branches of the popular media in constructing women – or femininity – culturally. It is important and relevant for this debate to extend to the ways in which clothes play a key part in our acts of self-presentation. Dress is especially interesting as a representational field for the very reason that it is not merely imposed from without: we necessarily use dress ourselves in daily acts of self-creation, behaving individualistically in this respect whether we like it or not. Some resent it, some enjoy it, perhaps most of us have a varying and ambivalent relationship to our appearance. Escape it we cannot.

In the late 1980s it increasingly seemed that lesbians were experiencing a freedom and a pleasure in dress that was denied heterosexual feminists, if not heterosexual women in general. The dyke event of the year in London in the winter of 1986/7 was a glamour ball,

'Come Dancing', at which women who had for years followed the self-denying ordinance of sober-coloured casual wear appeared in frocks, high heels, lipstick and *décolletage* – items they would not have even thought of wearing in the 1970s. Tickets were like gold dust.

By contrast, many feminists still fight shy of 'fashion' and are suspicious of any form of self-adornment that seems to suggest complicity with mainstream norms of the feminine, since this is associated with the sexual objectification of women. In the spring of 1989, an event to celebrate twenty years of feminism was held at the Institute of Contemporary Art in London. There, a session on dress was dominated by a view of fashionable underwear which came close to equating it with pornography. One speaker launched an attack on the lingerie department of that well-known British chain Marks and Spencer and exhorted us all to wear instead 'serviceable cotton knickers'. As one who haunts the temple of silk at London's Marble Arch I had to disagree, but when another lesbian asked why it was politically incorrect for a lesbian to wear a silk camisole in order to look attractive to another woman, the original speaker implied that such a move would have something to do with S/M practices. Another woman spoke of her sense of threat when standing near a Knicker Box shop in a lonely railway terminal, as she felt the proximity of frilly underwear would tempt a man to rape her. Many women present seemed to share these views. While it is understandable and rational for women to fear male violence, the idea that it is provoked by items of dress seems to come close to the establishment, judiciary view of the 'provocative' nature of women's clothes, and that women who do adorn themselves are 'asking for it'. Surely we should hold on to the idea that whatever we wear, it is the responsibility of men to control their feelings, and the idea that women 'cause' rape by bodily self-display is a hoary old excuse that no feminist should countenance.

It is not just 'provocative' dress to which some feminists (and radical men) object. Many assume that what is meant by 'fashion' is *haute couture* – the original high cost creations designed in Paris, Tokyo and Milan for at most a few thousand women worldwide. This then becomes a second reason to reject traditional forms of self-adornment – it is just one more manifestation of exploitative capitalism, creating in us 'false' needs which we should resist. Yet although 'high fashion' is generated to a large extent through the work of *haute couture* designers, it is disseminated through every level of reproduction and expense, to appear at length in the high street and the down-market mail order catalogues. *Haute couture* is also influenced by street fashion, and the existence of street fashions demonstrates that a desire to adorn one's body is not simply the result of having been duped by the fashion industry and capitalism.

What the development of capitalism, since pre-industrial times but especially since industrialisation, has done is to make *all* dress

fashionable. That is to say that in the contemporary western world the dress of all of us is determined by a fashion cycle, and rapidly changing styles cater to a desire for novelty and individualism. Whether this is viewed as creating 'false needs' or not, it means that even the most fervent anti-fashion dresser is in danger of creating a fashion precisely by producing a new and different appearance.

There were some feminists in the 1980s who tried to view fashion in a more complex way, as one cultural vehicle among others, and as a cultural practice that should be at least taken seriously instead of being merely denounced, just as feminists were taking Mills and Boon romances and television soap operas seriously, analysing their contradictory appeal. This enterprise has recently been attacked by Sabina Lovibond who accuses Suzanne Moore and myself of celebrating suspect pleasures and, by implication, women's subordination.[1]

Although it is undeniable that many members of both sexes do enjoy clothes and obtain pleasure out of self-adornment, the intention – mine at least – was never a mere celebration of dress. All I argued – and still believe – is that dress should be taken seriously as a cultural form and analysed as such. Dress and adornment contribute, after all, to self-representation, and the feminist debates of the 1980s placed representation at the core of feminist concerns. Nor is there any sign of this changing as the 1990s begin.

One of the problems with the feminist approach to fashion has been to contrast fashion – by implication artifice – with a 'natural' appearance. We should not follow 'fashion's dictates', the argument goes, but dress either to 'please ourselves' or in a 'natural' way. Rejection of cosmetics will reveal a 'natural' beauty, simple clothes devoid of the exaggeration of high heels, tight skirts and other constricting details will permit the natural movements of the body.

It is true that some exaggerated fashions do impede movement, but reliance on a notion of what is 'natural' obscures the truth that all dress is cultural and constructed. It has long been a standard figure of speech to refer to the way in which individuals of both sexes take a 'pride in their appearance'. The word 'appearance', so taken for granted as a part of the vocabulary of grooming and fashion, actually acknowledges this constructed element in dress. In our hairstyles, our choice of clothes and our use (or not) of cosmetics, we create an 'appearance' for public and private consumption; an image whose relationship with some implied 'reality' beneath it is by no means straightforward. Many feminists *do* assume that there is a 'real self' beneath the artifice of fashion and that the feminist's duty is simply to allow this 'real self' to 'come out', but no such distinction between artifice and nature can long be maintained.

Indeed, culture enjoins each of us to construct an 'appearance' of some kind, preferably consistent with our social role. It is really only the mad or those naked, crumpled figures in photographs of concentration camps, that have abandoned or been forced to abandon the attempt – and with it, in a horrible way, their very humanity. Even a baby is tagged and assigned an outfit which grants its gendered entry to the human race immediately it is born. The western stereotype of the 'naked savage' was always a myth; there has never been a culture without adornment, without some modification of the raw material of the body.

The feminist belief that a right-on woman can somehow escape fashion altogether is therefore mistaken, nor is it true that women are uniformly oppressed by a totalitarian dictatorship of fashion. As Kaja Silverman has expressed it:

> The male subject, like the female subject, has no visual status apart from dress and/or adornment . . . Clothing and other kinds of ornamentation make the human body culturally visible . . . clothing draws the body so that it can be culturally seen, and articulates it as a meaningful form . . .
> Even if my sympathies were not fully on the side of extravagant sartorial display, I would feel impelled to stress as strongly as possible that clothing is a necessary condition of subjectivity – that in articulating the body, it simultaneously articulates the psyche. [2]

A further reason for the feminist suspicion of fashionable dress is that it 'objectifies' women and defines them exclusively as sexual objects. It is questionable whether this is the only or even the main purpose of fashionable dress, but it is clearly one component. Today it is not just the clothes themselves but to an even greater extent the photographic representation of fashion and the fashionable body that draw on sexual appeal. Fashion photography has utilised sub-soft porn scenarios, and there is often a kind of 'seduction' in the fashion photography layout.

How does overtly lesbian photography make a difference? It forces us to question our assumption that 'objectification' is always objectionable. It forces us to consider the possibility that anyone who fancies another human being 'objectifies' them, at least momentarily. Is the gaze inherently sadistic? If a (heterosexual) woman admits 'I like men's bottoms', is she metaphorically cutting men up into bits? Is it in the nature of physical desire to distance, reify and create obsessions out of aspects of another person's body? These are questions we should ask.

The representation of gender has been an especially important feature of western dress since the eighteenth century. Gender differences are part of bodily representations in all cultures, and this was true in the West as well. But what was particularly marked in western dress in the late eighteenth century was an intensification of masculinity in the styles that men wore. Under the influence of Beau Brummell and other dandies, men gave up powdered hair, cosmetics, high heels and brightly coloured silks and satins. Henceforth, sobriety of style was the hallmark of the elegant man. Soon, manliness itself came to be associated with sober dress, and by the end of the nineteenth century, flamboyant clothing for men was coded as irredeemably effeminate, and associated with homosexuality. Oscar Wilde's interest in dress reform and aesthetic dress was, in 'the eyes of society at the time, not the least unsavoury aspect of his reputation as it deteriorated in the 1890s from the merely provocative to the absolutely sinister. [3]

In the nineteenth century, any rejection by a woman of traditional feminine attire was equally apt to attract ridicule and disgust. The 'mannish woman' was a phobia of bourgeois Victorian society and many were the *Punch* caricatures of this unlovely creature. By the early twentieth century, male dress for women was clearly associated, at least in France, with lesbianism. Upper-class lesbians, such as 'Missy', woman lover of the writer Colette, wore 'drag' as a badge of sexual identity, despite the rigours of the law, which apparently forbade this. [4] (French women bicyclists, on

the other hand, wore 'rational dress' – breeches – for cycling, more frequently than English women.)

By the Radclyffe Hall period of the 1920s, masculine garb was a clear indication in a woman of a preference for her own sex. [5] Yet mainstream fashion was also extremely boyish – the 'garçonne' look was one of the major fashions of the twenties.

Mainstream fashion certainly continuously changes its own definitions of masculinity and femininity and plays with gender all the time. Throughout the twentieth century the tides of masculinity and femininity have ebbed and flowed in the fashion world. After the Christopher Robin look for women in the 1920s came the sleek sinuosity of the 1930s. The feminist (and possibly lesbian) writer Winifred Holtby viewed this with alarm. She wrote – anticipating more recent debates:

> The post-war fashion for short skirts, bare knees, straight, simple, chemise-like dresses, shorts and pyjamas for sports and summer wear, cropped hair and serviceable shoes is waging a defensive war against [the] powerful movement to reclothe the female form in . . . frills and flounces, to emphasise the difference between men and women. [6]

Before the outbreak of war in 1939, Paris had turned away from the narrow, sloping-shouldered, droopy styles of the thirties. Wide, built-up shoulders and pinched-in waists were introduced in 1938. Although this prefigured Christian Dior's ultra-feminine 'New Look', which was to burst upon the world in 1947, the big shoulders and tighter waists were equally compatible with the military look of the war years. In the USA, the uniforms of the armed forces were designed specifically to appeal to women and to give a smart appearance; they provided a glamorously modified military look. In the USA and Britain, shortages and restrictions dictated that skirts were skimpy. [7] Wartime fashions, therefore,

Coasting – Wheeling from the Pegs.
Photograph by Alice Austen,
undated (Slaten Island Historical Society).

From Comrades In Arms, *directed by Stuart Marshall, 1990. Stills photographer: Sunil Gupta.*

Sabrina Fair [an Audrey Hepburn film] had made a huge impact on us all at college: everyone walked around in black sloppy sweaters, suede low-cut flatties and gold hoop earrings . . . Audrey Hepburn and Givenchy [her Paris designer] were made for each other. His little black dress with shoestring straps in *Sabrina Fair* must have been imprinted on many teenagers' minds forever. [8]

These fashions were not just about youth, they represented youth in rebellion against the conservatism of cultural life in the fifties – in France, the USA and Britain. Lesbian and gay subcultures could not but be influenced by this strange atmosphere of rebellion in the midst of the cold war. In the repressed atmosphere of those times, Princess Margaret broadcast to the British nation, promising not to marry a divorcee, and the official discourse concerning homosexuality was gradually moving it away from its connotations of criminality and treason towards concepts of sickness, neurosis and the medical model.

The butch and femme modes of dress in the 1950s need to be set in this context and are not exactly the same phenomenon as Radclyffe Hall in the 1920s and 1930s. Radclyffe Hall seems to have perceived herself as a member of the 'third sex', an 'invert', influenced by the belief, widespread in the early twentieth century, that homosexuality was an inborn condition. There was much less certainty about this in the 1950s.

By this time, mainstream fashion styles were in any case more various and relaxed, and in order to look truly different, a lesbian had to go to greater lengths to distance herself from them. Before the Second World War, for example, even the most masculine lesbians, such as Radclyffe Hall, wore trousers only on informal occasions – as did daring heterosexual society women; by the 1950s 'slacks' were widely worn; in 1969 they were permitted in the Royal Enclosure at Ascot racecourse.

combined an echo of pre-war Paris with militarism and austerity to produce a style that was slightly masculine yet also at its best both sexy and elegant.

In spite of the exaggerated femininity of the New Look and then of film stars such as Monroe, it was in the 1950s that youth and the youth market began to be taken seriously. The resulting casual look traded on a *gamine* rather than an exaggeratedly feminine appearance. American styles – jeans, Westerns, rock 'n' roll – were important; so was the Paris Left Bank, a look that was popularised in several Hollywood films which starred Audrey Hepburn. Her style in turn influenced Barbara Hulanicki, creator of the important Biba shops in Britain in the 1960s:

For me at this time, a gay identity, although more than tinged with transgression – or for that very reason – offered hope. Edmund White has captured, in *The Beautiful Room is Empty*, the way, at that time, all deviant identities were collapsed into one another, so that bohemianism, left-wing radicalism and homosexuality seemed naturally and inevitably connected. 'Things were simpler, clearer then.'[9] Although the general view might still be that lesbians dressed like men and/or went about in couples as a 'man' and a woman, bohemian dress offered another option:

> I met Maria during my next-to-last year in prep school . . . I see her even now striding along in black pants and a man's white shirt . . . her hair slicked back behind her ears . . . a sailor's pea-coat and no make-up, although her eyebrows have been slightly plucked. She looks very scrubbed . . . but also faintly glamorous; the glamour clings to her like the smell of Gitanes in wool. Is it the hard defiance in her eyes or just the slicked-back hair with its suggestion of the high-school bad girl that lends her this dangerous aura?[10]

By the early 1960s, when I started to frequent the Gateways lesbian club in Chelsea, the two modes, the bohemian and the traditional butch/femme, coexisted but had a distinct class meaning. The more casual bohemian style was associated with the middle-class teachers, journalists and artists whom my lover and I got to know; strict butch/femme styles were working class. Or that is how it seemed. On the other hand, two of the then aspiring writers we knew maintained strictly butch roles in their relationships even if they dressed in the casual leather jacket and jeans style that seemed the height of chic.

What was changing was mainstream fashion itself. In 1964 the Beatles, in Mod suits and little-boy fringes, first hit the charts, and the pop world began to develop a widely-copied androgynous look for men. This made heavily butch styles look simply out of date.

Countercultural and deviant styles – from Teddy boys' drapes to CND duffel coats – were familiar in the 1950s and 1960s. 'Alternative' styles, whether intentionally or not, undermined the way in which early twentieth-century fashion in Britain had expressed in a completely taken-for-granted 'unconscious' way class and gender belonging.

After the Second World War, however, the expansion of bohemianism (and its marketing via films and other media) and the development of working-class youth styles signifying rebellion contributed to a different view of dress and adornment. Unlike the movements to reform dress in the nineteenth century,[11] these new alternative styles had nothing to do with 'the natural' or with comfort; they expressed allegiances and social attitudes.

Bohemianism in the late fifties and androgyny in the sixties represented a rejection of the general conservatism of the first post-1945 decade. For this reason, and because of its association with youth, androgyny was a highly sexualised mode of self-representation in the 1960s. In Paris, the designer Courrèges developed the archetypal sixties' fashions of trouser suits, miniskirts and flat boots. In London Mary Quant, who came from the bohemian 'Chelsea Set' of the fifties, built her style around the beatnik look of black stockings, 'off' colours and simple, rather childish shapes in clothing; the pinafore dress, for example. To me at the time, these up-market ready-to-wear clothes seemed wonderful: they expressed bohemianism and boyishness simultaneously. Biba, whose clothes were cheaper but very trendy, likewise emphasised cropped hair (although very long straight hair was also the height of fashion), a flat, narrow body and a 'natural' look in make-up (although it doesn't look very natural today!). With the emergence of these styles, the lesbian could slip into the mainstream.

In the late 1950s, I was wearing the tight black velvet or Black Watch tartan 'drainpipe' trousers, the flat ballerina shoes and big sweaters of the art schools as an alternative form of dress. By 1966, these styles had modified into high fashion. In 1969 I even started to wear trousers to work (as a social worker). At the time this was certainly frowned on, yet two years later social workers were roaming the inner cities in torn jeans, gym shoes and bra-less t-shirts.

By this time, androgyny had shifted towards styles that were effeminate rather than boyish – the long hair and droopy clothes for both sexes popularised by the hippies. Whether boyish or effeminate, I could no longer easily appear as an 'obvious' lesbian. Indeed, with my long curls, I was sometimes mistaken for a (very) young gay man.

This reworking of gender in 'unisex' style had at the time an erotic charge which is now hard to recapture. Partly this was because it was associated with general social rebellion and sexual radicalism. Partly it was because it messed up gender so much more threateningly than the scrubbed little boy-look of the early Beatles and Quant. Also, androgyny was not then, as it became for the feminism of the 1970s, a denial of difference and desire.

The androgyny of the 1960s has usually been discussed in terms of the feminisation of men. When I look back, though, what I remember is the floridly macho look of long hair with flared trousers, boots, wide-brimmed hats. These made both men and dykes look powerful, not wimpy.

Despite the influence of Christian Lacroix minicrinolines and 'Dallasty' glamour looks, the masculinisation of all fashion has continued into the 1980s. Fashion has promoted a hard, tough image for women, and the fashionable body of today is increasingly a masculine body: muscle vests for both sexes reveal actual muscles, put there by weight training. Female models gel their schoolboy locks and even on occasion wear clothes that appear to have

stepped straight out of Chain Reaction – while some of the outfits seen at Chain Reaction look like the latest fashion.[12] Miniskirts worn with thick black tights and a leather jacket suggest freedom and even aggression rather than passive display. Punk, which gave shaved necks and spiked hair, hard make-up and urban aggro to fashion, the Japanese designers whose influence extended to heavy, muffled styles and black everywhere, and the Italians who popularised masculine tailoring – together they created an eighties fashion image that was really quite lesbian, even S/M. On one occasion *Vogue* used a model dressed in studded leather and a peaked cap to show off a diamond dog collar.

In this context, femininity is more obviously a 'masquerade' than ever; Madonna sleaze (denim skirts with lace frills, heavy 'fifties' lipstick in deepest crimson) creates a different appearance from the Marilyn Monroe image of the 1950s; more camp, a parody, a pastiche. In the 'postmodern' 1980s, countercultural fashions lost a good deal of their power to shock, being rapidly assimilated into media and then high-street culture. To some extent this has always been the fate of alternative dress; but never so quickly as today. Today fashion styles are not taken so seriously as they once were. On the other hand the pastiche and parody of the postmodern sensibility has acted to deprive fashion of its 'naturalisation of the arbitrary'. There is a parody of gender along with everything else. This must inevitably influence the way in which lesbians and gay men can and will represent themselves and inscribe their deviant sexual identity on their bodies. Clothing naturalises gender in the sense that we feel that it is 'natural' for girls to wear pink, just as it is 'natural' for them to be less aggressive than boys. But how can the lesbian or gay male gender be naturalised when it is a challenge to the very notion of a 'natural' sexuality neatly matched to biological sex?

Photographic representations by and of lesbians, and lesbian forms of adornment and self-display, constitute an exploration of the forms that desire may take in a same-sex relationship. When Sheila Jeffreys asserts that all lesbians must eroticise sameness, she pronounces a grotesquely narrow moral code which implies that sex with anyone of a different (how different) age, class or race must always be 'wrong'.[13] This is clone love with a vengeance. It assumes – mistakenly – that two women of the same age, class and race therefore necessarily experience themselves – each other – as 'the same'. Furthermore, in describing heterosexual relations as the 'eroticisation of power differences', Sheila Jeffreys makes a number of assumptions that appear not to be born out by the facts.[14] For her, erotic love premised on differences is never more than, less than or other than the flip side of the coin of cruelty, rape and sexual abuse. If you are turned on by Mills and Boon you will 'learn' to enjoy rape or sexual abuse. Yet from the evidence she discusses in her book *Anticlimax*, it appears that women do not learn to enjoy these experiences. Fantasy is not reality.

In any case, when lesbians explore lesbian desire it is precisely that: an exploration of the power generated by sexual attraction itself. In an erotic encounter two individuals may mutually exert a form of power over each other, and this may be played out in a variety of ways. Lesbians and gay men are bound to be concerned with difference and its effect on sexual desire. We live in a heterosexual culture in which it is taken for granted that sexual desire arises as an effect of the 'natural' difference between the sexes. Lesbian and gay desire challenges this assumption. Yet we are still left with a problem. As I have argued elsewhere, 'it still seems as if heterosexuality sets the parameters of the terms in which lesbians and gay men may be defined and define themselves.'[15] Lesbian spectatorship, lesbian photography and lesbian self-adornment may be seen as an attempt to cross this boundary. The investigation of desire and its construction is likely to start from or at least to include some of the trappings of heterosexual desire, but the lesbian artifice of leather, silk and make-up uses it as the *bricolage* of a dominant culture it challenges by subverting a language we had thought was familiar, but which is now made strange.

The lesbian gaze is a transgressive act.[16] And transgression is the first step towards a new definition and a new boundary.

NOTES

[1] Sabina Lovibond, 'Feminism and Postmodernism' in *New Left Review*, no. 178, November/December, 1989.

[2] Kaja Silverman, 'Fragments of a Fashionable Discourse' in *Studies in Entertainment: Critical Approaches to Mass Culture*, ed. Tania Modelski (Indiana: Indiana University Press, 1986), pp. 145, 147.

[3] Richard Ellmann, *Oscar Wilde* (London: Penguin, 1988).

[4] Elyse Blankley, 'Return to Mytilene: Renée Vivien and the City of Women' in *Women Writers and the City: Essays in Feminist Literary Criticism*, ed. Susan Squier (Knoxville: University of Tennessee Press, 1984); Shari Benstock, *Women of the Left Bank: Paris 1900–40* (London: Virago, 1987).

[5] Katrina Rolley, 'Cutting a Dash: The Dress of Radclyffe Hall and Una Troubridge' in *Feminist Review*, no. 35, Summer 1990.

[6] Winifred Holtby, *Women and a Changing Civilisation* (Chicago: Academy Press, 1978; originally published in 1935).

[7] Elizabeth Ewing, *Women in Uniform* (London: Batsford, 1974); Elizabeth Wilson, *Adorned in Dreams: Fashion and Modernity* (London: Virago, 1985); Elizabeth Wilson and Lou Taylor, *Through the Looking Glass* (London: BBC Books, 1989).

[8] Barbara Hulanicki, *From A to Biba* (London: Hutchinson, 1984), pp. 54, 61.

[9] Edmund White, *The Beautiful Room is Empty* (London: Picador, 1988).

[10] ibid.

[11] Stella Mary Newton, *Health, Art and Reason: Dress Reformers of the Nineteenth Century* (London: John Murray, 1974).

[12] Chain Reaction was a lesbian S/M bar and disco with cabaret events held in South London. It closed in the summer of 1990.

[13] Sheila Jeffreys, *Anticlimax: A Feminist Perspective on the Sexual Revolution* (London: the Women's Press, 1989), p. 301.

[14] ibid., p. 229.

[15] Elizabeth Wilson, 'Chic Thrills' in *Hallucinations* (London: Radius Hutchinson, 1988), p. 55.

[16] Michel Foucault, 'A Preface to Transgression' in *Michel Foucault: Language, Counter Memory, Practice: Selected Essays and Interviews*, ed. Donald F. Bouchard (New York: Cornell University Press, 1977).

CONSPIRACY OF SILENCE

Nina Levitt

. . . lesbianism may be tolerated as an exotic activity but it remains a forbidden identity, and an artist stands to lose both privilege and authority if she is public about lesbian activity. But, when living in a culture in which sexual practices are frozen into identities and these identities then bound within representational stereotypes, it is necessary to restate the obvious when speaking from such a site.[1]

The photographic work *Conspiracy of Silence* (five, 30" × 40" colour prints) appropriates front and back covers of pulp novels from the 1950s and 1960s in order to critique and disrupt a specific genre of cultural depictions of lesbians that serve to uphold heterosexual morals. Embodied in a framework of heterosexual 'normalcy', lesbians are fictionally constructed as 'lonely' yet 'fearful of men'; 'tormented' by our 'warped passions', we are 'savage' and 'incorrigible' because we 'desire the forbidden'. On the one hand, lesbians are sexualised and appropriated for male consumption and fantasy, and on the other hand, socially condemned as sexual deviants and rendered powerless. It is through the authority of the narratives constructed on these bookcovers that women (and men) are offered frozen, patriarchal definitions of female sexuality; yet for many women these novels were one of the few available sources of lesbian representation.

'Inversion' had become a characteristic view of homosexuality in popular culture. Our presence is equated with inherent perversity. My use of the negative (as opposed to a positive print) inverts and alludes through a technical inversion, to this representation of homosexuality. The piece literally makes a negative of the patriarchal representation of the lesbian body.

I photographed existing lesbian pulp novels onto slide film and then printed them on colour photographic paper, and in some cases, I added colour and/or photograms. The effect of the negative and resulting colours adds to this sense of 'otherness'. In two of the images, I incorporated photograms of clothing into the issue of public lesbian identity, echoing the semi-clad lesbians on these particular covers.

The title of the piece refers to the circle of silence that prevents the valorisation of lesbian identity. In turn, this 'conspiracy' is perpetuated by lesbian invisibility, a result of social and self-imposed oppression.

Conspiracy of Silence was first exhibited in *Sight Specific: Lesbians and Representation* (A Space, Toronto, 1987), a landmark Canadian exhibition which sought to 'address the absence of specific lesbian imagery in both the mainstream and alternative communities, issues of representation of difference and the political implications of the absence or presence of images'.[2] Due to the collective courage of the artists in this exhibition, I was able to come out in my work, to an art community that at the time was busy hailing the work of feminist and gay male artists. Much to my delight, this work has since been included in exhibitions and publications outside of a lesbian context, which gives me hope that finally, the silence is beginning to break.

Toronto, 1990

NOTES
[1] Lynne Fernie, *Sight Specific: Lesbians and Representation* (Toronto: A Space, 1988), p. 5.

[2] Press release for the exhibition by Lynne Fernie, curator.

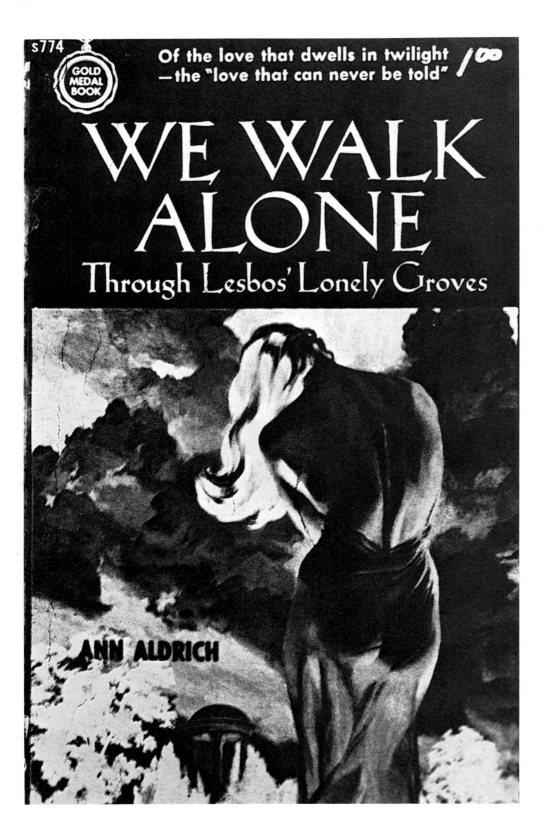

How does a girl know whether or not she is a lesbian?

Probably the question never would have occurred to Mavis Harris if she had not wanted to help Tom, ... the business backing he ... ded to the twisted de- ... ad access to influence

... neglected his wife for ... visiting motels with ... thing Mavis had once ... now had to get from the arti ...

Could ... free herself from Louise's kind of love? C ... he become an incorrigible lesbian? To find out, Mavis would have to throw the other two women at each other, thus releasing Tom for herself ... But did she want to?

THIS FRANK AND UNUSUAL NOVEL TELLS HOW THE SEEDS OF WARPED PASSION SPROUT—HOW THEY ARE NUR- TURED—HOW, SOMETIMES, THEY CAN BE UPROOTED!

ONE SISTER WAS NORMAL, THE OTHER WAS NOT—

Strange Sisters

ROBERT TURNER

They were both indescribably lovely—
yet one wanted a man's love...while
the other craved a woman.

THE SAVAGE NOVEL OF A LESBIAN ON THE LOOSE!

B526F   50¢   K   BEACON SIGNAL

Desire and Torment

swept through Joyce's trembling young body at the gentle touch of Edith's cool hand upon her face. She had never felt like this before. It frightened her ...and filled her with a terrible excitement!

Joyce was eighteen, a freshman at a fashionable school for girls. Suddenly all that mattered to her was a woman twice her age.

A haunting and shocking story of how a young girl's hunger for love made her prey to tormented and forbidden passions. Only a writer as skillful and sensitive as Valerie Taylor could have taken such a daring subject and fashioned it into a stirring novel as WHISPER THEIR LOVE.

THE SAME DIFFERENCE:

ON LESBIAN REPRESENTATION

Martha Gever and
Nathalie Magnan

We've taken as our topic lesbian representation, feminist politics and psychoanalytic theory. These are not necessarily overlapping problems, but they are problems which resonate in the discussion we've had about our work and lives – long before we decided to do this collaboration. We are differently situated in the world: one of us a writer and the editor of a magazine on independent video and film; one of us a photographer and graduate student. We are two friends who have been writing and talking to each other, comparing ideas and asking questions.

This essay will not outline *a* theoretical position, *a* political practice or *a* lesbian aesthetic. We will consider some moments in lesbian history, in feminist history, some questions posed for feminists by lesbians and the politics of representation as framed within feminism and within theories of sexual difference.

We *are* different. Lesbians aren't a coherent type or one variant category of the straight norm. Nor do we represent lesbians.

Representation, however, is central to any public statement concerning lesbians. Stereotypes plague us, as does invisibility. An enormous rift exists between how we are portrayed and portray ourselves as deviant women in patriarchal, heterosexist societies and how we function and represent ourselves within our own subculture. Not that these are independent social systems, nor are lesbian identities free from gender-based definitions and descriptions. This category, which is sexual, is also social, as any lesbian knows. Our caricatured personae and lives become the subject of voyeurism, displayed in order to be exorcised. We encounter hostility; we see lesbians pictured as vampires, witches, predatory beasts, sadists, murderers, lonely spinsters and sexual conquests. These lesbian types function as pictorial codes and narrative agents; we rarely see anything else. While we won't discuss photography as a specific cultural form, what we have to say about feminist theory and lesbians has many implications for feminist photographic criticism and practices.

Of course, the social meanings attached to lesbians and representations of lesbians vary from place to place, from time to time, and our experiences differ immensely. But there can be no doubt that feminism, at least in North America and western Europe, cannot marginalise lesbians.

THE LESBIAN MENACE

In the midst of the period of social upheaval known as 'the Sixties' – remembered by some of us as an important time of political education and by some of us as severely Utopian – women's liberation re-emerged as a political movement. At the same time, the label 'lesbian' also assumed political currency. The dreaded term was invoked by anti-feminists to dismiss what they judged to be unfeminine ideas and political activities, challenging the privileges associated with maleness: lesbians were castrating bitches, aberrant women incapable of accepting their natural function as wives and mothers, or old maids who can't attract a man. The ignominy of lesbianism was powerful enough to put fear into those feminists who largely sought reforms within the existing social order. But the loosening mores of the period also inspired some bravery among lesbians and gay men: the 1969 Stonewall rebellion led to the formation of the gay liberation movement, allied to the civil rights movement, the anti-Vietnam War movement and the more radical segments of the women's liberation movement. Lesbians conscious of their oppression as women and as homosexual outlaws became active in both gay and women's liberation groups, though in many cases they found support in neither.

In the USA, the story of the NOW/Lavender Menace controversy has become legend. In 1969 Rita Mae Brown charged NOW with homophobia. NOW founder Betty Friedan responded by denouncing those who insisted on bringing lesbian rights to the NOW platform, calling them the 'lavender menace,'

and NOW proceeded to systematically purge its lesbian members. The effect of this strategy was not exactly what Friedan intended: a group called Radicalesbians formed and appeared at a major feminist conference in 1970 wearing Lavender Menace t-shirts. They seized – or, as one account reported, liberated – the microphone and read a manifesto titled *The Woman Identified Woman*. Although the Lavender Menace numbered about thirty, that document was reproduced and circulated widely; it introduced a programme for lesbian feminism which deeply influenced the direction of the women's liberation movement, as well as the lives of many lesbians.[1] The Radicalesbians didn't limit their political goals to obtaining civil rights, but advocated a complete commitment of women *to* women in order to overthrow patriarchy. And, as women who loved women, not men, lesbians were upheld as the prototypical revolutionary feminists:

> As the source of self-hate and the lack of real self are rooted in our male-given identity, we must create a new sense of self. As long as we cling to the idea of 'being a woman,' we will sense some conflict with that incipient self, that sense of I, that sense of a whole person. It is very difficult to realise and accept that being 'feminine' and being a whole person are irreconcilable . . . It is the primacy of women relating to women, of women creating a new consciousness of and with each other, which is at the heart of women's liberation, and the basis for the cultural revolution.[2]

Once lesbian feminism had been formulated, feminists had to come to terms with lesbians, and more lesbians became active feminists. But there has been tension ever since. Lesbian separatism – modelled on various nationalist movements, especially Black nationalism – was adopted by some as the practical alternative to patriarchy. Needless to say, straight women weren't welcome. Patronymics were abandoned and new spellings of 'woman' and 'women' were deployed. As a member of the Furies, a Washington-based group, Rita Mae Brown advocated collective organisation as the ideal lesbian, feminist, political and personal form of social organisation.[3] Collectives sprung up, as did lesbian businesses, publications, music festivals and artistic communities. Portraits of lesbians began to circulate, as affirmative actions by and for real, live lesbians. Whether imagined strategically or romantically, women's culture and women's communities were proposed as possible here and now.

The obvious opposite of woman-identified is male-identified, and this epithet entered the lesbian feminist vocabulary. Traditionally, however, many lesbians had either rejected or embraced feminine identity; the lesbian subculture was populated by butches and femmes. But lesbian feminist definitions of lesbianism proclaimed such roles as male-identified. In a 1971 essay, Anne Koedt, author of the influential article 'The Myth of the Vaginal Orgasm', wrote, *All role playing is sick,* be it "simulated" or "authentic" according to society's terms.'[4] On the front line of the attack on gender roles, lesbian feminists should be neither butch nor femme, but something else.

We admit that this chronology is somewhat simplistic. What should be emphasised is that radical feminist and lesbian feminist analyses of sexual politics have irreversibly altered concepts of social behaviour and of sexuality. Coming out after 1970 was made less difficult, less painful due to the gay and women's liberation movements. We no longer must accept our sexual desires as pathological. But, as many of us have learned, sexual politics and gender identity are extremely complex constructs that resist simple corrective measures. In the cultural realm, for instance, replacing sexist stereotypes with 'positive images' or admitting more women artists to the art world has left most sectors of patriarchal and capitalist ideology untouched. We are not

prepared to indict the Radicalesbians, lesbian separatists and other 'women identified women' as insidious reactionaries, as some have proposed in recent years. However, we do not accept political analyses based on idealised female identity as theoretically sound or sufficient explanations of sexual differences.

VOCABULARY

The notion of sexuality as we understand it today is fairly recent. It was constructed by male scientists such as Charcot, Freud, Ellis, Krafft-Ebing and Hirschfield at the end of the last century.[5] As suggested by Foucault, the rules of the game between power and pleasure had changed, and the concept of perversion became established.[6] This new consciousness generated a norm with its opposite, a difference. When the medical discourse normalised difference, modern homosexuality became possible. Lesbians encode their own social position verbally, visually and gesturally. Thus, there are two realities, medical and lesbian, that barely coincide. Some recognisable signs are shared but an opposition exists between the hegemonic and the perverse, the dominant and the deviant within a shared social territory.

Naming is not neutral: it establishes categories, a hierarchy, a place for the lesbian within the social order. Names carry moral judgements. In the medical definition of the word 'lesbian' the *inversion* of desire is central. (Around the turn of the century, lesbians were actually called 'inverts'.) This should be seen as one attempt by the medical institution to control what has obviously escaped them. Science defines lesbian desire in terms of pathological deviation.

The notion of perversion leads to the term 'queer', defined by Webster as:

> differing from what is usual, ordinary, odd, singular, strange, slightly ill, giddy, doubtful, suspicious. Having mental quirks, eccentric, not genuine, counterfeit [and, at last] homosexual.

This terminology applied to homosexuality relegates the term 'queer' to negativity, as opposed to normality. In this relationship, the counterfeit Other only reinforces. But gay men and lesbians sometimes manage to construct subcultures that present a resistance to neat notions of normality instead of accepting the negativity of deviance.

The second type of words applied to gay women are exotic – 'lesbian' and 'sapphic'. Lesbians come from Lesbos, Sappho's island, situated in faraway Greece. This reference encourages multiple geo-historical projections. The exotic names connote antique times, enormous distances and long-past Utopias. Some lesbians even attempt to bridge this distance. As an adjective, 'sapphic' is one attribute among others, referring both to the exotic and the aesthetic. Since Sappho was an acclaimed poet, 'sapphic' often connotes a soft version of lesbianism. A light marking of sexual preference becomes a sign of good taste.

These meanings bring the 'lesbian' into an abstract, romantic territory – as a poetic artifact – which saves the word 'lesbian' from total social damnation. It is hardly coincidental that lesbians resurface in the literature of Romanticism and the attendant interest in Orientalism, most notably in Baudelaire and Courbet. The words 'sapphic' and 'lesbian' reappeared in the middle of the nineteenth century after four centuries of oblivion, replacing the mechanical words 'fricatrices' and 'tribades' (both share the common derivation meaning to rub). This exoticism, with its suggestion of artiness, still haunts concepts of lesbianism. Is this the reason why 'lesbian' is used by some as the least offensive of our names?

In the English-speaking world in the latter decades of the twentieth century 'lesbian' is the word that most lesbians have to take on in order to name their social/sexual position. This word appears and becomes meaningful in the lesbian's self-referential vocabulary during the coming-out process. In other words, the identity of a woman who loves women parallels a linguistic history from deviant to lesbian, from shame to affirmation to proclamation, in that order and all at once.

Another exotic but more aggressive name regularly associated with 'lesbian' is 'amazon'. Monique Wittig and Sande Zeig provide a fictitious origin to this term in their splendid dictionary, *Lesbian Peoples*:

> Amazon: In the beginning, if there ever was such a time, all the companion lovers called themselves Amazons . . . Then with the settlement of the first cities, many companion lovers disrupted the original harmony and called themselves mothers. Thereafter, amazon meant for them daughter, eternal child, she who does not assume her destiny. Amazons were banished from the cities of mothers.[7]

In lesbian subcultures, historical references have value since they construct a historical destiny.[8] Wittig and Zeig, though, contest and thus destabilise 'lesbian' as a concept. More conventional efforts have been made towards an empirical historical account of lesbianism, such as Lillian Faderman's book, *Surpassing the Love of Men*.[9] However, the practice of systematic erasure of lesbian texts and images guarantees immense gaps in the reconstruction of any heritage while abetting the inflation of mythic key moments like the revival of goddess cults. On the other hand, establishing a valid historical past can allow the projections of a continuous and homogeneous social and personal identity.

But language depends on who speaks. This is exemplified by varying uses of the word 'dyke'. In the *Roget's Thesaurus* we have 'dyke' or 'bull dyke', both of which are derogatory. But in *Lesbian Peoples* the connotations are more subtly established:

> If you're poor/then you're a dyke/if you're rich/you're sapphic//but if you're neither one, or the other/a lesbian a

lesbian is what you'll have to be/If
you're strong/then you're a dyke and if
you're weak/you're sapphic//but if you're
neither one or the other//a lesbian, a
lesbian is what you'll have to be.

Clearly, the language depicting lesbians is never objective or stable.

Nor within lesbian subcultures are voices united. Differentiation within 'lesbianisms' might subvert the notion of perversion. Heterogeneity should be acknowledged. We do not have to understand our sexuality within the boundaries marked by medical or legal or religious institutions. While these institutions control the social order, our sexuality cannot be regulated.

Words alone don't describe the cultural boundaries experienced and to some degree maintained by lesbians. One way of neutralising the supposedly dangerous deviation from the heterosexual ideal is representing lesbians as heterosexual mimics, which is reminiscent of the old strategy of inversion. Perhaps assigning a familiar gender position calms the anxieties provoked by physical similarity in sexual relationships. Isn't the anxiety of 'no man' based on the failure of biology to explain the lesbian attraction? Biology legislates sexual difference by the naturalness and the unnaturalness of roles and sexual preference.

Clothing is a metaphor for gender identity. Traditionally, trousers and masculinity – as in the question, 'Who wears the pants?' – were synonymous. But since the sixties, western dress has become more and more unisex. In a bourgeois society that marginalises feminist demands, one possibility for public rebellion is what one can buy: the costume. Mode of dress has been a contested tactic in sexual politics, as with the androgynous 'new woman' who appears at the turn of the century.[10] In the 1950s, a sign of resistance to the reconfirmation of the heterosexual ideology – a resistance that based itself on the memories of the Second World War where women's primary social identity was not based only on reproduction but also on production – was the act of wearing pants. Does the androgynous fashion of the early 1980s signify the integration of feminism into the normative social order? In symbolic terms, the equal rights movement was redefined by some as a right to wear men's clothes, but it is noteworthy that androgynous fashion always tends toward male dress conventions. This is hardly surprising, since clothes often imply power, or at least the *appearance* of power.

So butch dress became socially acceptable. Yet with 'real' butch the body is present, the play is for real. In sexual relationships the power is encoded through clothing. Blatant cross-dressing as a social phenomenon appeared in western society around the turn of the century. Thus, the 'manish lesbian' surfaced when lesbianism was medically declared deviant. Rich women were able to be flamboyant – some members of Natalie Barney's circle in Paris for example – without having their existence endangered by their erotic choice. And again in the 1950s, the only recognised lesbian was the mannish one. Socially, there are few representations of the 'femme' part of the story. Although many feminists declared butch-femme roles regressive, the late 1970s saw the arrival of outrageous and organised S/M lesbians who celebrated overt power.

Some of us might want to consider a sexuality not defined by the dichotomy male/female. Some of us might want to consider a sexuality that could take into account a constant negotiation for power. This understanding of sexuality subverts systematic encoding.

It is different.

THE SAME DIFFERENCE

We've leapt from gender and sexual politics to gender and social codes – especially language – and its correlate, silence. We've tried to disturb the silence, to introduce women who contradict neat gender and sexual dichotomies. Here we meet up with psychoanalytic theory, as employed to explain the different positions of male and female subjects within patriarchy and to explain sexuality in representation. This direction is not arbitrary; we're talking about feminist cultural and theoretical strategies that renounce much feminist art and the surrounding feminist theories prevalent in the early and mid-1970s: the articulation of female identity, feminine sensibility, woman-identified imagery.

A woman's discovering or revealing her natural, biologically-based identity – her feminine essence – has been called essentialist. Those feminists who took this route, it's been said, fell into a trap laid by patriarchal ideology, which naturalises sexual difference rather than analysing difference as a function of representational systems. To a degree, this evaluation is apt if applied to work with specific feminine iconography: Judy Chicago's or Tee Corinne's cunt/flowers, Barbara Hammer's women-as/in-nature movies, or Mary Beth Edelson's shamanistic photo cycles, for example. Still, much feminist culture of the past decade – including literature, music and performance as well as visual art, film and video – asserts varieties of female experience rather than feminine nature. These efforts have also been faulted because, according to feminist psychoanalytic thought, difference isn't represented; it abides in representation itself. Thus the need for a 'politics of representation'.

Also suspect in art circles is much feminist historical research and writing as well as sociological studies about women. [11] According to Kate Linker, writing on 'Representation and Sexuality':

> . . . equal rights or gender equity strategies . . . based in the elimination of discrimination and in equal access to institutional power, in no way attempt to account for the ideological structures of which discrimination is but a symptom . . . They leave untouched the integrated value system (of patriarchal ideology) through which feminine oppression is enacted. And it is with the aim of understanding the construction of sexed subjectivity so as to disarm the positioning of the phallocentric order that artists have turned to psychoanalysis. [12]

Which artists? Well, certainly those Linker included in the exhibit *Difference: On Representation and Sexuality* at the New Museum (Winter, 1985) among them Mary Kelly, Barbara Kruger, Sherrie Levine, Judith Barry, Victor Burgin, Max Almy, Dara Birnbaum, Sylvia Kolbowski. [13] Representation here was framed as reproduction – of ideology and images. Two notable sexual differences not represented were female and male homosexuality. This absence, of course, is not exceptional: in the proliferating texts on psychoanalysis and feminism, difference is decidedly singular – masculine or feminine – the same difference.

Keeping in mind that the foundations of psychoanalytic critiques of representation are derived from Freud, who theorised lesbians as women who reject femininity, assuming masculine identification instead, [14] and Lacan, who theorised lesbians as women who refuse to recognise castration, [15] we encounter a theoretical crossroads. Should we interrogate what seems to be a theoretical inadequacy from inside or outside the theory? Can the 'politics of the unconscious', in Peter Wollen's words, be a feminist politics that admits lesbians? [16] (After seeing Wollen and Laura Mulvey's videotape, *The Bad Sister*, we'd say no.) And what about politics? Can we ignore this interpretation of feminism, without which, it's said, we cannot understand our oppression, without which feminism – including feminist artistic practices – can only address symptoms?

Psychoanalytic descriptions of patriarchy – following from Lacan – propose sexual identity – masculine or feminine – as the primary social division. And this division forms the basis of a system of signification, including all representation, and language in particular. The central instance of differentiation – of division – which allows each subject's entry into the symbolic order which underlies society occurs when the child recognises the mother's lack of a penis. One has one or one hasn't. This basic division determines sexual positioning and results directly from Freud's castration complex: one either risks castration or one is castrated.

Now, Juliet Mitchell and Jacqueline Rose, the British feminist editors of Lacan's writings on feminine sexuality, agree that this division is not identical with anatomy – not a biological difference. But phallic lack is the characteristic of femininity; in other words, a negative position. Lacan said, 'Woman does not exist,' Mitchell writes, 'the girl will desire to have the phallus and the boy will struggle to represent it'.[17] Mitchell takes care to point out that no individual actually has the phallus, since the phallus is a psychic construct. But various feminists, among them Mary Ann Doane, Teresa de Lauretis and Jane Gallop, have problematised the confusion between phallus and penis. Strict Lacanian feminists assert that this is a confusion; no human individual really possesses the phallus: this is a masculine mystique, a masculine conceit.[18] But this confusion isn't coincidental: the phallus wields power and so do men.

In the psychic economy described by Lacan and his followers, the unconscious is structured like a language. Desire resides in the unconscious; the unconscious is governed by repressions of key events associated with the subject's entry into the symbolic order – separation from the mother and the castration complex; the child's demand for love can never be satisfied; unsatisfied demand is desire; the phallus, which is missing, is the object of desire; the phallus is the measure of desire. All desire is masculine, while femininity is constructed on not having – absence, lack, negativity. Thus feminine identification is a masquerade, a mask shaped by masculine desire. Who looks? Who's looked at? Voyeurism is domination. This logic, then, positions the woman outside language, outside desire, outside the symbolic order, leading some concerned with the question of feminine sexuality and representations of women into the black hole that is femininity.

Artists and critics who take this direction have arrived at various conclusions about what artistic practice is required: counterlanguage, women assuming the phallus critically so as to erode its power;[19] unmasking patriarchal structures supporting oppression;[20] giving voice to the repressed maternal;[21] acknowledging feminine masquerade;[22] a radical heterosexuality, an other bisexuality.[23] The feminist cultural project, then, becomes aligned with elaborations of feminine sexuality. That's what's meant by the 'politics of the unconscious.'

The contradiction in the psychoanalytic explanation of sexual difference that assigns woman to a purely negative position is, as Mary Ann Doane put it, that 'She *can* speak.' What we need, she writes, are 'theories which attempt to define or construct a feminine specificity (not essence) . . . which work to provide woman with an autonomous symbolic representation'.[24] But even though natural femininity has been debunked and the hopelessness of making representations of women has been challenged, in this system feminism remains tied to femininity. Heterosexual difference remains the only sexual difference – and the basis for all social difference. To quote Jacqueline Rose paraphrasing Lacan: 'individuals must line up according to an opposition (having or not having the phallus)'.[25]

As we said, we will not leave the authority of Lacanian psychoanalytic theories on sexual difference unquestioned. Here we will cite Monique Wittig's provocative and pertinent essay, 'The Straight Mind.'

> The discourses which particularly oppress all of us, lesbians, women and homosexual men, are those discourses which take for granted that what founds society, any society, is heterosexuality. These discourses speak about us and claim to say the truth in an apolitical field . . . as if, in what concerns us, politically insignificant signs could exist . . . The concept of difference has nothing ontological about it. It is only the way that the masters interpret a historical situation of domination. The function of difference is to mask at every level the conflicts of interest, including ideological ones.[26]

For all dominated peoples – the Others, the different ones – an analysis of power that is experienced economically, politically, as well as psychologically, must be incorporated in any analysis of social relations. For women, lesbians and homosexual men, difference is not a neutral concept. Can we overcome psychological oppression and exploitation without confronting institutionalised power – for instance, the institution of psychological 'treatment'? Is ideology generated by inherent, ahistorical, immutable psychic processes alone? If so, in the Lacanian scheme, patriarchy cannot be subverted, deconstructed or in any way undone. The phallus remains primal and primary. Patriarchy, as defined within Lacanian theory, is monolithic, unchanging from culture to culture, without a history. This ignores women acting as historical subjects, as participants in social struggles.

What political action can be taken to realise a politics of the unconscious? Can this attempt to bring art into feminist political struggle avoid replicating the fate of earlier avant-garde art movements? Will these representational strategies, too, become subversive moves divorced from political discourse, eventually subsumed by dominant art discourse? Do ruptures in the symbolic order – deconstruction of media images, for instance – disrupt mechanisms of power? Is simply unhinging gender positions, bisexuality, the most radical goal for feminist artists? For feminism?

Lacanian theory or a practice based on this theory cannot account for lesbian sexuality outside femininity, but lesbian experience tells otherwise. Lesbian experience and lesbian critiques of heterosexuality, along with critiques of heterosexual categories, troubles the essence of femininity far more than bisexuality can. Throughout psychoanalytic literature, the basic question recurs: 'What does woman want?' Wittig comments:

> What is woman? Panic, general alarm for an active defence. Frankly, it is a problem that the lesbians do not have, because of a change of perspective, and it would be incorrect to say that lesbians associate, make love, live with women, for 'woman' has meaning only in heterosexual systems of thought and heterosexual economies. Lesbians are not women.[27]

Lesbians find ourselves outside heterosexual systems, placed there by history and, sometimes, by choice. Yet, we should add, lesbians do not live on an isolated island. We often mingle in the heterosexual world. Indeed, there is no escape. We rejoin women – we are women – when we participate on many fronts of feminist struggle. But in the particular struggle against the institution of heterosexuality – representations, ideology and all – lesbians are not women.[28]

NOTES
[1] Anne Koedt, 'Lesbianism and Feminism' in *Radical Feminism*, ed. Ann Koedt, Ellen Levine, Anita Rapone

(New York: Quadrangle Books, 1973); Ann Snitow, Christine Stansell, Sharon Thomson, eds, *Powers of Desire: The Politics of Sexuality* (New York: Monthly Review Press, 1983).

2 Koedt, op. cit.

3 Nancy Myron and Charlotte Bunch, eds. *Lesbianism and the Women's Movement* (Baltimore: Diana Press, 1975).

4 Koedt, op. cit.

5 Ann Ferguson, Jacquelyn N. Zita, Kathryn Pyne Addelson, 'On ''Compulsory Heterosexuality and Lesbian Existence'': Defining the Issues' in *Feminist Theory: A Critique of Ideology*, ed. Nannerl O. Keohane, Michelle Z. Rosaldo, Barbara C. Gelpi (Chicago: University of Chicago Press, 1982).

6 Michel Foucault, *The History of Sexuality, Volume I: An Introduction* (London: Penguin, 1984).

7 Monique Wittig and Sande Zeig, *Lesbian Peoples: Materials for a Dictionary* (New York: Avon, 1979).

8 Adrienne Rich, 'Compulsory Heterosexuality and Lesbian Existence' in *SIGNS*, Summer 1980; Ferguson, op. cit.

9 Lillian Faderman, *Surpassing the Love of Men: Romantic Friendship and Love Between Women from the Renaissance to the Present* (London: The Women's Press, 1985).

10 Carroll Smith-Rosenberg, *Disorderly Conduct: Vision of Gender in Victorian America* (New York: Knopf, 1985).

11 Ruby B. Rich, 'Cinefeminism and its Discontents' in *American Film,* December 1983.

12 Kate Linker, 'Representation and Sexuality' in *Parachute,* September/October/November 1983.

13 Kate Linker, *Difference: On Representation and Sexuality* catalogue, New Museum of Contemporary Art (New York: The New Museum of Contemporary Art, 1985).

14 Juliet Mitchell, *Women: The Longest Revolution* (London: Virago, 1984).

15 Juliet Mitchell and Jacqueline Rose, eds, *Feminine Sexuality: Jacques Lacan and the Ecole Freudienne* (New York: W.W. Norton, 1982).

16 Wanda Bershen, 'Scenes of the Crime: An Interview with Peter Wollen' in *Afterimage*, February 1985.

17 Mitchell, *Women: The Longest Revolution.*

18 ibid.

19 Annette Kuhn, *Women's Pictures: Feminism and Cinema* (London and New York: Pandora Press, 1990).

20 Linker, 'Representation and Sexuality'.

21 E. Ann Kaplan, *Women and Film: Both Sides of the Camera* (London and New York: Methuen, 1983); Mary Kelly, *Post-Partum Document* (London: Routledge, 1983).

22 Sylvia Kolbowski, 'Representation's Reproduction' in *Wedge*, Winter 1984.

23 Jane Gallop, *The Daughter's Seduction: Feminism and Psychoanalysis* (New York: Cornell University Press, 1982).

24 Mary Ann Doane, 'Women's Stake: Filming the Female Body' in *October*, Summer 1981.

25 Mitchell and Rose, *Feminine Sexuality*.

26 Monique Wittig, 'The Straight Mind' in *Feminist Issues*, Summer 1980.

27 Wittig, ibid.

28 This paper was originally delivered as part of the Women's Caucus programme at the 1985 National Society for Photographic Education Conference in Minneapolis. It was first published in *Exposure*, vol. 24, no. 2, Summer 1986.

CELESTIAL BODIES

Jean Fraser

'This Sister Benedetta, then, for two continuous years, at least three times a week, in the evening after disrobing and going to bed would wait for her companion to disrobe, and pretending to need her, would call. When Bartolomea would come over, Benedetta would grab her by the arm and throw her by force on the bed. Embracing her, she would put her under herself and kissing her as if she were a man, she would speak words of love to her. And she would stir on top of her so much that both of them corrupted themselves. And thus by force she held her sometimes one, sometimes two, and sometimes three hours . . . to entice her and deceive her further, Benedetta would tell her that neither she nor Benedetta were sinning because it was the Angel Splenditello and not she that did these things . . .'

Testimony of Sister Bartolomea Crivelli against Sister Benedetta Carlini c.1623. [1]

But Ruth clave unto her . . . And Ruth said, Entreat me not to leave thee, or to return from following after thee: for whither thou goest, I will go; and where thou lodgest, I will lodge: thy people shall be my people, and thy God my god: where thou diest, will I die, and there will I be buried: the Lord do so to me, and more also, if aught but death part thee and me.

Holy Bible, Book of Ruth, verses 14 to 18.

Eager to enter religious life, most of us blissfully embraced our new family when we were safely behind the novitiate walls. The initial joy beyond belief of finding ourselves gathered into a family of loving and generous, beautiful and brilliant women often contributed to our first and major trial: constant struggle against particular friendship. Many of us mention discovering the taboo against p.f.'s as we and our peers called them, by unwittingly violating it. Our superiors described particular friendships as exclusive intimacy with another sister, drawing us away from total dedication to God and community. Ideally we were expected to love all of our sisters equally . . . As a safeguard we were advised to recreate in groups of three or more and with as many different sisters as possible. Although our superiors did not state that particular friendships left unchecked might become Lesbian love affairs, the official caveats were so cloaked with an aura of forbidden, dangerous, and vague evil that we feared them as serious violations of the religious rule and probable grounds for dismissal.

Rosemary Keefe Curb (formerly Sister Mary Geralda). [2]

The bells ring out on the damp sea air. It is Sunday morning. The nuns will walk along the cliff path from the convent, singly and in two's. The convent was a castle a long time ago. It is surrounded by a high stone wall, from where nuns had leapt with broken hearts, they said. It clings to the cliff and dominates the prom with an ineluctable silence. I cannot enter it. It is an ancient place where rituals unfold in holy tongues, tongues I have never been taught.

One early summer evening you hand me something in a white bag. 'Put it on. It will suit you.' You stand tall in the doorway, your hip tilted, a dry, cynical smile pulling the corners of your mouth, testing me. I take off my rings, leaving faint white circles on the skin. I remove my jeans and shirt. 'Help me,' I say quietly. You come behind me and fasten the strings, hook the eyes. You tell me to wipe off my lipstick and pass me a tissue. Then, as arranged, I go out into the street. You follow five steps behind.

The habit drops from my neck like a cape, effacing the curves of my body. I sin as I walk. I think about my nipples being grazed by the rough cotton. Leicester Square parts like the Red Sea. I float guiltlessly among them as voices fall, eyes are averted and apologetic.

My face is serene. I am purged of perversity. The wimple pulls tightly across my forehead. The constraint gives me pleasure, makes me graceful.

You follow, invisible, five steps behind. Your eyes are burning into my back, my broad shoulders, the place where my ass moves under the habit. You are watching their faces. I wonder if you are as wet as I am, and if, later, you will make me sit down on the edge of our bed, lift the layers and lick my inner thighs . . .

Forbidden Grace, **Cherry Smyth.** [3]

If . . . a nun should be in the slightest degree remiss, [the Mother Superior] sends for her, treats her harshly, orders her to undress and give herself twenty strokes with the scourge. The nun obeys, takes off her clothes, takes up the scourge and chastises herself, but scarcely has she given herself one or two strokes than the Superior comes over all compassionate, snatches the instrument of penitence away from her, bursts into tears and says how dreadful it is for her to have to punish anybody, kisses the nun on the forehead, eyes, mouth and shoulders, caresses and flatters her: 'But what a soft, white skin she has! such a lovely figure! lovely neck and hair! Sister Sainte-Augustine, you really are silly to be so bashful, slip off your chemise, I am a woman, dear, and your Superior. Oh what a beautiful bosom! And so firm! And could I let it be torn by spikes? No, no, nothing of the kind' . . .

The Nun, **Denis Diderot, 1760.** [4]

A car pulls up, Mother Ethel steps out – a vision in black habit and wrinkled wimple, adorned with a collection of gay liberation badges, a silver whistle and a pair of nipple clamps.

'Our mission,' [he says], 'is the promulgation of universal joy and the expiation of stigmatic guilt . . . the guilt attached to labels like ''homosexual''. It is often what prevents people from coming out . . . it isn't the fear of other people's immediate reactions that frightens them so much as the fear of living long-term with the label ''gay'' . . . Stigmatic guilt is something the Church and other social institutions have used to keep people in line. It isn't meant to stop their behaviour, but to control it. When you speak to a right wing fascist, especially those in the Church, you find that they don't actually expect their laws to stop people from having sex. What they want to do is stop the legitimisation of it . . . We've taken the dingo as our totem, because it's the most stigmatized animal in Australia.'

Paul Burston interviews Mother Ethel-Dreads-a-Flashback, Sydney Order of the Sisters of Perpetual Indulgence. [5]

'Ah Sister Suzanne, you don't love me!'
   'I don't love you, dear Mother?'
   'No.'
   'Tell me what I must do to prove it to you.'
   'That you will have to guess.'
   'I am trying, but I cannot think of anything.'
   By now she had raised her collar and put one of my hands on her bosom. She fell silent, and so did I. She seemed to be experiencing the most exquisite pleasure. She invited me to kiss her forehead, cheeks, eyes and mouth, and I obeyed. I don't think there was any harm in that, but her pleasure increased, and as I was only too glad to add to her happiness in any innocent way, I kissed her again on forehead, cheeks, eyes and lips . . . and she gasped as she urged me in a strange, low voice to redouble my caresses, which I did. Eventually a moment came, whether of pleasure or of pain I cannot say, when she went as pale as death, closed her eyes, and her whole body tautened violently, her lips were first pressed together and moistened with a sort of foam, then they parted and she seemed to expire with a deep sigh. I jumped up, thinking she had fainted, and was about to go and call for help. She half opened her eyes and said in a failing voice: 'You innocent girl! It isn't anything. What are you doing? Stop . . .'

The Nun, **Denis Diderot, 1760.** [6]

When I was young I loved a man . . . and I had shown I loved him. I had to get away . . . It was a strange way of bringing me in but God works in strange ways. I had work to do and I had the life. No-one on the outside can possibly know what that means . . . I had forgotten everything until I came here . . . I've been drifting and dreaming and now I seem to be living through the struggle and the bitterness again . . . I couldn't stop the wind from blowing and the air from

being clear as crystal and I couldn't hide the mountains.
Sister Clodagh in *Black Narcissus*. [7]

Michael's mother was out of breath by the time they reached Union. 'I've never seen a street like that in my life, Mikey!'

He squeezed her arm, taking sudden pleasure in her innocence. 'It's an amazing city, Mama.'

Almost on cue, the nuns appeared.

'Herb, look!'

'Goddamnit, Alice! Don't point!'

'Herb . . . they're on roller skates.'

'Goddamn if they aren't! Mike, what the hell . . .?'

Before their son could answer, the six white-coifed figures had rounded the corner as a unit, rocketing in the direction of the revelry on Polk Street.

One of them bellowed at Michael.

'Hey, Tolliver!'

Michael waved half-heartedly.

The nun gave a high sign, blew a kiss, then shouted: '*Loved* your jockey shorts!'

(Michael shows his middle-American parents round San Francisco) *Tales of the City*, Armistead Maupin. [8]

NOTES

[1] Judith C. Brown, *Immodest Acts: The Life of a Lesbian Nun in Renaissance Italy* (Oxford and New York: Oxford University Press, 1986), p. 117.

[2] Rosemary Keefe Curb, 'What is a Lesbian Nun?' in *Breaking Silence: Lesbian Nuns on Convent Sexuality*, ed. Rosemary Curb and Nancy Manahan (London: Columbus Books, Florida: Niaid Press), p. xxvii.

[3] *Forbidden Grace* is a work currently in progress (1990).

[4] Denis Diderot, *The Nun* (1760) (London: Penguin, 1974), p. 122.

[5] 'Entertaining Mother Ethel', interview by Paul Burston in *Capital Gay*, 17 August 1990.

[6] Diderot, op. cit., p. 137.

[7] *Black Narcissus*, directed by Michael Powell and Emeric Pressburger, 1947.

[8] Armistead Maupin, *Tales of the City* (San Francisco: Chronicle Publishing Company, 1978), p. 193.

ACKNOWLEDGEMENTS
Models: Jo Buxton, Nasreen Memon and Cherry Smyth – many thanks. And special thanks to Cherry Smyth for ideas and feedback.

TRANSGRESSION

DEVOTION

SUBLIMATION

SANCTITY

BLASPHEMY

COMMUNION

PROFANITY

REVERENCE

REVELATION

CHASTITY

SACRILEGE

ABSOLUTION

DEAR SHIRLEY

Hinda Schuman

Dear Shirley,
I've gone from a married woman to a sexual minority in one
embrace.
Love, Hinda

Dear Shirley,

At work those who know that I am a lesbian seem to imagine that
my life is a series of wild parties and strange doings.

Those who think that I am single imagine my nights at the bars,
full of strange doings and wild parties.

Love, Hinda

Dear Shirley,
How come you stopped writing?
Why do I suddenly feel so isolated?
Why is my life a whisper when I'm feeling so happy?
Love, Hinda

Dear Diary,

My friend Shirley just freaked out.

All my letters are coming back 'return to sender'. Now that I have another woman instead of another man, she seems to think that I will start to make weird noises and cause her sink to clog. I miss my best friend.

I do not understand this.

Love, Hinda

Dear Diary,
Being a lesbian is like being rich. You're never sure if people stay
away from you because you are; or if they move closer because it's
(politically) correct.
Love, Hinda

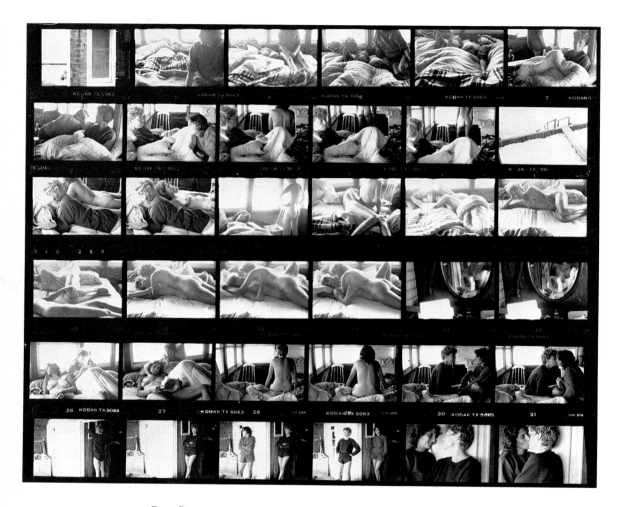

Dear Diary,

Some lesbians assume that because I am, that I believe what they believe, vote as they vote, read what they read, wear what they wear, and want what they want.

Sometimes this is true. Sometimes it is not.

Love, Hinda

18   ALICE IN WONDERLAND

"I wish I hadn't cried so much!" said Alice, as she swam about, trying to find her way out. "I shall be punished for it now, I suppose, by being drowned in my own tears! That *will* be a queer thing, to be sure! However, everything is queer today."

Just then she heard something splashing about in the pool a little way off, and she swam nearer to make out what it was; at first she thought it must be a walrus or hippopotamus, but then she remembered how small she was now, and she soon made out that it was only a mouse, that had slipped in like herself.

'DON'T SAY CHEESE SAY LESBIAN'[1]

Rosy Martin

CONTEXT – THE FAMILY ALBUM

Be it a leatherbound book or a rag-bag of undated, unsorted pictures in a shoe box, most families keep an album, which is a key part of the 'unconscious' myth of the 'happy family'. Photos of weddings, new babies, holidays and celebrations abound; well, photography is even more popular than home decorating and Do-It-Yourself as a 'leisure' pursuit, and shares with them a desire to gloss up the surface of things – a wallpapering over the cracks, divisions and discontents that always threaten to erupt.

Photos are too easily read as evidence. The acts of construction, framing and editing slip from memory: 'Move over there a bit, put your arm around . . . smile!' The conventions of picture-making that we absorb through popular culture, magazines, advertisements and television are also occluded, as is the question of 'who took the picture', for what reason and in what context. Viewing the 'family album' often activates a response of nostalgia – the return 'home' to an idealised golden past, an imaginative past, free of conflict, where everyone had a place, everyone knew their place and 'reality' was 'real'.

Mothers most often take on the role of the archivists and guardians of the family history. They use their editorial power to validate their own good mothering and to deny that which they don't want to accept – and this leads to structured absences. The family album represents the ultimate 'pretended family relationship'.[2] Notions of 'normalcy' are privileged, and a kind of overarching, happy heterosexuality is enshrined in this document, which leaves no room for a representation of the complex, varied, struggling, contesting, power-contained group that makes up 'the family'.

The institutions of photography – from the multi-national corporations such as Kodak and Fuji, to the High Street chemists – are linked to recycle notions of what constitutes a 'good' photograph, within a narrow range of criteria that reproduce the dominant cultural, sexual and ideological systems of society:

> Photographs are no more, and no less, than fragments of ideology, activated by the mechanisms of fantasy and desire within a fragmentary history of images.[3]

Whilst the very popularity of photography – half of the adult population in Britain own a camera – and the relative cheapness of the high technology available, could enable the practice to be a democratising activity, it is still packaged around notions of the audience which are prescriptive and gender specific. The technical, amateur market talks, in advertisements and magazines, to a presumed male audience in terms of 'quality, precision, excellence, mastery, control and creative self-expression'. 'Snap-shooters', however, are presumed to be female; advertisements which target this market stress notions of passivity and the lack of skills: 'fool-proof, anxiety removed, the camera makes decisions for you, forget the technology, just enjoy it'. This echoes the advertisement which accompanied the invention of the Kodak camera in 1888: 'you press the button, we do the rest'.

In the face of this ideological onslaught, how can we re-view these fragments, these scraps of fading yet oh so precious paper, so loaded with significance for us as individuals, so repetitive when viewed *en masse* as 'social documents', so slippery in meaning that they now can be extracted and recycled as part of the 'Heritage Industry'.[4]

Starting with existing family album pictures, working with a sympathetic listener, it is possible to expand the reading and to unmask memories. However, the agenda is set by the context, degree of trust and the goals envisaged. The project for an oral historian is to retrieve and record a dissenting history *vis-à-vis* class, race, gender and sexuality.[5] Within a therapeutic context, in which feelings, previously blocked or repressed, are the focus, it is possible to use these pictures as keys to the unconscious. Since the early 1970s, in North America, photographs have been used in

therapy in various ways.[6] When we look at photographs we actively create meanings from what is perceived, hence a skilled therapist can use photographs as tools, in working with clients, to encourage and support those clients' own insights into their lives.

IDENTITY AND NOTIONS OF THE SELF

> The self is a text – it has to be deciphered . . . The self is a project, something to be built.[7]

We are not born into the world as a little 'self' which grows to form the adult subject, instead:

> We become who we are only through our encounter, while growing up, with the multitude of representations of what we may become – the various positions that society allocates to us. There is no essential self which precedes the social construction of the self through the agency of representation.[8]

Identity is not inborn, pregiven or 'natural'. Subjectivity is fractured, contradictory, ambiguous and disrupted. It is striven for, contested, negotiated; it is not achieved by an act of will, nor discovered in the inner recesses of the soul, but rather put together in historical circumstances, in collective and individual experiences, and subject to challenge and change:

> As individuals we are not the mere objects of language, but the sites of discursive struggle which take place in the conscious [and unconscious] of the individual.[9]

As defining adults crowd round the cradle of the new-born, cooing 'isn't she pretty' or 'isn't he strong', the biological sex of the baby is overlaid with the cultural expectations of gender. Like it or not, the little girl embarks upon her life's journey within the discourses of 'femininity', to which she must perforce adapt, or risk exclusion, ostracisation and the loss of parental love. The notion of 'femininity' is built upon traditional verbal and visual representations of women, and what is expected of women within the various overlapping institutions that make up society. Representations cannot simply be tested against the real, since everyday, common-sense 'reality' is based upon and formed through a pre-existing overlay of existing representations.

So what about the lesbian? Whilst the cultural industries are awash with images of prescriptive 'femininity', there is a dearth of images of the lesbian. She is under-represented, silenced and denied. What we do have, however, are perjorative myths.

SELF-IDENTITY AND PHOTOGRAPHY

Much of the original work on identity sought to find 'positive images' for those who are outside of dominant culture, including women, Black and ethnic minority groups, people with disabilities, working-class people, lesbians, gays and elderly people. However, this work was founded on the premise that by creating a fixed 'positive' image it was possible to overturn negative stereotypes. This premise assumes that a photographer can create and fix a particular meaning and reading within an image – that somehow intent is all. But this ignores the context for viewing the image: where it is seen, what words accompany it, what other pictures frame it. It ignores the role of the audience: what particular viewers may bring with them in order to interpret an image in terms of ideas, other pictures seen before, their visual vocabulary and other points of view. It also ignores any unconscious readings and responses to images. There are ways in which identity-work always does link back into stereotypes for the audience, since these are the short-hand versions of the world that people use to categorise diverse and complex ranges of meanings in order to make 'common sense' of them. Stereotypes are linked to underlying power relations, and call up an intuitive belief in their generalised prejudicial assumptions:

> As feminists we take it for granted that current dominant images of women should continually be questioned and if necessary challenged, but we find the notion of 'positive' images a limited one in that it ignores how meaning is constructed or subjectivity produced. [10]

I have been working, along with Jo Spence, on exploding the myth of fixity of meaning to encompass a whole range of subject positions, exploring our fragmented identities and disrupting closed, simplistic readings.

PHOTOTHERAPY

The photographic practice we have been developing since 1983 we call phototherapy. [11] Our work comes out of photographic discourses, and the links between images and image-making and notions of conscious and unconscious identities, to which we have added therapeutic skills. Using the techniques of co-counselling, Gestalt, visualisation and psychodrama, we have worked together, having first established a deep sense of safety and trust. We offer each other non-judgemental, good-quality listening, reflection and reframing of belief systems which have become stuck and self-punishing. We have taken as our therapeutic model the work of Alice Miller:

> It was the child in me – condemned to silence long ago, abused, exploited, and turned to stone – who finally found her feelings and along with them her speech and told me, in pain, her story . . . I was amazed to find that I had been an abused child, that from the very beginning of my life I had no choice but to comply totally with the needs and feelings of my mother and to ignore my own. [12]

The phototherapist becomes the advocate for the client's own 'hurt inner child', and encourages her to recreate, represent and witness her own history, to learn to protest about it, and finally to be able to nurture herself. Our work is a collaboration between equals, in which we take turns to be client and phototherapist. In this exchange of power relationships, the sitter/director explores her story, determines the subject, the props and the image, facilitated by the phototherapist, who gives permission, support and reflection, and uses role-play, gentle encouragement, provocation and contradiction to enable the sitter/director to get deeply in touch with feelings she has learnt to hide. Our therapeutic style is 'playful' and offers release from stored tensions, traumas and grief:

> It is in playing, and only in playing, that the individual child or adult is able to be creative and to use the whole personality, and it is only in being creative that the individual discovers the self. [13]

All our work is about process, change and transformations. It draws upon memory, tiny yet significant details from the past, 'gestes', things that were said to us or about us, belief systems that have got stuck, old patterns, that may once have been useful and adaptive, but which now limit or deny our ability to make appropriate choices. We look behind the 'screen memories', [14] the simplifications and myths of others we have for too long accepted as our histories, to at last tell our own stories, from our points of view. It is not a search for an authentic 'real me', but a mapping out of the intricacies and multiplicities of our identities. We are exploring our 'psychic reality' in a form of 'unconsciousness raising'. Our ultimate aim is self-acceptance.

ONE PARTICULAR STORY OR MY 'SELF' AS CASE HISTORY

Although, in one sense, all the work I have done in phototherapy as sitter/director is lesbian work, I have selected here those pieces which are the most clearly about my lesbian identity. All the work is done initially for myself and only when it feels safe enough, when I have dealt with the feelings brought up, have I decided to make it public. The work was not made to show, although it has subsequently been used within gallery and community spaces, and in running workshops, when I thought that what I was trying to unearth would be useful to share with others – to open up debates, questions and feelings.

THE CONSTRUCTION OF HETEROSEXUALITY

> Standing at the bar in Rackets, [15] alternately sipping my drink and inhaling my ciggy, wondering if I'll see anyone I know to take refuge from this old anxiety which surfaces; I'm so acutely aware of how I may be seen. I long for the floor to swallow me up, to be only the 'fly on the wall', to see and not be a potential object of another woman's gaze – 'not good enough, not lesbian enough, not stylish enough, not . . . enough'.
> It's a familiar old pain, I rush back in time, like flipping through a book of pictures, to my teenage, wallflower past.

I chose to look at my adolescence, since on reflection, it appears to have been a time when my identity was most influenced by the institutions – school, the communications industry, class dynamics and compulsory heterosexuality in which I either sought a 'mirror' or against which I rebelled. I was either actively colluding in or refusing the agendas set, testing out the taking-up of differing positions, and reacting to expectations expressed by others.

To highlight my identity formation in conflict, I chose to work through 'A day in the life of a schoolgirl – circa 1962'. [16] In doing this work, in 1986, I also wanted to challenge essentialist notions about sexuality. I wanted to explore the ways in which sexuality is constructed at the level of culture and history, through complex interactions, to challenge essentialism's assumption of continuity in behaviour and subjective meaning, and to show how the social construction model opens up the possibility of change and discontinuity.

My own shift from heterosexuality to woman-identified to lesbian, within the context of feminism, and my own particular need to make sense of the world as I experienced it, left me with no 'natural' to fall back upon, but rather a constant questioning, oscillating between theory and practice, and the imperative to deconstruct my own heterosexual formation. In showing the work I also wanted to open up a dialogue with the heterosexual members of the audience – who could engage with it at the level of their own memories, identification and embarrassed

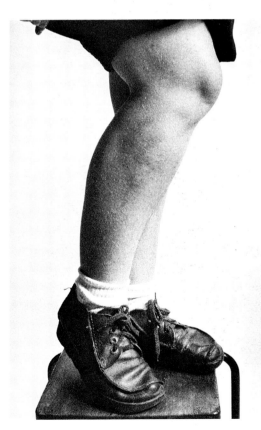

'Even the plumpest girl can stand with poise and elegance.' Anne Webb, Growing Up Gracefully (1965).

amusement – and who I hoped would then take the risk to look at their own positions and assumptions more critically.

Since photographs are mimetic, it was important to provide a recognisable cultural and historical frame that was specific to my story. My parents are hoarders, an attribute partially conditioned by living through two world wars, which taught 'make-do-and-mend' attitudes, and so I was able to find make-up and clothes from 1962, and contemporary magazines. I found these objects very evocative: 'Teenage Spot Creme', 'Angel face' powder by Outdoor Girl, 'Batwing' eyelashes, 'Vitapoint', kirby-grips, cotton wool stuffing for my circular-stitched black bra, the 'roll-on', narrow pointed stiletto-heeled shoes, a photograph of Dusty Springfield. I explored the process of transformation. Issues of 'the good schoolgirl' and my working-class identity in crisis contextualised my flight into heterosexuality as a form of escape (!), and my taking on working-class street-style as an act of rebellion against my parents and my middle-class, academic, achievement-fixated school.[17]

My feeling now is one of compassion for the me-of-15, as well as surprise at how easy to recall, how deeply ingrained, were the skills I had learnt: creating a 'beehive', applying those layers of make-up with such precision, dressing in my armoury of containment and learning how to present myself, 'sitting pretty' or balancing upon one judiciously placed high-heeled shoe.

Unnatural, extraordinary, bizarre behaviour (when seen out of context), the rituals of an anthropological subject, learning to be a gendered 'object-of-the-male-gaze', to present myself as a woman, and ending up looking more like a pastiche of my mother. That I chose then to replace my glasses, to see rather than be looked at, was already the clue that I enjoyed creating the masquerade but was ultimately more comfortable as an observer.

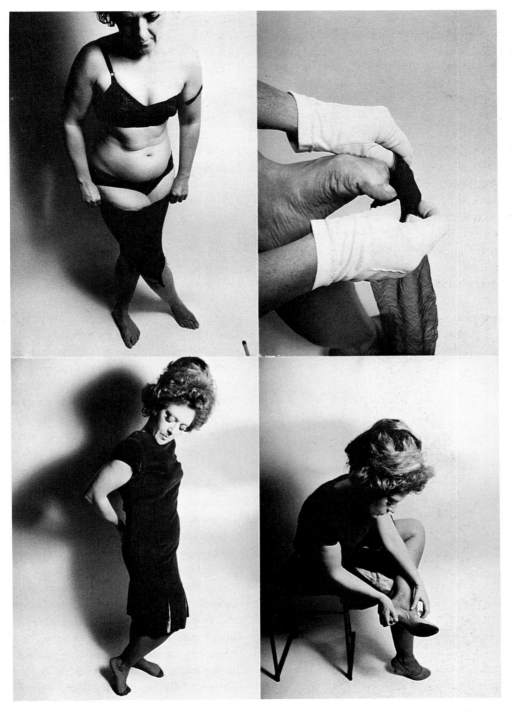

'Women use their bodies far more than men to support their personality, even when they have a pretty face to attract attention. The fact is that the female shape is basically photogenic.' Liselotte Strelow, Photographic Portrait Management *(1966)*.

WHAT DO LESBIANS LOOK LIKE? TRANSFORMING THE SUIT

In the nineteenth century, the mania for classification led to a 'scientific' study of sexuality based upon the confessional model. Havelock Ellis based his work on his acquaintance with six women, one of whom was his wife, and in it codified as 'scientific wisdom' contemporary myths about lesbian sexual practices, a stereotype of the lesbian (see caption below right) and the 'pseudo-homosexual' woman, and categorised women's passionate friendships as female homosexuality.[18] Hitherto women's same-sex friendships had been tolerated, or even

Transforming the Suit – Part 1
'Obsessed by their unobtainable goals to be men, they wore the most sombre uniforms: black tuxedos, as though they were in mourning for their ideal masculinity.'
Brassaï, *'Sodom and Gomorrah'* in The Secret Paris of the Thirties *(1932).*

Transforming the Suit – Part 2. What do Lesbians look like?
'When they still retain female garments, these usually show some traits of masculine simplicity, and there is nearly always a disdain for the petty feminine artifices of the toilette. Even when this is not obvious, there are all sorts of instinctive gestures and habits which may suggest to female acquaintances the remark that such a person "ought to have been a man".

'The brusque energetic movements, the attitude of the arms, the direct speech, the inflections of the voice, the masculine straight-forwardness and sense of honour, and especially the attitude towards men, free from any suggestion either of shyness or audacity, will often suggest the underlying psychic abnormality to a keen observer.

'In the habits not only is there frequently a pronounced taste for smoking cigarettes, often found in quite feminine women, but also a decided taste and toleration for cigars. There is also a dislike and sometimes incapacity for needlework and other domestic occupations, while there is some capacity for athletics.

'She shows, therefore, nothing of that sexual shyness and engaging air of weakness and dependence which are an invitation to men.' Havelock Ellis, Sexual Inversion *(1897).*

encouraged,[19] but with the rise of feminism, and the economic options opening out to (primarily middle-class) women, so that they no longer had to marry to survive, the sexologists raised the stigma of 'lesbianism' against independent women. Labelled as congenitally defective, the 'invert', with her 'unnatural and depraved' desires, was cast in a pathological and morbid light. By the early twentieth century, European popular culture was linking love between women with disease, insanity and tragedy (see over).

Photography played its part too in this classification process and the search for 'objective scientific facts', since photographs were seen as embodying a 'true' image of reality, and even reality itself. Since the body, and particularly the face, were thought to show innate characteristics, scientific photographs of particular 'types' were collected, analysed and drawn upon as evidence of social deviance to support the theories of eugenics.[20]

The medical-psychological discourse, in which power is granted to the 'experts', served to create a particular identity: 'the lesbian'. As sexuality was constructed as the key to an individual's 'true nature', the definitions were used to limit and prescribe those defined. However, as Foucault has argued, once a category has been set up, those defined may group together and use it to speak for themselves, creating a 'reverse discourse'.[21] Radclyffe Hall in her novel, *The Well of Loneliness*,[22] expanded and transformed the theory of the 'invert' to speak as one herself, and, on the basis of innateness, to plead for tolerance.[23] This strategy for social acceptance was a timely use of contemporary theory, but what if the feminists of the nineteenth century themselves had been able to be the definers of a lesbian identity, as lesbians now demand?

In rejecting the conformity of a 'compulsory heterosexuality'[24] I found myself confronting a series of perjorative myths as to what a lesbian could and should be: myths arising from fear, ridicule and contempt, and perpetrated as a means of social control of all women. Heterosexism is an institutionalised system that promotes the idea that only heterosexuality is 'normal' and 'natural', and supports sexism in that it maintains rigid and limiting sex-role stereotypes. The dominant ideology of representation naturalises *hetero*sexual difference, leaving only stereotypes of 'perversion', 'exotica' or 'predator' for the lesbian.

So how did I, in the early 1980s, fit into all this? There was a current lesbian feminist stereotype on offer: very short hair, checked shirt, men's trousers, loads of 'right-on' badges with a strident, assertive personal style, but although she was an 'alter ego' beside her I always felt inadequate and judged. She was, somehow, this 'real lesbian', an ideal against whom I (and so many others I've later discovered) just didn't make it. But it was she who set me off researching all the other stereotypes of what a lesbian 'should' and could be.

Using the same man's suit in every photograph, with a few key additional signifiers, I placed myself within a range of roles and 'definitions by experts'. I re-staged, examined and exploded the mythologies of the lesbian, butch/femme and masculine/feminine, my 'alter ego', and the lesbian still closeted within a heterosexual marriage. My aim was to challenge any reductavist notions of my 'identity-as-a-lesbian', to break the concept of a fixed immutable sexuality, to destabilise female/male stereotypes, to decode role play, and to foreground ambiguity.[25] Doing this work was part of freeing myself from other people's versions of who I am, and a move towards self-acceptance.

So, what does a lesbian look like?

UNWIND THE LIES THAT BIND
A Coming-Out Story . . .
No, I didn't immediately rush out and tell the world how happy I was, even though I couldn't quite believe how a friendship had heated up to such passion. But it didn't last long; she

found someone else, and I had to come to terms on my own with the identity I'd been taught to despise, whilst continuing to love and desire her, but only being the one she turned to in her hard times. Self-doubt and insecurities resurfaced, but I had, eventually, made *the* decision.

But still, didn't I believe that 'the personal is political'? Even if I felt then that I was coming out as a failure – celebrating a relationship of rejection *is* more difficult – blocking off such an important part of my identity was self-

Transforming the Suit – Parts 3 and 5.

An Alter Ego

'With flower-sweet finger-tips, they crush the grape of evil till it is exquisite, smooth and luscious to the taste, stirring up a subconscious responsiveness, intensifying all that has been, all that follows, leaving their prey gibbering, writhing, sex-sodden shadows of their former selves, conscious only of one ambition, one desire in mind and body, which, ever festering, ever destroying, slowly saps them of health and energy.' G. Sheila Donisthorpe, Loveliest of Friends *(1931)*.

destructive. So, I took the risk to come out to my friends, which proved relatively easy: 'I always thought you probably were', 'well, actually . . .'

Family Matters?
But coming out to my parents? I thought it was better to leave well alone since they are very old, with dyed-in-the-wool value systems. But I peppered my conversations with them with what I thought were large hints, clues, ideas which could have been taken up but never were . . . When I showed them the early phototherapy work, my father would discuss the clothes in great detail. He happily parted with trousers, shirts and jackets which no longer fitted him, even his cuff-links. As a tailor, a creator of key signifiers, was he aware of the look he was helping me create? My mum, however, would search through the pictures looking for images of me appearing suitably feminine, passive, pretty, in the endless search for her 'sweet little girl'.

Finally, I couldn't stand the duplicity anymore. My decision to contextualise my phototherapy practice with my lesbianism in a television programme forced my hand.[26] I could hardly let my parents, all pride in their daughter's achievements, telling all their friends, relatives and neighbours to watch, learn of my lesbianism from the television screen. I had to speak with them separately. I was seriously ill at the time and so accepted my mother's offer to nurse me. I didn't edit my pinboard or my bookshelves before she came, it was time she knew . . . This was far from ideal, since my illness rendered me vulnerable, but time was running out. One morning I found her reading my statement about my lesbianism.[27] She was in a state of shock, both tearful and angry. I was not prepared for the force of her fears and there was no way she was able to listen to any cogent arguments. 'It makes my flesh creep', she said, 'unnatural, perverted, evil . . . you are such a worry to me', and she hoped so much that it was 'just a phase'

that I was going through. Against the force of her revulsion, I could only hold onto and repeat that 'it was my choice, and my responsibility'. She searched round for people to blame for my 'corruption', for the loss of her 'sweet girl, who loved getting dressed up, posing, [her] delightful (dutiful) daughter'.

She never saw the television programme, commanded me never to tell my father, and she has never seen any phototherapy exhibitions or articles I've written. It's a closed book, which she does not choose to open. Sadly, I have had to come to terms with that.

Clause 28
During the struggle against Clause 28, my mother's rejections resurfaced; I had not fully realised before how deeply homophobia was ingrained in society. While the demos were

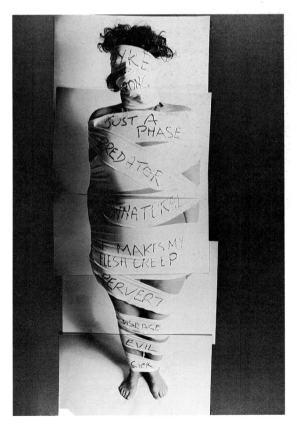

Unwind the Lies that Bind.

good and the organising, resisting and
solidarity amongst lesbians and gays against
institutionalised bigotry were empowering, I
also spent time compulsively reading *Hansard*
in my local library.[28] In order to begin to work
through my internalised oppressions using
phototherapy, I collected together all the
quotes from Members of Parliament that I
found the most painful. To make visible how it
felt to have the negative projections of others
stuck upon me, Jo wrapped me in binding rags,
thus blinding me, gagging me and tying me
down, and wrote upon them the perjorative
myths that were currency at this homosexual-
baiting time, together with my mother's words.
I struggled, pulled and stretched myself free –
for a moment. No, phototherapy is not a magic
cure, but it does help to say the unsayable, to
make visible to others what they are doing,
and to make visible to myself how my
internalisation of hatred, disgust and fear
silences and contains me. And how it could
feel to break out of these projections.

So this work was both a highly personal and
political response to Clause 28, and it enabled
me to make a forceful statement, publicly.

CONCLUSION
Whilst we know, intellectually, that
photographs are constructed, frozen, framed
moments pulled out of a continuum of
possibilities, yet we invest them with fixed
meaning. When confronted with hundreds of
different images of the 'self', where can one find
the 'truth'? By choosing to make visible aspects
of my life which out of self-protection have
been repressed from popular and personal
memory, the scenarios of shame, internalised
oppression and isolation may be witnessed,
recognised and mourned, with the
phototherapist acting out the role of the
'maternal gaze'.[29] This enables me to move
towards a freedom from the 'power of the
compulsion to repeat'. Rejecting the search for
the fixity of an 'ideal self', I can enjoy 'self' as
process and becoming.

By using phototherapy to map both my
psychic and social construction, I am
highlighting both the specificity of the
formation of my subjectivity and the wider
discourses which frame it. I thereby become
the subject rather than the object of my own
histories:

> The aspects of play, dress-up and
> period props signifying era, class,
> occupation and sexual identity bridge
> the social and the intra-psychic, the
> social and the political, and the personal
> and political.[30]

My father died on 4 July, 1990, giving me a
new meaning to 'independence'. I never did tell
him of my lesbianism, although I'm sure he
guessed. I dedicate this text to my memories of
him, his questioning and challenging mind,
and his sensitivity to non-verbal clues, which I
learned and have incorporated in this practice.

NOTES
[1] The then British Environment Minister, Kenneth
Baker, on a photo-call in March 1986, suggested to
the waiting press photographers that instead of
'saying cheese, you should say lesbian – it makes
people laugh.'

[2] Section 28 of the Local Government Act of 1988 in
Britain states that:
A Local Authority shall not:
a) Promote homosexuality or produce material for the
   promotion of homosexuality.
b) Promote the teaching in any maintained school of
   the acceptability of homosexuality as a pretended
   family relationship by the publication of such
   material or otherwise.
c) Give financial or other assistance to any person for
   either of the purposes referred to in paragraphs (a)
   or (b). Nothing of the above shall be taken to
   prohibit the doing of anything for the purpose of
   treating or preventing disease.

[3] Simon Watney, 'On the Institutions of Photography'
in *Photography/Politics: Two*, ed. Pat Holland, Jo
Spence, Simon Watney (London: Comedia Publishing
Group, 1986).

4 Allan Sekula, 'Reading an Archive: Photography Between Labour and Capital' in *Photography/Politics: Two*.

5 Jeremy Seabrooke, 'My Life Is In That Box: Photography and Popular Consciousness' in *Ten.8*, no. 34, Autumn 1989; Hall Carpenter Archives, Lesbian Oral History Group, *Inventing Ourselves* (London: Routledge & Kegan Paul, 1989).

6 David A. Kruass and Jerry L. Fryrear, eds, *Phototherapy in Mental Health* (Illinois: Charles C. Thomas, 1983); Judy Weiser, 'Phototherapy: Using Snapshots and Photo-interactions in Therapy with Youth' in *Innovative Interventions in Child and Adolescent Therapy*, ed. Charles Schaefer (New York: Wiley, 1988);Weiser, 'More Than Meets The Eye: Using Ordinary Snapshots as Tools For Therapy' in *Healing Voices: Feminist Approaches to Therapy with Women*, ed. T. Laidlaw and C. Malmo (London and New York: Jossey-Bass, 1990).

7 Susan Sontag, 'Under the Sign of Saturn' in *A Susan Sontag Reader* (London: Penguin, 1983).

8 Victor Burgin, 'The Absence of Presence' in *The End of Art Theory* (London: Macmillan, 1986).

9 Chris Weedon, *Feminist Practice and Poststructuralist Theory* (Oxford: Blackwell, 1987).

10 Rosy Martin and Jo Spence, 'Phototherapy: New Portraits for Old' in *Putting Myself in the Picture*, Jo Spence (London: Camden Press, 1986); Martin and Spence, 'New Portraits for Old: The Use of the Camera in Therapy' in *Looking On: Images of Femininity in the Visual Arts and Media*, ed. Rosemary Betterton (London: Pandora, 1987).

11 Rosy Martin and Jo Spence, 'Phototherapy – Psychic Realism as a Healing Art?' in *Ten.8*, no. 30, October 1988.

12 Alice Miller, *The Drama of Being a Child* (New York: Basic Books, 1981); see also Miller, *For Your Own Good* (London: Faber, 1983).

13 D.W. Winnicott, *Playing and Reality* (London: Tavistock Publications, 1972).

14 J. Laplanche and J.B. Pontalis, *The Language of Psychoanalysis* (London: Karnac, 1988).

15 A Lesbian bar in North London, now defunct.

16 Rosy Martin and Jo Spence, 'Double Exposure – the Minefield of Memory' in *Photographs in Context* (London: Photographers' Gallery, 1987).

17 Rosy Martin, 'Phototherapy – Transforming the School Photo. Happy Days are Here Again' in *Photography/Politics: Two*; Martin, 'Unwind the Ties that Bind' in *The Family Snaps: The Meanings of Domestic Photography*, ed. Patricia Holland and Jo Spence (London: Virago, 1991).

18 Havelock Ellis, *Sexual Inversion*, (London: Wilson and Macmillan, 1897).

19 Lillian Faderman, *Surpassing the Love of Men* (London: Junction Books, 1981).

20 David Green, 'Veins of Resemblance: Photography and Eugenics' in *Photography/Politics: Two*.

21 Michel Foucault, *The History of Sexuality* (London: Penguin, 1984).

22 Radclyffe Hall, *The Well of Loneliness* (London: Virago, 1982).

23 Sonja Ruehl, 'Inverts and Experts: Radclyffe Hall and the Lesbian Identity' in *Feminism, Culture and Politics*, ed. Rosalind Brunt and Caroline Rowan (London: Lawrence and Wishart, 1982).

24 Adrienne Rich, *Compulsory Heterosexuality and the Lesbian Continuum* (London: Onlywomen Press, 1981).

25 Rosy Martin and Jo Spence, 'What Do Lesbians Look Like?' in *The Body Politic* (London: Photographers' Gallery) and *Ten.8*, no. 25, June 1987; Martin, 'How Does the Lesbian Gaze?' in *Outlook*, Winter 1990.

26 Jo Spence, Rosy Martin and David Roberts in 'Putting Ourselves in the Picture', *Arena*, BBC 2, directed by Ian Potts.

27 Rosy Martin and Jo Spence, 'Phototherapy: New Portraits for Old' in *Putting Myself in the Picture*.

28 *Hansard*: official report of the proceedings in Parliament.

29 Rosy Martin, 'Dirty Linen' in *Ten.8*, no. 37, Autumn 1990; Martin, 'Unwind the Ties that Bind' in *Family Snaps*.

30 Jan Zita Grover, 'Phototherapy: Shame and the Minefields of Memory' in *Afterimage*, vol. 18, no. 1, Summer 1990.

THE SOIL IN MY BLOOD

Jackie Kay

THE SOIL IN MY BLOOD

I was pulled out with forceps
left a gash down my left cheek
and pus that took months
to dry up – I nearly died
four months inside a glass cot
but

She came faithful
from Glasgow to Edinburgh
and peered through the glass
I must have felt somebody
wanting me to survive
she would not *pick another baby*

She brought me up
on cuddles and Campsie Glens
Burns suppers and wild mountain thyme
Glaswegian humour and all the blooming heather
the moors empty as after
the bloody thing out of the womb
how I travelled to get here.

II

I don't know what diseases
come down my line
when dentists and doctors ask
the old blood questions about family runnings
I tell them: I have no nose or eyes or mouth
to match, so spitting image or dead cert
my face watches itself in the glass

Pull it out – the matter
matted as unoiled locks
my dread needs some grease to shine
these way past midnight hours
when the loneblood takes me

I have my parents who are not of the same tree
and my brother that is not of my blood
though he is my bloodbrother and
you keep trying to make it matter
the blood, the tie, the passing down
generations

I am like my mother and father
I have seeped in Scotland's flavours
sizzling oatcakes on the griddle
I am like the mother and father
who brought me up and taught me
not how to be Black but
how not to be grateful

We all have our contradictions
the ones with the mother's nose and father's eyes have them
the blood does not bind confusion
yet I confess to my contradiction
I want to know my blood.

III

I know my blood.
It is dark ruby red and comes
regular and I use Lillets
I know my blood
when I cut my finger
I know what my blood looks like

It is the well the womb the fucking seed
Here I am far enough away to wonder
what were their faces like
Who were their grandmothers
What were the days like
passed in Scotland
The land I come from
the soil in my blood

AFTER MAMMY TOLD ME SHE
WASNIE MY REAL MAMMY

I was scared to death she was gonnie melt
or something or mibbe dissapear in the dead
of night and somebody would say she was a fairy
godmother. So the next morning I felt her skin
to check it wis flesh, but mibbe it was imitation
how could I tell if my mammy wis a dummy
with a voice spoken by someone else?
So I searches the whole house for clues
but I never found nothing. Anyhow after
I got my guinea pig and forgot all about it.

ANGELA DAVIS

On my bedroom wall is a big poster
of Angela Davis who is in prison
right now for nothing at all
except she wouldn't put up with stuff.
My mum says she is only 26
which seems really old to me
but my mum says it's young
just imagine she says being on
America's Ten Most Wanted People's List at 26!
I can't.
Angela Davis is the only female person
I've seen (except for a nurse on TV)
who looks like me. She has big hair like mine
that grows out instead of down.
My mum says it's called an Afro.
If I could be as brave as her when I get older
I'll be OK.
Last night I kissed her goodnight again
and wondered if she could feel the kisses
in prison all the way from Scotland.
Her skin is the same too you know.

I can see my skin is that colour
but most of the time I forget
so sometimes when I look in the mirror
I give myself a bit of a shock
and say to myself *Do you really look like this?*
as if I'm somebody else. I wonder if she does that.
I don't believe she killed anybody.
It's all a load of phoney lies.
My dad says it's a set up.
I asked him if she'll get the electric chair
like them Roseberries he was telling me about.
No he says the world is on her side.
Well how come she's in there then I thinks.
I worry she's going to get the chair.
I worry she's worrying about the chair.
My dad says she'll be putting on a brave face.
He brought me a badge home which I wore
to school. It says FREE ANGELA DAVIS!
And all my pals says – who's she?

THE VISIT

I thought I'd hid everything
that there wasnie wan give-away sign
left

I put Marx Engels Lenin (no Trotsky!)
in the airing cupboard – she'll no be
checking out the towels surely!

All the copies of the Daily Worker
I shoved under the sofa
the dove of peace I took down from the loo

A poster of Paul Robeson
saying give him his passport
I took down from the kitchen

I left a bust of Burns
my detective stories
and the Complete Works of Shelley

She comes at 11.30 exactly.
I pour her coffee
from my new Hungarian set

And foolishly pray she willnae
ask its origins – honestly!
This baby is going to my head.

She crosses her legs on the sofa
I fancy I hear the Daily Workers
rustle underneath her

Well she says you have an interesting home.
She sees my eyebrows rise
It's different she qualifies

Hell and I've spent all morning
trying to look ordinary
– a lovely home for the baby

She buttons her coat all smiles
I'm thinking
I'm on the Home Run

But just as we get to the last post
her eye catches at the same time as mine

a red ribbon with twenty world peace badges

Clear as a hammer and sickle
on the wall
Oh she says are you against nuclear weapons?

To Hell with this. Baby or no baby.
Yes I says. Yes yes yes.
I'd like this baby to live in a nuclear free environment

Oh her eyes light up.
I'm all for peace myself she says
and sits down for another cup of coffee.

LESBIAN FAMILY ALBUM PHOTOGRAPHY

Cathy Cade

The great advantage of presenting images of
lesbians in the form of a family album is that,
in the face of prejudice and stereotypes that
state otherwise, lesbians can be presented as
fully human. Family albums of our growing-up
years show that we were born to certain
parents, in a given place, time, and ethnic class
or religious group. We may or may not have
defined ourselves as lesbians when we were
youngsters, but we all grew up to be complex
adults with many roles and identities. Family
albums also encourage us to investigate the
interweave of differences and similarities
between and among lesbians. This was my
purpose in creating the book *A Lesbian Photo
Album: The Lives of Seven Lesbian Feminists.*[1] The
women of the book are Black, white, Asian,
Jewish, Roman Catholic, middle class, working
class, rural, urban, some are disabled, and
many are mothers. Using archival and
contemporary photographs combined with
edited interviews, I was able to present a rich
celebration of lesbians' lives for both a lesbian
and a non-lesbian audience.

*'This was taken at the penny
arcade. At 12 I was sneaking around
to the corner drug store to read
lesbian paperback novels' (1955).
Jeri in* A Lesbian Photo Album.

'Shalea and Omar, my New York and California babies, the constants in my life' (1982). Jeri in A Lesbian Photo Album, *photograph by Cathy Cade.*

Having completed *A Lesbian Photo Album* and thinking about the term 'family album photography', three different kinds of albums come to mind: firstly, the gathering of photos and stories from when lesbians were growing up; secondly, photographic and written descriptions of the lives and 'chosen' families of adult lesbians; and finally, presentations of what the mothering lesbians are creating for *their* children. Each of these provides different opportunities and difficulties for a photographer.

First, the archival collecting, interpreting and presenting is very important, for there is so much we do not know about the history of lesbians as a group and as individuals. The role of the photographer here is to choose: to find lesbians able and willing to be open, who have photographs of their growing up, and then to choose among these women and their pictures. This work will be limited by the pressures that don't allow all lesbians to be totally public and the circumstances relating to whether photographs are available. I'll never forget one woman saying, 'my mother's life was so hard there was no way she could have held on to the few pictures she had'.

In the archival work, the photographs were created by someone with one set of values and chosen by a lesbian feminist photographer with another. It would be interesting to know who is the family photographer: male or female? mother or grandfather? What values were important to them? Families may have very limited ideas about what is suitable to photograph. For example, are you supposed to be smiling or looking serious? Should you be photographed in a work context? I found pictures of people at work among working-class, but not middle-class, families.

I included myself in *A Lesbian Photo Album* as a way of informing the reader about who was selecting the photos and editing the interviews. I also included myself so that I would have a sense of what it was I was asking of the other women in being a part of this book and so open about their lives.

I included stories as well as the photos, for there were not always pictures of the important aspects of a lesbian's life; some photographs needed interpreting, and often the way a woman told her story was too wonderful to leave out.

I was able to show lesbians in the complexity of their adult roles: as workers, lovers, perhaps mothers or political activists, artists, and so on.

'Although I walked with a severe limp, I loved to run and jump and clown around' (1946). Jill in A Lesbian Photo Album.

'I love fancy canes' (1982). Jill in A Lesbian Photo Album, *photograph by Cathy Cade.*

This recording forms the second kind of family album that I have already defined. Now that I was taking the pictures, the women and I were much freer to decide on and make the images we wanted. I had also hoped to show current 'chosen' families. Many lesbians, in the USA at least, like to refer to their closest friends as 'family'. The problem is that the term is used loosely with no agreed rules of who is included. Also the people who a lesbian gets her support from may change quite frequently, especially if she lives in an urban area. Another problem is that the various individuals in most friendship/family groups have made different decisions about being public or open about their sexuality. Many lesbians get significant support from non-lesbians and some of these people may not be ready to be in a lesbian book. One of the women in my book had an incredibly rich life, encountering almost daily brothers, grown children, old factory friends, newer feminist lesbians and neighbours. Many of these were lesbians and gay men, or knew of her lesbianism, but not all. There was no way they would all get together or be in a lesbian book. The result is that some of the women of my book look more isolated as adults than they really are.

The question of who adult lesbians call their family and where they find support is interesting and important. In *Making a Way*, JEB (Joan E. Biren) has photographed a wide variety of lesbian institutions and support structures, although the images are not organised as the family and support system of any one lesbian.[2] For the time being we probably still need to look to novels and essays for this information.

I'm not sure that family album photography can present our sexual lives. Perhaps this is my timidity, a reflection that growing up in *my* family we weren't supposed to talk about sex. Although I presented the lesbians in *A Lesbian Photo Album* as sexual, I did not really present their sexuality. I included a fair amount of nudity, especially breasts – a personal bias no doubt. I did this even though I thought it might keep the book out of some libraries, and getting it into libraries was a high priority. I included the nudity because I felt that being at home in our bodies is central to lesbian feminism.

A third kind of lesbian family album could focus on how lesbians raise their children. Lesbian mothering is the focus of my current work. I'm addressing the questions: 'What do lesbian mothers do?', 'How are they similar and different from other mothers?', 'What is mothering a baby, a 7-year-old, a 17-year-old, a 37-year-old, like for a lesbian?'

As a photographer working with a lesbian and her family, I'm able to plan to be at certain events, and according to my values and interests, choose what to photograph. With

*Kimi, Lesbian Mothering series, 1990.
Photograph by Cathy Cade.*

some of the younger families, where lesbians
are deciding to have children after they have
become lesbians, I'm able to photograph their
pregnancies and births. I don't always know
what I'll photograph before I meet a family, but
my experiences as a lesbian, feminist and
mother are clearly evident to me when I look
back on what I've photographed. Thus I notice
the butchness of Kimi holding her 3-year-old
on the jungle gym; as a mother I celebrate
Dana's first skin-to-skin kiss of Max.

It is necessary to include a few words about
ethics and getting permission to publish family
photographs. A central tenet of feminism is

*Max's First Kiss, Lesbian Mothering
series, 1990. Photograph by Cathy
Cade.*

that women have the right to control their
lives, and by extension, images of their lives.
On the other hand, you do not need to allow
another person's homophobia to prohibit the
sharing of knowledge about lesbians and our
cultures. In practice, this can get tricky and
frustrating. Sometimes the issues of permission
feel like the hard dues I have to pay for all the
fun I have photographing. In *A Lesbian Photo
Album* no one was named specifically as a
lesbian without her permission and there was a
disclaimer in the beginning of the book
instructing people not to assume someone was
a lesbian unless so specified. I got permission
from the lesbian who was the subject of a given
chapter to use her archival photographs, and
went along with each lesbian's sense of what
was acceptable use of them. Last names weren't
often used. However, we didn't, for example,
ask everyone's permission to be shown as a
relative of a lesbian.

With several women I pushed a bit to get to
include some pictures they were hesitant about
– especially nudes. I convinced one woman but
failed to persuade two others and had to forego
the use of the photographs. I might ask them
again when we're all in our eighties.

I try to pay particular attention to getting
permission to publish from children after
they're old enough to understand the question
. . . about 6 years old? It is easy to get scared
that a child who gave you permission to take a
photo of her with her lesbian mother when she
was 6 won't let you publish it when she's 13. It's
especially scary if this mother has been telling
you her daughter is giving her a hard time for
being a lesbian. And yet, I've found some kids
able to give permission and proud to have their
picture published, even if they are giving their
mom a hard time. I suspect these struggles are
more about independence than anything else.

Lesbian family photography is very
important, in spite of the limitations I've been
discussing, most of which are reflections of our
oppression as lesbians. Lesbian family
photography is much more than just a

documentation of how we grew up, our adult chosen lives and families, or the way we mother. For the photographs make visible the support we have and the new families and cultures we are creating. These possibilities then become available to others and we can educate our allies. Family albums remind us of what we have accomplished despite the many voices, including some deep within ourselves, telling us we can't make changes. It is a spiral; lesbians create the cultures which make possible the creation and dissemination of the photographs, which in turn help promote the cultures.

NOTES
1 Cathy Cade, *A Lesbian Photo Album: The Lives of Seven Lesbian Feminists* (Oakland: Waterwoman Books, 1987). You can order the book from Cathy Cade, 3022 Ashbrook Court, Oakland CA 94601, USA ($14.95 plus postage for a book weighing one pound in weight).
2 JEB (Joan E. Biren), *Making a Way* (Washington, DC: Glad Hag Books, 1987).

FAMILIAR NAMES AND NOT-SO-FAMILIAR FACES

Lynette Molnar with Linda Thornburg

'They have a compulsion to flaunt their
sex in public.'

David Ruben, MD, *Everything You Always
Wanted To Know About Sex*

The impetus for *Familiar Names and Not-So-Familiar Faces* (originals in colour) came out of a conversation with a friend who had just read the book *Everything You Always Wanted To Know About Sex*. At issue was the chapter on homosexuality which contained a diatribe on 'blatant homosexuals'. We found the indictment of 'blatant homosexuality' ludicrous in a culture where most lesbians and gay men, if not closeted, are certainly discreet (especially in public). We marvelled at the conviction that an increased awareness of the existence of homosexuals, since the 1969 Stonewall riots, somehow makes us blatant.

We began to strategise about a way to object to the ironic, irrational charge of 'blatant homosexuality' in a world whose entire economy is based on blatant displays of heterosexuality and the invisibility of Other. Our problem became twofold: how to exemplify the obvious invisibility of lesbians and gay men, and how to subvert the all pervasive, traditional heterosexist images of love, sex, sales, authority, ownership, news, politics and entertainment. We've attempted to illustrate what a culture could resemble if it were not so anti-gay and homophobic and more tolerant of difference.

George Lupo/Pasadena, California

Martha Woodward/Pasadena, California

Martha Woodward/Pasadena, California

If this is what a beginner can do with a Nikon FG,
imagine what you could do with a little practice.

With Pope John Paul II in Fairbanks: "A long journey for peace"

Molnar's *Familiar Names and Not-So-Familiar Faces* consists of a series of photomontages in which images of the photographer and her female lover are stripped into already-existing reproductions. The montage is deliberately not very convincing: it's quite obvious that the two figures have been imported from some other world and pastiched into these mainstream settings. The scale, the repetitiveness of these same figures embracing in a variety of commercial settings enforce the artificiality of the insertion, producing a sense that this is an act of defiance, a clumsy and not-altogether-successful fusion of two different universes. Anyone living the life of an informed outsider will recognise that this is precisely the position that we occupy – culturally and politically, if not economically. Molnar's work struck me as a clever objectification of both the present aspiration and reality of the uncloseted lesbian.

The reaction of the other two Ohio Arts Council jurors was very different. Looking at the work primarily *in terms of what lay within the frame*, they rejected it on the basis of its technical flaws ('She hasn't even varied the size of the two female figures,' 'The figures don't look as if they are really integrated into the scene') and formal deficiencies ('Why didn't she change the pose of the two figures? It's too repetitive'). When I objected that these seeming limitations became challenges and virtues, given the paucity and distortions of most images depicting lesbians, my fellow jurors' resistance took the form I've described above: *We're judging photographs, not social revolutions.* And, of course, photographs are never instruments in/of social revolutions: they exist in a world apart.

The misunderstanding Molnar encountered in taking her work before the general public, even as they 'read' fluently to members of her subculture, is a common experience among lesbian photographers addressing lesbian issues in work that they exhibit outside their communities.

Jan Zita Grover, 'Dykes in Context' in *Ten.8*, no. 30, 1988, pp.44-5.

WHICH ONE'S THE PRETENDER?

SECTION 28 AND LESBIAN REPRESENTATION

Anna Marie Smith

Section 28 of the British Local Government Act 1987-8 prohibits local authorities from 'intentionally promot[ing] homosexuality or publish[ing] material with the intention of promoting homosexuality' and 'promot[ing] the teaching in any maintained school of the acceptability of homosexuality as a pretended family relationship'. The Section came into effect in May 1988. While no local authority has actually been prosecuted under this legislation, its impact has been considerable. Commenting on the cancellation of programmes by local authorities relating to homosexuality, a spokesman for the National Council of Civil Liberties stated, 'It's the self-censorship, the decisions taken by councils behind closed doors that make Section 28 so dangerous.'[1] Section 28 does not constitute a typical juridical prohibition. It does not say 'no', to specific persons (homosexuals) or acts (sodomy). It refers instead to conceptual entities, 'promotion', 'homosexuality' and 'pretended family relationship'. Its effectiveness is symbolic rather than juridical.

What, then, does discourse on the prohibition of the promotion of homosexuality *do*, if anything? And, if Section 28 is so 'vague' that it is virtually 'useless' as a law, what is its relevance to a discussion on lesbian representation?

LESBIAN REPRESENTATION: RE-PRESENTING THE LESBIAN

Section 28 would be irrelevant to lesbian representation if lesbian representation kept its promise. That promise, which is common to all representations, is the complete, unaltered and fully accessible presentation of an original within an enclosed space.[2] In this case, the original would be 'the Lesbian' 'our true selves', 'our true meaning', 'our true desire', constituted prior to any encounter with outside discourses. Ideally, we would enjoy 'our own' images of this original in 'our own' separate space purified of difference; the not-lesbian would be entirely absent. Actual men, and the 'male-identified element', would be excluded. And because nothing but lesbian-ness constitutes this space, we would immediately grasp the meaning of these images;[3] there would be no gaps in understanding, only immediate recognition of ourselves. This ideal lesbian representation would take the form of collective soliloquy: it would be about us, by us and for us. Ethical and political problems would only emerge when either an external reference contaminated our space ('that representation of lesbianism is illegitimate because it is male-defined') or our own internal expression was presented to the outside ('men might enjoy and consume our own images').[4]

We may say that this ideal is possible and that we have already achieved this ideal, but everything we *do* in terms of lesbian representation shows us its impossibility. If our representations were merely the presentation

An example of different lesbian identities. © *Alison Bechdel, 1990.*
Dykes To Watch Out For *Calendar, Firebrand Books, New York.*

of an original which we, as lesbians, immediately recognised as our true selves, then there would be no gap between the original concept, its expression and its reception, and no difference between the first presentation of the original concept and subsequent (re-)presentations. Actual lesbian discourse, like all discourses, shows the failure to achieve these conditions of ideal representation. We engage in numerous, almost obsessive attempts, time and time again, to show to ourselves what we mean by lesbian-ness, to make the invisible visible, and the unspoken spoken. We are always trying to talk to ourselves about ourselves. The point is that if a perfect presentation of an original which we all immediately recognised were possible, there would not be this urgency to speak lesbian-ness, for the meaning of lesbian-ness would already be clear to us before we had even begun. How can we account for this urgency to explain that which we should already understand except by recognising that we are always distanced from this original lesbian-ness, that this origin never took place? Furthermore, if all presentations were purely a re-enactment of the original, a pure repetition in which nothing is ever added or changed, how do we account for the tremendous heterogeneity in our own images of lesbian-ness(es)?

Pro-censorship lesbians have attempted to answer these questions, indeed, to close the debate. Whenever there is a 'deviation' from the 'lesbian norm', perverse lesbian practices (butch/femme, sado-masochism, fetishism, and so on) or imagery (*On Our Backs*, *Quim*, or the film, *She Must Be Seeing Things*, for example), they speak as if a true original lesbian-ness is corrupted through these illegitimate representations. The other lesbians involved in these deviations are accused of violating boundaries and of illegitimately importing 'male-defined' codes into the lesbian space. And, with the assumption that lesbian-ness is absolutely contradictory to the explicit sexuality of these images, the deviant lesbian producers themselves are named 'male-defined'. These answers, however, are insufficient in terms of the richness and complexity of our experiences. If there is one true lesbian-ness, why do we have this differentiation in our community in terms of race and class, let alone sexual expressions? Taken to its logical conclusion, there would be no plurality whatsoever in the pro-censorship lesbians' ideal lesbian image; there would be only the reproduction of a singular, universal essence, purified of all differences, including race and class.

An alternative approach to lesbian-ness, and to representation in general, would be suspicious of any promise of the full re-presentation of an original. Instead of a singular, universal essence, a true lesbian-ness, our lesbian identity is always differentiated, constituting a group of identities which only resemble one another. There is always this differentiation because the lesbian space, like any other space, is never purified of difference. For example, a lesbian-ness is not first a true lesbian-ness which later acquires a particular race or class externality. Like any other identity, the only lesbian identities which we can have are identities which have meaning in specific contexts, the specific configurations of multiple codes. (Con-)texts of lesbians: the meaning of lesbian-ness for the black DJ at a South London nightclub is not exactly the same as its meaning for the single mother in the dole queue in Belfast is not exactly the same as its meaning for the closeted Oxford graduate in the City is not exactly the same as its meaning for the American sex trade worker in London's Soho, even if each of these individuals identifies as a lesbian. Contexts are not external; they are central to the meaning of identities.

SECTION 28 AS CONTEXT

If we can never have a purely separate space for the production of 'our own' images, and if contexts are central to our ongoing struggle for/obsession with/enjoyment of representation, then official discourse on homosexuality, such as discourse on Section 28, is never external to 'our' representations. An examination of the speeches in the Houses of Parliament by the supporters of this legislation is useful and relevant in two ways. First, the speeches on Section 28 are important because they constitute an organised body of expressions which reflect some of the most influential thinking on homosexuality in contemporary Britain. Second, these speeches are not simply expressions of absolute intolerance of gays and lesbians, but instead take the form of a remarkable body of complex metaphors about homosexuality. The debates revolve around the construction of conflicting versions of gayness and lesbian-ness through representation, and not simply around prohibition.

Discourse on Section 28 is therefore about context, the contexts of 'our' representations of 'our own' lesbian-ness, in that it reflects part of the context in which our struggle to represent lesbian-nesses is situated, and in that discourse on Section 28 contributes to the ongoing creation of that context. The influential 'weight' of these speeches, as official discourse, is such that they cannot be disregarded. For all our dreams of separate spaces, our own lesbian discourses are always engaged with 'outside' discourses; the traces of 'outside' representations of lesbian-ness will always affect our soliloquies within.

HOMOSEXUALITY AS INVADER AND SEDUCER
How are gayness and lesbian-ness represented in the parliamentary speeches on Section 28? First, homosexuality is situated as an equivalent element within a chain of signifiers. Advances on the Left are equated with excessive local government initiatives which are in turn equated with a promotion of homosexuality which is in turn equated with the destruction of the social order. In this sense, homosexuality is used as an equivalential signifier which facilitates the equation: the advance of the Left and unlimited local government = destruction of the social order.[5]

In addition to this construction of equivalences, however, these speeches are also organised around a complex deployment of metaphorical representations. The figures of invasion and seduction are prominent in this play of metaphors. The invader script is 'borrowed' from AIDS discourse. Dame Jill Knight, for example, states that the promotion of homosexuality must be prohibited because 'AIDS starts with and mainly comes from homosexuals [and then] spreads to others'.[6] This is, of course, a strategic (mis-) interpretation of AIDS; attempts to locate an origin of the HIV virus in gayness or blackness are 'grounded' in strategies of exclusion and disavowal rather than neutral scientific fact.[7] Knight's statement is not, however, isolated; it is located in what we could call the hegemonic discourse on AIDS. The metaphorical representation of homosexuality in this statement is therefore a particularly influential representation. Homosexuality is presented as external to a space, which we shall call 'the norm', and as an element which attempts to enter that space in the form of a contaminating disease. We are not given the image, then, of a simple opposition, 'homosexuality versus the norm'. Instead we are given a complex of spaces, the invader from the outside, and the threatened norm. Speakers such as Knight are no longer 'those people opposed to homosexuality' but become instead 'defenders' of the norm against the 'invaders'. Images about 'invaders' and 'defenders' are particularly effective in the British context because they are situated in a tradition of similar representations, such as discourse on various diseases, communist infiltration, immigration populations, crime 'waves' and drug 'crazes'. In each case, an invasion script is used so that opposition to these elements is represented as a heroic defence of a threatened space rather than a simple opposition.

When speakers such as Knight find homosexuality in the classroom, through accurate or inaccurate depictions of actual curricula, they speak as if homosexuality has invaded that space. In other statements, they speak as if homosexuality has also taken the form of a seducer, illegitimately tempting vulnerable children. All the supporters of Section 28 take the view that no one's sexuality is fixed at birth; for them the possibility of seduction is universal. The Earl of Halsbury quotes from *The Wolfenden Report*[8] and argues that because '"people's sexual orientation [is] not fixed at any particular stage, but is stabilised around the middle twenties"', school-leavers are still 'open to seduction' and must be protected until that age.[9]

The problem for the supporters of Section 28 is not simply the existence of a homosexual community, or the acts of consenting adults in private. Homosexuality constitutes a threat, in their terms, when it operates as a con-taminating invader, or as a corrupting seducer. The dangerous potential of homosexuality is realised in so far as its circulation is made public, encouraged and legitimated, that is, in so far as it is 'promoted'.

LESBIAN-NESS AS THE EXCEPTION:
THE GOOD HOMOSEXUAL AND GOOD
LESBIAN VERSUS DANGEROUS GAYNESS
Through the examples and direct references in the Section 28 debate, however, it is clear that this representation of homosexuality as invader and seducer pertains to only some forms of homosexuality. Lord Halsbury, for example, says that it is important to distinguish between 'responsible' homosexuals and their 'exhibition[ist]', 'promiscuous' and 'proselytising' counterparts.[10] There is a distinction here, which runs throughout the discourse of the supporters of Section 28, between the 'good homosexual', a law-abiding and not-diseased character who restricts her

homosexuality to a monogamous relationship with one other adult behind closed doors, and what we could call 'dangerous gayness', an unfixed, excessive, contaminating element driven by a desire for expansion and unlimited pleasure.

For our purposes, it is important to note that lesbians and lesbian-ness are never referred to in the context of the invader and seducer representations; only some aspects of *male* homosexuality are depicted in this manner. Lord Halsbury in fact explicitly locates lesbian-ness in the 'good homosexual' category. He says that in contrast to the excesses of some male homosexuals, lesbians are 'not a problem':

> They do not molest little girls. They do not indulge in disgusting and unnatural acts like buggery. They are not wildly promiscuous and do not spread venereal disease.[11]

He concludes that gay men attempt to conceal their dangerous excessiveness by placing the term 'lesbian' before the term 'gay' in the naming of the homosexual community, such that the 'relatively harmless lesbian leads on to the vicious gay'.[12]

This conception of lesbian-ness as relatively harmless in contrast with the dangers of male homosexuality is repeated elsewhere in right-wing discourse. Roger Scruton, editor of the influential New Right journal, the *Salisbury Review*, argues that there must be a moral distinction between heterosexuality and homosexuality. He recognises that this distinction cannot be made in terms of reproductive and non-reproductive intentions, since this would locate intercourse between infertile heterosexuals on the same moral plane as homosexual practices. He suggests the lack of an 'inner restraint' in homosexual practices, due to the lack of the moderating effect of female otherness on male desire, as the basis for this distinction. However, he then differentiates between male and female homosexuality. In terms of male homosexuality:

> Sexual desire is revealed as an imperative force, stayed only by social barriers and rushing forward quickly to its satisfaction as soon as they are breached.[13]

The danger of male homosexuality is understood as unlimited excess: the 'natural predatoriness' of male desire is not restrained by female desire. As a result, male homosexual desire takes the form of immediate gratification and promiscuity. Female homosexuality is likewise defined in terms of gender. The promiscuous impulse is neutralised, and there is no emphasis on sexual organs or sexual excitement. The need for a lasting partner is supposed to 'take precedence in a woman's sentiments over the immediacy of sexual excitement'.[14] For Scruton, female homosexuality is, 'an extremely poignant, often helpless, sense of being at another's mercy'.[15] He claims that female homosexuality must take this form because a lesbian 'cannot act like a man' without compromising the gender identity which makes her attractive to another woman.[16]

This New Right depiction of lesbian sexuality as harmless is a thoroughly strategic construction. First, the exclusion of any element is always twinned with the inclusion of a neutralised and yet similar difference. This representation of lesbian-ness cannot be taken in isolation; it is the support for the demonisation of male homosexuality. Second, this representation of lesbian-ness is based on a conception of female gender as passive, moderate, non-assertive, and so on. This is of course exactly the representation of 'woman' which has been criticised extensively by feminists. It is also assumed that gender determines sexuality, that maleness is the defining character of male homosexuality, and that femaleness defines lesbian sexuality. Indeed, given the presupposition of femaleness as passivity and as that which neutralises

excess, any female sexuality, lesbian or otherwise, becomes an impossibility. Defined by femaleness, lesbian sexuality erases itself at the moment that it attains a specificity apart from male homosexuality.

Some aspects of lesbian and gay discourses demonstrate the opposite, namely the failure of the determination of sexuality by gender. Our discourses sometimes establish pluralities of male homosexualities and lesbian sexualities, and construct equivalences across gender divisions and across the homosexual/heterosexual divide. For example, a lesbian who wears a leather jacket, rides a motorcycle and enjoys nightclubs and rough sex may have more in common with some gay men and heterosexuals than with other lesbians, but this common 'ground' does not make her a 'false' lesbian or a 'pretend' man. The multiplication of differences and the expansion of the complexity of the gender-sexuality terrain is always countered, however, by discourses in which difference is neutralised and positions are rigidified. Right-wing discourse makes every attempt to rescue patriarchal familial values from disintegration. In terms of the Right's attack on sexual minorities and the gains won by feminism, the patriarchal definition of gender, the conception of sexuality as determined by gender and the

An official Conservative Party poster from the 1987 election campaign. Photograph by Simon Watney, 1987.

erasure of the possibility of female sexuality are critical strategic manoeuvres.

LESBIAN-NESS AS THE DANGEROUS PRETENDER

In discourse on Section 28, lesbian-ness is excluded from the invader and seducer scripts. Throughout the speeches, the word 'lesbian' is generally used only in compound names designating concepts such as 'gay or lesbian love',[17] 'gay and lesbian rights' and 'Lesbian and Gay Pride Week',[18] 'homosexual or lesbian [teachers]',[19] 'lesbian and gay youth groups',[20] and 'lesbian and gay existences'.[21] These references are important, in that they constitute official recognition of the existence of lesbians which has been previously denied. Lesbian practices were not referred to in the 1533 Act of Henry VIII on sodomy, the 1861 and 1885 laws on sodomy and gross indecency, the 1898 Vagrancy Act or the 1967 Sexual Differences Act which decriminalised some homosexual practices. The attempt in 1921 to include lesbian practices in the category of acts of gross indecency failed because it was believed that such legislation would bring these practices '"to the notice of women who [had] never heard of [them], never dreamed of [them]"'.[22]

The use of the term 'lesbian' in the Section 28 speeches is historically significant, even as an imaginary goodness against which male excesses appear to be all the more excessive, or as a term in a compound name without its own specificity. In some cases, however, lesbian-ness is also portrayed as a specific and *dangerous* element. Howard, as Minister of the Environment (which includes local government affairs), presented a list of examples of the alleged promotion of homosexuality. One of his examples is the inclusion in an Inner London Education Authority bibliography of texts for children of the book entitled *Faultlines*. Quoting from the bibliography, he says that it is a 'hilarious story of a lesbian mother who lives with her lover and their children, a black gay male child

minder and three hundred rabbits'.[23] Baroness Blatch, a leading member of a right-wing lobby on 'family values', states that because male *and* female homosexuality is antithetical to the family, they constitute serious threats to the entire social order. She says, 'There is no future in society in women with women and men with men.'[24]

Lesbian-ness is similarly represented as a dangerous element in the context of legislative discourse about donor insemination. Conservative Party MP, Ann Winterton, tabled a motion in the House of Commons on 26 October 1989, in which she expressed 'profound concern' that lesbians had received artificial insemination by donors at a London pregnancy advisory service clinic. In an opinion poll taken in February, 1990, 49 per cent of Conservative MPs and 33 per cent of all MPs said that they would support a legal ban on lesbians receiving artificial insemination from clinics.[25] Winterton and other Conservative representatives, Wilshire and Lady Saltoun, attempted to amend embryo research legislation to prohibit access to insemination services for lesbians, but their motions failed. However, a Labour amendment which would have guaranteed equal rights to access to donor insemination also failed. A carefully-worded Government clause, ordering clinics to assess the welfare of children born as a result of their services, was passed. According to Government officials, the stability of the marriage of prospective parents and the availability of a 'male role model' are to be taken into account in this assessment. A spokesperson for the Campaign for Access to Donor Insemination states, 'It is clear that the "welfare" clause will have virtually the same practical effects as Lady Saltoun's and Ann Winterton's amendments would have, but in a more insidious and politically acceptable manner.'[26]

Lesbian-ness has therefore been recognised in New Right discourse, but it is generally portrayed as relatively harmless in comparison with the invading and seducing excessiveness of some aspects of male homosexuality. Where lesbian-ness is represented as a dangerous element, however, this representation takes the form of a third metaphorical structure, the representation of lesbian-ness as a dangerous pretender. *Both* male homosexuals and lesbians are represented as dangerous pseudo-parents of children. *Both* male homosexual and lesbian relationships are depicted as dangerous pseudo-norms and pseudo-families. The second part of Section 28 concerning homosexuality as a 'pretend family relationship' addresses this specific danger. It is supposed to make illegal any local authority discourse which 'portrays' homosexuality as 'the norm',[27] grants homosexuality a 'more favourable treatment, a more favourable status, or wider acceptance [than heterosexuality]',[28] or suggests that the '[homosexual] lifestyle is desirable over another'.[29] When asked by Lords Henderson and McIntosh about the precise meaning of the term, 'pretended', the Earl of Caithness says:

> The word 'pretended' . . . relates to the concept that a [homosexual or lesbian] relationship is a conventional family relationship or the portrayal of it as equally valid as the traditional family relationship.[30]

The Earl of Halsbury agrees with this definition and adds that 'pretended' means 'someone who is claiming to something', like a 'pretender to the throne'.[31]

Section 28 is therefore an attempt to eliminate the possibility of deception, the possibility that the corrupted image, gayness and lesbian-ness, of the original relationship, the heterosexual-patriarchal family, may be accepted as a legitimate re-presentation of the original. That deception is itself understood as the result of illegitimate representation, the 'portrayal' of gayness and lesbian-ness as a norm. The crisis is that the false representative, the 'pretender' to the throne,

The mere existence of this and other sex education texts was used as 'evidence' of the promotion of homosexuality by the Right. Dame Jill Knight described this book as a 'pile of filth' and said that its 'promotion' by local councils was 'terrifying' (Official Report, House of Commons, 8 May 1987, col. 998). From Jenny Lives with Eric and Martin *by Susanne Bösch, photographs by Andreas Hansen (Gay Men's Press, 1983).*

may be mistaken as a true version of the original. Section 28 attempts to name gayness and lesbian-ness as the false simulacra, and attempts to distinguish between the pretender and the true original. Logically, the very necessity of such a distinction is indicative of its impossibility, but, for our purposes, this dimension of the Section 28 discourse is critical. Only in the form of the pretender to the original is lesbian-ness specifically portrayed as a dangerous element in New Right discourse.[32]

This inconsistency in the representation of lesbian-ness is nonetheless coherent. Male homosexuality is depicted as invaderness and seducerness in so far as it exceeds proper boundaries, in so far as it 'thrusts itself down the throats' of the normal and the innocent.[33] The point is that we lesbians are generally thought to be lacking anything that could be thrust down anyone's throat, lacking the possibility of disrupting the social order by penetrating proper boundaries. The lesbian with a child, however, does have something dangerous in the terms of New Right discourse. The lesbian with a child shows the possibility of a family which is not based on patriarchal and heterosexual principles, the very principles which are supposed to be universally necessary. It is by her displacement of the married man as the head of the family that she becomes a pretender to the throne.

The lesbian with a child, however, is still not a *sexual* subject. The New Right discourse remains consistent in its erasure of the possibility of lesbian sexuality. Lesbian-ness becomes dangerous not as a sexuality but as a displacement of the traditional family, like female heterosexuality becomes dangerous not as a sexuality but as a displacement of the patriarchal control of female sexuality and reproduction, in the form of prostitution and abortion. The various possibilities for sexual subversion by women are not recognised.

PRO-CENSORSHIP LESBIAN DISCOURSE AS AN IMAGE OF NEW RIGHT DISCOURSE
The implications of the fact that this New Right discourse on lesbian-ness partially constitutes the context in which lesbian representation takes place are complex. Clearly, a defence of lesbian mothering is a priority. The demand for free access to insemination should be regarded as a logical equivalent of the demand for free choice on abortion. [34] In terms of imagery, the depiction of lesbian parenting is in this context strategically significant – a refusal of the New Right claim that any parenting outside the traditional familial order is inherently corrupt.

Alternative imagery which contradicts the New Right conception of the lesbian as harmless difference, and which establishes the *sexuality* of lesbian-ness, also has a strategic importance in this context. Although pro-censorship lesbians demand the suppression of these representations, there is nothing positive

to be won through their concealment. Not only is the suppression of alternative lesbian imagery an illegitimate suppression of difference, it is also a collusion with the New Right demonisation of male homosexuality. The New Right's use of the image of lesbian-ness as harmlessness also constitutes an erasure of the sexuality of lesbian-ness. In this context, there is a tremendous subversive potential in alternative lesbian imagery which shows that which the New Right must conceal, the possibility of a subversive female gender and female sexuality which escapes the patriarchal logic. It is true that this refusal of the harmless and de-sexualised lesbian opens up the possibility of the increased scrutiny of lesbian spaces by right-wing elements. However, a retreat to a strategy of invisibility is no longer an option; the figure of the lesbian mother has marked out our place in official discourse.

The continuities between New Right discourse on lesbian-ness and pro-censorship lesbian criticism of alternative lesbian imagery are striking. In both cases, anxieties about difference are organised around questions of representation. Opposition to difference is represented in terms of the defence of an original against a dangerous pretender. The dangerous pretender, the lesbian mother for the New Right, and the corrupted representations of lesbian-ness for the pro-censorship lesbians, is portrayed as that which threatens to take the place of the original through its simulacra effects. The crisis for the New Right is that vulnerable children may accept the lesbian mother as a genuine parent, while the crisis for the pro-censorship lesbians is that we might tolerate these alternative lesbian-nesses as legitimate variations. The response in both cases is the same – the erasure of lesbian sexuality. [35]

Strategically, it is counter-productive to reproduce this argument about originals and pretenders. This metaphorical structure, and the conception of the harmless lesbian, should be abandoned to right-wing discourse. We should not be fighting for this-lesbian-ness-as-opposed-to-that-lesbian-ness. On the contrary, we should be struggling to create an environment in which different sexualities and identities can emerge to interrupt authoritarian discourses, rather than making claims about a true original. We cannot ask 'Which one's the pretender?' without engaging in an illegitimate suppression of difference and the censorship of alternative representations.

Tank Girl. Tank girl is © Jamie Hewlett.
Tank Girl appears in DEADLINE
magazine: 17 Leathermarket Street, London
SE1, UK.

NOTES

[1] The *Guardian*, 11 October 1989, p.27; for more information on the implications of Section 28, see M. Colvin, *Section 28: A Practical Guide to the Law* (NCCL, 21 Tabard Street, London SE1 4LA); *Section 28: A Guide for Schools, Teachers and Governors* (Stop the Clause Education Group, 26/38 Mount Pleasant, London WC1X 0AP); R. Glutch et. al., *Publish and Still Not Be Damned* (National Council for Voluntary Organisations, 26 Bedford Square, London WC1 3HE), and *Section 28 and the Youth Service: An Information Pack* (London Union of Youth Clubs, 64 Camberwell Road, London SE5 0EN).

[2] Throughout the western philosophical tradition, which Derrida calls the 'metaphysics of presence', there is a continuous privileging of the 'true original' over the 'corrupted' image. In Husserl's account, which Derrida understands as the highest moment in this tradition, the possibility of meaning and communication is grounded on ideal objects, original meaningful essences, which are necessarily prior to expression. A perfect expression is one in which nothing is added to the original sense. This pure reflection of the original is only possible where the expression and reception of the expression take place within consciousness, that is in the case of pure soliloquy (*s'entendre parler*). J. Derrida, *Speech and Phenomena* (Illinois: Northwestern University Press, 1973) pp.32-59.

[3] I am using the somewhat awkward term lesbian-ness rather than lesbian and lesbianism to suggest a quality or element which is not strictly bound to any empirical entity, such as actual people or communities. Technically, it is a floating signifier which is never in absolute proximity to a signified. I will also use the similar terms gayness and blackness below.

[4] The exclusionary strategies practised in the context of the representation of lesbian-ness can take many forms. A lesbian sexuality conference in London in the spring of 1990 excluded transsexuals and women who engaged in sexual practices such as sado-masochism, butch/femme, etc., on the grounds that they promoted sexism and racism. In more progressive contexts, however, the effects of exclusion are more ambiguous. For example, both men and women were invited to view lesbian erotic photography in a recent exhibition in Toronto, *Drawing the Line*, by the collective Kiss and Tell – Susan Stewart, Persimmon Blackbridge and Lizard Jones (an event in the Queer Culture Festival, April 1990). Women viewers were encouraged to write their comments on the walls around the photographs, such that their text became part of the exhibition. Men were asked to write in a traditional comment book. (See Jan Zita Grover's essay, p.000). The exhibition became for the women viewers an interactive experience, or, in other terms, a writerly text, a text which is perpetually re-written, a fusion of the 'original' and interpretation of the 'original', such that difference is multiplied, a text which is 'ourselves writing' (R. Barthes, *S/Z*, New York: Hill and Wang, 1974, p.5). This strategy is subversive in so far as it places women in the non-traditional positions of active consumer-producers. The division of women's and men's comments also encouraged interaction between different women viewers in the form of chains of commentary and counter-commentary; it is perhaps true that many women would not have participated in the same way if men's comments were included on the walls. Nevertheless, this division raises several problems. It is assumed that as a viewer of these photographs, each individual's identity as a woman or as a man is of paramount importance, and that each individual fully identifies with one of these two categories in the act of viewing. This strategy risks the reassertion of that which ought to be questioned, namely the claims to universality and essentialism of binary gender identities. Gender differences are not pre-given but are produced through systems of representation (Parveen Adams, 'A Note on the Distinction Between Sexual Division and Sexual Differences' in *m/f*, no. 3, 1979, p.52). A more 'writerly' representation of lesbianism would both reverse the traditional positions of women and men, and also challenge the conception that the world can be neatly divided into two opposed and separate realms, female experience versus male experience.

[5] Mathematically, if $a = b$ and $b = c$, then $a = c$. Term 'b' is the equivalential signifier. I have analysed the discourse on the prohibition of the promotion of homosexuality in more detail in 'A Symptomology of An Authoritarian Discourse' in *New Formations*, no. 10, Summer 1990, pp.41-65.

[6] *Official Report*, House of Commons, 8/5/87, col. 999.

[7] Simon Watney, 'Psychoanalysis, Sexuality and AIDS' in *Coming On Strong: Gay Politics and Culture*, ed. Simon Shepherd and Mick Wallis (London: Unwin Hyman, 1989), pp.33-4.

[8] *The Wolfenden Report*, the findings of a Home Office Committee on homosexuality, prostitution and the law, was published in 1957. Jeffrey Weeks considers the Report as a classic liberal text in that it proposed that the state should regulate the public sphere but that it should not intervene in the maintenance of moral standards in the private sphere. The effects of the 'Wolfenden strategy' are ambiguous. Both the reforms in the 1960s of the laws on obscenity, homosexuality, abortion, theatre censorship and divorce, and the simultaneous escalation in the policing of prostitution and homosexuality in the public sphere, can be traced back to the Wolfenden approach. Weeks, *Sex, Politics and Society* (London: Longman, 1981), pp.239-44.

[9] *Official Report*, House of Lords, 16/2/88, cols

593-4. Many of the politicians who opposed Section 28 chose to argue the opposite, that sexuality is fixed biologically at birth, that 'we are what we are'. They said that legislation against the promotion of homosexuality was absurd in that no sexuality can be promoted (*Official Report*, Standing Committee 'A', Roberts, 8/12/87, col. 1215; and in the House of Commons, Pike, 15/12/87, col. 1014, Hughes, 9/3/88, cols 340, 390, Livingston, 9/3/88, col. 417, Fisher, 9/3/88, col. 394). Where the New Right has grasped the importance of representation and struggles around identity, the arguments of these politicians, albeit well-intentioned and in some cases strategically necessary, implied that representation is irrelevant to politics. In the context of the New Right attack on sexual minorities, the belief that homosexuality naturally pertains to 10 per cent of the population could become a licence for complacency. Discourse organised around the conception of biologically-fixed sexualities negates both the value of building and expanding the lesbian and gay movement, and the strategy of challenging *everyone's* conception of sexuality and gender. This strategy of interruption is located precisely on the terrain of representation and the construction of identities.

10 *Official Report*, House of Lords, 18/12/86, col. 310.

11 ibid.

12 ibid.

13 Roger Scruton, *Sexual Desire* (London: Weidenfeld and Nicolson, 1986), p.308.

14 ibid., p.307.

15 ibid., p.308.

16 ibid.

17 MP Fisher, *Official Report*, House of Commons, 9/3/88, p.394.

18 Earl of Caithness, *Official Report*, House of Lords, 16/2/88, p.621.

19 MP Lestor, *Official Report*, House of Commons, 15/12/87, p.1023.

20 MP Wilshire, *Official Report*, House of Commons, Standing Committee 'A', 8/12/87, p.1206.

21 Baroness Blatch, *Official Report*, House of Lords, 16/2/88, p.600.

22 Lord Desart, House of Lords, quoted in J. Weeks, *Coming Out* (London: Quartet, 1977).

23 *Official Report*, House of Commons, Standing Committee 'A', 8/12/87, p.1209.

24 *Official Report*, House of Lords, 16/2/88, p.610.

25 The *Guardian*, 6 March 1990, p.5.

26 'Tories fail in bid to ban insemination', *The Pink Paper*, 2 June 1990, p.3.

27 Howard, *Official Report*, House of Commons, 15/12/87, p.1019.

28 Earl of Caithness, *Official Report*, House of Lords, 1/2/88, p.889.

29 Baroness Blatch, *Official Report*, House of Lords, 16/2/88, pp.599-600.

30 *Official Report*, House of Lords, 16/2/88, p.633.

31 ibid.

32 Lesbians are specifically *defended* only in terms of the dangerous pretender metaphor. Lord Rea attempted to amend the legislation to remove the prohibition of the teaching of homosexuality as a pretended family relationship. In his speech, he says that this phrase is 'particularly offensive' and adds that he was himself raised by his mother and another woman, who had a relationship which was 'not simply friendship'. He asserts that he had a 'good family', and had 'as rich and as happy a childhood as most children who are reared by heterosexual couples'. *Official Report*, House of Lords, 16/2/88, p.617-8.

33 Paraphrase of MP Dickens, who says: '[homosexuals] are only likely to get that support [against violent attacks] if they stop continuing to flaunt their homosexuality and thrusting it down other people's throats', *Official Report*, House of Commons, 9/3/88, p.417.

34 The rights of lesbian mothers, and of the children of lesbians, are not only threatened in terms of custody battles and access to insemination services. Questions about the official status of this parenting can also emerge in terms of the registration of the birth, the naming of the child, applications for social security payments and access to educational institutions. In applying for mother's allowance in Toronto, a lesbian friend was obliged to indicate either the name of the father of her child or that the father was unknown. She asked that the state officials recognise that she had used artificial insemination by an anonymous and private donor. In a court decision, it was determined that she had to choose one of the two existing categories to qualify for assistance. With her subsequent refusal to define her child in terms of a father figure, 'known' or 'unknown', she was denied mother's allowance.

35 For a critique of the discourse of pro-censorship lesbians on sexuality and censorship, see Margaret Hunt, 'The De-Eroticisation of Women's Liberation: Social Purity Movements and the Revolutionary Feminism of Sheila Jeffreys' in *Feminist Review*, no. 34, Spring 1990, pp.23-46.

THE CEREMONY

Della Grace

DREAM GIRLS

Deborah Bright

Untitled, from series Dream Girls *1989–90, photomontage.*

The impulse for a lesbian photomonteur (menteur) to paste (not suture, please) her constructed butch-girl self-image into conventional heterosexual narrative stills from old Hollywood movies requires no elaborate explanations. For a long time, I resisted doing such obvious 'one-liners' because my training as a fine art photographer had taught me to make only work that was indirect, densely layered, elliptical and metaphorical. On the other hand, I felt hobbled by various (and competing) tendencies among feminist film and photo theorists whose demands for analytical rigour on questions of gender and power I shared, yet in whose writings (and works) I found little that evoked my own experience as a lesbian.

Even as I submitted myself to the tutelage of strict mistresses such as Mary Ann Doane and Jacqueline Rose, I found myself envying the unabashed funkiness of contributors to lesbian porn rags like *On Our Backs, Bad Attitude* and *Outrageous Women* who brandished their strap-ons and wooed their lace-clad 'bottoms' with gusto, derisive of righteous feminist mafias. The montages, then, were conceived and made in the spirit of the latter – to construct 'scenes' and summon into material form these old fantasies for my own pleasure. But it is with a nod to my intellectual 'tops' and the serious context of this book that I attempt a brief archaeology of what preceded this work. I am also indebted to the work and example of Jo Spence, who showed me the importance of allowing myself to play, remember and reconstruct my social and psychic selves before the camera.

Though I represent my adult self in these altered stills, the fantasies are from my childhood and adolescence. I grew up in the white, white collar professional suburbs of Washington, DC, during the 1950s and 1960s, in a devoutly Christian family that very much resembled the conservative, Republican post-war ideal of the time. Because the values of my milieu were socially privileged (even divinely sanctioned, it seemed) and because I had little contact with those of different origins and beliefs, I had no perspective on their severity, intolerance and reductiveness until I left home at 18. Even then I spent another decade of unresolved passions for women, followed by a stint of heterosexual marriage, before I found the means to come out, both psychically and socially.

But thinking back over those years of childhood and adolescence, I recognise many signposts along the way that matched those of many of my lesbian friends: my intense attachments to particular girlfriends; a pugnacious contempt for things 'feminine'; the embrace of a tomboy identity (named 'Jack'); and the idealisation of older women who were intelligent, autonomous and spirited. None of these predilections particularly troubled my mother, who convinced herself (more than me) that I would outgrow them and that my desires would 'naturally' turn to boys. The power of parental suggestion is great when there are few visible alternatives. In the world of my adolescence, 'spinsters' were seen only as heterosexual women whose status was not chosen but given by unfortunate circumstances.

But it was clearly my adolescent fantasy life that kept me going when I lacked any knowledge of the realising of homoerotic desire, a fantasy life fed by images from my immediate environment. I didn't seek these from illicit or underground sources – they were the banal fare of everyday experience, the kinds of shows and novels most of my schoolmates also saw and read, the magazines that lined the coffee-tables of many middle-class, suburban living rooms.

My fantasy materials were highly particularised to my race and social class: I day-dreamed my narrow culture in the language of its signifiers, turned out to perfection in the cinematic narratives of MGM, Paramount and Warner Brothers. But subject-identification in the movies is a slippery thing, more complicated than most heterosexual feminist film theorists have acknowledged to date. So I'm going to try here to analyse the kinds of erotically satisfying subject-positions I achieved for myself in certain films in the 1950s and 1960s, positions that I might retrospectively call 'lesbian' without essentialising that relation in any way.

In classic Hollywood romances, reading a contradictory 'lesbianised' subject-position usually demands resisting the film narrative's resolution, which often culminates in the monogamous union of the hero and heroine. My resistant reading was often (though not always) triggered by a compelling erotic attraction to the heroine.[1] After informally polling a sample of lesbian friends of my general age-group who shared a similar socialisation in the pre-Stonewall USA, I found that female stars who attracted a dedicated following among us included Katherine Hepburn, Lauren Bacall, Greta Garbo, Marlene Dietrich, Maureen O'Hara, Barbara Stanwyck, Doris Day, Ann Southern, Julie Andrews, Vanessa Redgrave and Audrey Hepburn. Cinematic traits these stars shared in their films from the 1940s to the mid-1960s included supple, athletic bodies in tailored suits, strong facial features, dominant rather than subordinate body language, displays of superior intelligence and wit, and (by definition) roles that challenged conventional feminine stereotypes.[2] These transgressions of the norms of femininity were often 'punished' or regulated by the monogamous, heterosexual logic of the film narrative, but that did not matter much. For reception is driven by desire and what many young, middle-class proto-dykes 'saw' in these films in the early 1960s were concrete (if attenuated) suggestions of erotic possibilities that they could not name and that their own lived experience did not provide.

It seemed easy enough to fragment the narrative that evoked this desire and incorporate the desirable parts into a coherent day-dream where the heroines' 'potential/ potency' as homoerotic partners could be more fully and safely realised. These fantasy scenarios were of course far removed from the original narrative context of the film. Simon Watney has written of this kind of 'aggregation of sexual fantasy' around objects 'legitimated' by heterosexual culture for other purposes: the classic Hollywood Western as a staple scenario of gay male pornography, for example.[3] It is also testimony to the vitality and fluidity of desire that it so easily appropriates whatever channels are available to it, and certainly without requiring the kind of elaborate psychic calesthenics that some film theorists assign to any female spectator who possesses a desiring look.[4]

My pleasure in these montages is with the power relations among the characters they depict; with the sabotage of the heterosexual Hollywood set-up by a supplementary or substitute character of ambiguous gender who upsets the heterosexual economy of the scene. The montages undermine the function of the love triangle in the heterosexual narrative. For example, the lesbian 'driver' in Katherine Hepburn's car makes Spencer Tracy's kiss benign and impotent – little more than a grandfatherly peck on the cheek which Hepburn indulges. In the altered still from *The Sound of Music*, Christopher Plummer's character is apprehensive and protective of his 'property' in the presence of a potent (and equal) rival for her attention. Before its alteration, the dinner scene from *A Touch of Class* showed Glenda Jackson staring fixedly off-screen as George Segal held forth over his wine. I gave Jackson something more interesting to look at, leaving Segal firmly locked out of the visual loop. Other stills feature more conventional pairings (a lesbian inserted in place of the male partner as seducer/playmate), while several montages explore the eroticism of a drag identity. These are my fantasy postcards from childhood, sent with love.

'Lesbianised', these film stills raise a different set of expectations about the action that took place and the resolution of these stories. Their subversiveness is related to their time in history, a time when gender roles and sexuality in Hollywood cinema were strictly regulated by the Hays Code.[5] Before the 1970s, industry censors screened films for overt signs of homosexuality: 'fruity' men and 'dykey' women. Because they concentrated on flamboyant behaviours constructed by bigoted stereotypes, censors overlooked films with less explicitly coded signifiers of homoerotic bonding: for example, John Dall and Farley Granger in Alfred Hitchcock's *Rope* (1948), James Dean and Sal Mineo in *Rebel Without A Cause* (1955) and Shirley MacLaine and Audrey Hepburn in William Wyler's *The Children's Hour* (1962). Despite producers' and directors' public denials (when pressed by the Catholic Legion of Decency and other suspicious critics) that homosexuality was at issue in these films, it wasn't difficult to read such content into them. With the general loosening of sexual mores during the late 1960s and early 1970s and the emergence of the gay-rights movement, gay and lesbian sexuality began to be openly represented in Hollywood films, though to date it has been largely regulated by cinematic conventions of heterosexuality or those of 'sin and penance'. But because post-1960s films allow a new (if not altogether satisfying) visual explicitness, they don't offer me the same emotional charge or sense of discovery/trespass that I found in those earlier film images where my desire shaped the content to my own needs. In short, my film-still fantasies are constructed by (even as they deconstruct) the eroticised taboo and invisibility that were a part of their original context.

Finally, I should make some reference to the tactics of appropriation, pastiche and charade in postmodernist practice, particularly in the work of Cindy Sherman, Sherrie Levine and Barbara Kruger. Following Brecht's admonition that the structure of a representation be laid bare, revealed rather than mystified, postmodern appropriationists made their borrowings blatant and used the 'already-given' of their imagery to thwart conventional pleasures of fantasy and seamlessness. Like many feminist theorists of the 1970s and 1980s, they saw women's politicised appropriations of given signifying systems as a useful and sophisticated weapon against our invisibility (as well as a well-aimed blow at modernism's idealist aesthetics). Even if women could not stand outside masculine symbolic discourse, according to these theorists, they could use its gaps, contradictions and elisions to represent their own (feminine) identities and experience. Levine's rephotographing and repainting of canonical masterworks by male artists, Kruger's utilisation of gender-specified modes of address in her public signage and Sherman's apeing of a generic repertoire of stereotyped women's roles in high art, film noir, advertising, television soaps and other mass media sources were forceful, economical critiques of how the male-dominated sexual economy was reproduced at all levels of the culture industry.

While my strategy of photographer-as-performer in *Dream Girls* might recall Cindy Sherman's *Film Stills* of a decade ago, I have a different agenda which reflects the differing historical experiences of heterosexual women and lesbians. Sherman constructs images of femininity in her *Film Stills*, each frame producing a coherent 'cinematic' illusion channelled by our expectations of the familiar 'type' she represents for us ('dumb blonde', 'ingenue', 'seductress', 'working girl', 'teenybopper', and so on). Sherman's series is effective precisely because it is multiple; she (girl/woman) appears in each image, but she (Sherman) is not *in* any one of them. She is everywhere and nowhere simultaneously. But as Judith Williamson has observed, 'So strongly is femininity evoked in these situations that they have to be *sexual* – is there any definition of femininity that isn't?'[6]

In conventional representation, 'woman' equals sexuality (that *is* her 'difference' from men) and Sherman reproduces and records this governing equation in her many guises. Sherman's *Film Stills* are grounded in heterosexual definitions of femininity, which are largely male-defined and regulated. She brilliantly exposes the constructed nature of our culture's 'essences' of femininity (a condition that can only exist in relation to an equally imputed essence of 'masculinity'), but she does not challenge the universality of heterosexuality as a governing discourse. But heterosexuality and its discontents are problems most lesbians do not have.

As the title *Dream Girls* suggests, my work is about fantasy. The lesbian subject roams from still to still, movie to movie, disrupting the narrative and altering it to suit her purposes, just as I did when I first watched those films. This lesbian subject is herself constructed: a partial, fragmented representation of someone who may or may not correspond to the historical Deborah Bright who dreamt her into being. But what matters is that she's having a good time and that she's doing it with Julie, Vanessa, Glenda and Kate. To the lesbian friends who've seen them, these *Dream Girls* have provoked a whoop of recognition and pleasure, and that is satisfaction enough.

NOTES
[1] My identification always incorporated elements of both conventional gender roles: I fantasised pursuing, courting and making love with the heroine, while at the same time, I also fantasised *being* (like) her.

[2] The impulse to search for any apparent continuity between such cinema-inspired fantasies and the lives of the actors who played them is quickly discouraged. In the case of Katherine Hepburn, gay film historian Vito Russo recounts her horror at the very thought of homosexuality, flatly refusing to believe that such people existed. 'In later years, she has been a vocal opponent of homosexuality, linking it with other "social ills" of society,' Vito Russo, *The Celluloid Closet* (New York: Harper and Row, 1987), p.116.

[3] Simon Watney, *Policing Desire* (London: Comedia Publishing Group, 1986; 1987), p.73. Watney introduces this point to argue that such wholesale appropriations from the banal image-banks of everyday experience put to naught efforts by anti-porn interests to designate certain genres as inherently 'pornographic'.

[4] For example, Constance Penley quotes Mary Ann Doane's account of 'the convoluted means' by which a woman might assume a centred position of spectatorship in 'women's films' like *Rebecca*: 'I am looking, as a man would, for a woman'; or else, 'I submit myself, as if I were a man who thought he was a woman, to a woman who thinks she is a man'. Constance Penley, *Feminism and Film Theory* (London and New York: Routledge, 1988), p.16.

[5] The Hays Code, or Motion Picture Production Code, was formulated by the industry under the leadership of Will Hays, Hoosier Presbyterian elder and head of the Motion Picture Producers and Distributors of America. It was designed to protect the industry from outside censorship in the 1930s and remained in effect until the late 1960s. After some daring experimentation with gender roles in films of the 1920s and early 1930s, religious and civic pressure groups had demanded reform, particularly the banning of homoeroticism and 'deviant' sexuality on screen. Hays also inserted morals clauses into actors' contracts and kept a list of 'those deemed "unsafe" because of their personal lives'. See Vito Russo, op.cit., pp.31, 45.

[6] Judith Williamson, 'Images of "Woman"' in *Screen*, vol. 24, no. 6, 1983, p.104.

ACKNOWLEDGEMENTS
I would like to thank Jean Hardisty, Nancy Gonchar, Jan Grover, Jean Fraser and Tessa Boffin for their encouragement and suggestions as I wrote this essay. Nancy also deserves special thanks and credit for her help with the photography in *Dream Girls*.

COMING OUT TWICE

Jacqui Duckworth

Coming Out Twice is based loosely on a film I am currently directing. The film is a fictionalised account of my personal experience of multiple sclerosis and attempts an insight into the traumatic nature of the disease. Using surrealism to evoke an increasing sense of unreality as the disease inexorably enters daily life, the narrative highlights the psychological and emotional effects of MS.

This photo-essay is an assemblage of stills from the film taken by Sandra Hooper, Nigel Maudsley and Rachel Taite. The text has been written in collaboration with Jean Fraser.

I was diagnosed as having MS in 1984. I have what is known medically as an intentional tremor. This means that, although I am still when I am relaxing, I cannot move my limbs without shaking.

Having come out as a lesbian over twenty years ago, I have been surprised at how that earlier 'coming out' is mirrored in people's reactions when they realise I have a disability and their previous assumption of normality is shattered.

Surrounded by language,
unable to move,
words fail her.

*In a dark room she measures herself
against a forgotten and idealised self-image.
Her desire for wholeness is dislocated.
Fragments of a former existence haunt her.*

She experiences the unreality
of everyday things made strange.
Does she imagine the flea
which crawls out of the fur cup and saucer
and hops with great vitality beyond her reach?

Bound over to communicate
an experience too uncomfortable to hear:
Expectations are unreliable.

Alone, at a table set for others,
she tries to make order out of chaos,
and yet, with their own purpose,
the peas keep jumping off her fork.

She has a vision where unfamiliarity will recede.
A future where she will again
make friends with her body.
An acceptance purged of anger and uncertainty.
It will not matter if people stare.

ACKNOWLEDGEMENTS
Thanks to Adjoa Andoh who appears in these stills, to
Sandra Hooper, Nigel Maudsley and Rachel Taite, and to
Jean Fraser.

UNKNOWN DEVIANCIES (WHAT A DISH!)

Kaucyila Brooke

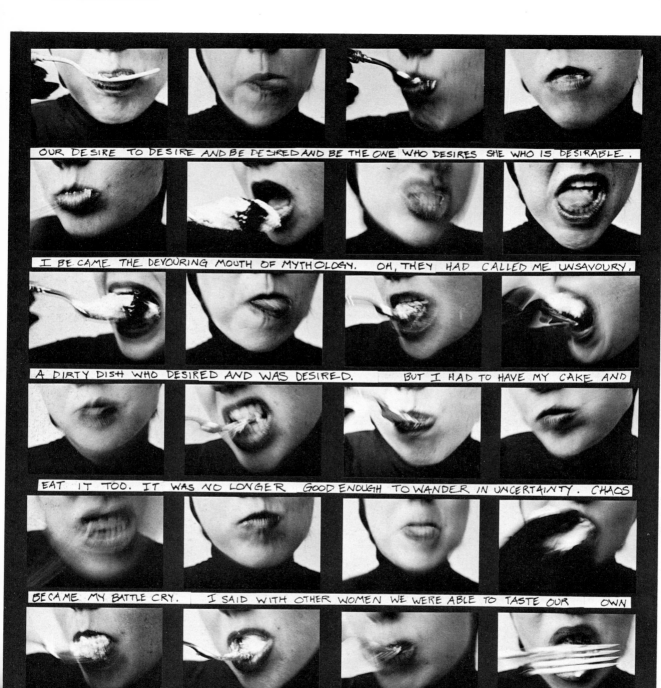

OUR DESIRE TO DESIRE AND BE DESIRED AND BE THE ONE WHO DESIRES SHE WHO IS DESIRABLE.

I BECAME THE DEVOURING MOUTH OF MYTHOLOGY.   OH, THEY HAD CALLED ME UNSAVOURY,

A DIRTY DISH WHO DESIRED AND WAS DESIRED.   BUT I HAD TO HAVE MY CAKE AND

EAT IT TOO. IT WAS NO LONGER GOOD ENOUGH TO WANDER IN UNCERTAINTY. CHAOS

BECAME MY BATTLE CRY.   I SAID WITH OTHER WOMEN WE WERE ABLE TO TASTE OUR   OWN

TEXTUAL BODY.   WE WOULD NOT BE VOMITED OUT. IT WAS A TOUGH BATTLE.

San Diego photographer Kaucyila Brooke makes what she describes as 'wall-size photographic sequences in comic-strip format that consider lesbian relationships within American popular culture.' Produced over the past five years, Brooke's large scale photo-text installations look at aspects of lesbian culture and alternative communities. Wry and often quite critical, they probe some of the ways lesbian relationships both challenge and reproduce the power relations and narratives of the wider culture. Situating her lesbian narratives within popular cultural contexts – the comic book, the Western, the photo-novella – Brooke dislodges some common but less-and-less productive modes for lesbian cultural practice. Interrupting conventions of documentary and autobiographical authority, and the ways they have been used to ground oversimplified and ahistorical models of 'personal experience', Brooke explores the intense mediation present in any effort to construct, much less communicate, a sense of self or identity . . .

Yet throughout Brooke's works we find the constant return to and reworking of interrelated questions – about power, sexual identity and how individuals navigate conflicting cultural codes. Brooke's work is also centrally 'about' how the works themselves navigate the borders between conflicting cultural worlds, how they represent lesbian subjectivities and issues within a gallery context, and articulate subcultural positions within a pervasively homophobic artworld.

Liz Kotz, 'Strategies for Lesbian Representation: Kaucyila Brooke's Photography' in *S.F. Camerawork Quarterly,* vol. 17, no. 2, Summer 1990.

LESBIANS, PHOTOGRAPHY AND AIDS

Deborah Bright

My interest in looking at examples of lesbian photographers' work around AIDS is not to acknowledge any distinctly lesbian aesthetic response to the epidemic. Nor am I proposing that lesbians and lesbian artists have any more righteous or profound a perspective on this issue and its meanings than do other groups. Also, to reduce the discussion to one medium – photography – is quite arbitrary, but I do so only because of space constraints and because photography is my particular area of practice and expertise. In many ways, I think the most powerful and effective work across the issues of gay and lesbian sexualities and AIDS has been done in independent video and film. [1] Nonetheless, I see some interesting developments among lesbian communities and among the photographers working within them that have been influenced by the cultural analysis around AIDS and the issues it has raised.

AIDS has touched lesbians in irrevocable ways, even those who have remained aloof from direct involvement in AIDS activism. As for gay men born before 1970, the epidemic has scored an ineradicable boundary line in our collective consciousness. We live in a 'post-AIDS' world, and with daily realities of living as a lesbian or gay man in that world which have changed profoundly. Although the media ignored us, lesbians were on the frontlines from the very beginning of the epidemic and the struggle over its representations. *Sex and Germs*, the first book to analyse the social and political ramifications of AIDS for the gay community, was written by a lesbian community activist in the Boston area, Cindy Patton. [2]

Other lesbian writers, art critics and activists, including Amber Hollibaugh, Paula Treichler, Jan Zita Grover and Martha Gever have made major contributions to the literature on the cultural analysis of AIDS in the USA. This is not surprising because it was clear to lesbians who were active in feminist politics before AIDS that the fall-out from the public hysteria and bigotry that came in the wake of sensationalistic media coverage of the epidemic would not be directed exclusively at gay men, but would fuel an already rolling conservative backlash against tolerance for social diversity, alternative family and sexual values, and women's – especially poor women's – rights to control their own sexual and reproductive choices.

Indeed, the anti-abortion movement and the right-wing campaigns against homosexuality in the USA, including Reverend Lou Sheldon's 'Coalition for Traditional Values', Oliver North's 'Freedom Alliance' and Reverend Donald Wildmon's 'American Family Association', should be understood as part of an organised conservative offensive against 'non-procreative', 'permissive' sexualities. The AIDS epidemic has been more than useful for raising the spectre of divinely sanctioned punishment for 'unnatural' sex. And it is women's immoral desire for 'free sex' (that is, sex without procreation), according to these same critics, that has brought about the supposed epidemic of abortion since the US Supreme Court's 1973 decision legalising the procedure (*Roe* v. *Wade*).[3] The last decade has seen a rollback of abortion rights at federal and state levels and repeated efforts to reinstate draconian laws around parental consent for abortion or to abolish it outright, to preserve state sodomy statutes (a right upheld by the Supreme Court in *Bowers* v *Hardwick* 1986), to repeal anti-discrimination laws for gays and lesbians, and to refuse public funding for clean needle distribution, condom distribution and safer-sex education which have been proved to be the most effective ways to date to halt the

Carol LaFavor and Allyson Hunter, two lesbian PWAs, at the National Association of People With AIDS Conference held in Dallas, 1987. Photograph by Jane Rosett.

Spread of HIV infection.[4]

Certainly many heterosexual women have been active around AIDS issues as well, as demonstrators, organisers, caregivers, fund-raisers, consciousness raisers and artists, and it has been much remarked that the group that has been conspicuously absent from the scene of AIDS activism has been the socially dominant one – heterosexual men. But in the art photography world, ironically, it has been a straight, white man who has been given the most acclaim and public space to represent his morbid vision of the AIDS epidemic. I am referring to Nicholas Nixon's much-exhibited portraits of People With Aids (PWAs), such as his series on Tom Moran. I do not want to take time to review Nixon's work or critique it here; that's been done quite effectively elsewhere.[5] But this kind of work and its cultural authority is a useful baseline to keep in mind when considering the kinds of practices that follow.

Understandably, the initial instinct for AIDS activists and sympathisers, both gay and straight, was to counter directly both mass media and high cultural representations like Nixon's which isolated their subjects and emphasised external signs of degeneracy and wasting. The incessant parading of 'before-and-after' photographs of bodies ravaged by Kaposi's sarcoma and weight loss allowed entrenched cultural stereotypes to supply their own bigoted explanations for these 'facts'. Thus the earliest kinds of images that appeared in the wake of the AIDS crisis, made by activists and those who cared for PWAs, were 'positive images' of gays and lesbians who were HIV antibody positive, shown without visible signs of wasting or disease, frequently in the company of loving partners or as part of a strong, defiant community. Jane Rosett's photographs made for the *People With AIDS Coalition Newsletter* are good examples of this

PWA Vera Ajanaku participating in her first 'Die-In' at a demo which took place during a speech by the Director of the Food and Drug Administration, Frank Young, 1988. Photograph by Jane Rosett.

approach. Within the strategic context of the activist network, Rosett's pictures served the valuable function of documenting a community in crisis and acting on its own behalf. Though she makes her living as a freelance photojournalist, Rosett has not hesitated to pull her photographs from national mass media circulation when she has felt they were being used to support a homophobic slant on a story.

However, it is when photographs were made with higher, artistic pretensions, rather than for local, instrumental purposes, that the inadequacy of 'positive images' as a re-presentational strategy became clear. Raised to the level of art, where individual expressions are automatically assumed to have the status of universal utterances and are exhibited in gallery settings, images of PWAs or even the subject of AIDS itself frequently took on a loaded sentimentalism reminiscent of *The Family of Man*.[6] These people deserve the empathy and pity of the non-afflicted because they are 'human' – they love, they laugh, they cry, they die.

The title of a recent AIDS benefit exhibition, *The Indominable Spirit*, says it all. Curated by art impresario Marvin Heifferman and exhibited at the International Centre for Photography in New York, it was a tasteful show, that is, it had few works by PWAs, 'out' gay artists or AIDS activists, and none that called into question the spectator's privilege or complicity in the appalling social indifference to the majority of the afflicted. In fact, very few of the works addressed AIDS at all. This is the 'suitable way' to approach AIDS, the *New York Times* tells us – not like those rabble-rousing ACT-UP people, or angry, accusatory works like those shown in the Artists' Space exhibition that so offended National Endowment for the Arts' director John Frohnmayer. *The Indominable Spirit* was the show financed by corporate dollars with big-name artists and a glossy catalogue with a self-congratulatory essay by the *New York Times'*

photography critic, Andy Grundberg.

The Indominable Spirit strategy also characterises the work of straight photographers like Sage Sohier, but with a twist.[7] Instead of it being a matter of the 'indominable spirit' of her subjects, gay couples living and loving in the Age of AIDS, it is more the 'indominable spirit' of the photographer who ventures into exotic and dangerous territories on self-imposed assignments. I say 'dangerous' because in 1986 when Sohier began making her portraits of gay and lesbian couples, there was a great deal of public misinformation and fear about how the virus could be transmitted; mosquito bites, public toilets, sneezing, coughing and spitting were all suspect. While she expresses an awareness of the renewed attacks on gays aroused by fears about the epidemic, her interest was not in producing 'positive images' for use by gays or educating her public about how gay and lesbian relationships were being affected by this crisis. She frankly admitted in an interview that she was not interested in anything more than producing a 'compelling' picture of her subjects, a picture that was psychically 'provocative' – even if it consciously played on old, stereotyped notions among heterosexuals about what homosexuals do in bed. 'I guess I like the idea of giving people (that is, heterosexuals) a glimpse into lives they wouldn't normally get', she says.[8]

But her chosen glimpses are purged of any emotional effect among the partners depicted; the touching is timid, reserved, uneasy, embarrassed, ambivalent. Gays and lesbians find these representations disappointing indeed. How sad and tense we all look – depressed and even guilty. And art galleries are only too happy to show work like Sohier's, and arts agencies to fund it, because it gives the appearance of being politically hip and liberally tolerant toward the reductive range of gay subjects documented (who are almost uniformly white and middle class, as well as monogamous), while preserving a safe and sanitary distance from them.

Gay activists responded with angry critiques of such paternalistic and 'yellow-gloved' responses from the liberal establishment – as well as the more blatantly sensationalistic images of Nixon and photojournalist Rosalind Solomon.

We rejected the implicit assumption that if we looked, behaved and comported ourselves just like straights, our 'crisis' (our very survival) would be worthy of acknowledgement. In addition, the careful decorum and propriety of such images re-established a new 'old' norm for homosexuals. Monogamous couplehood and domestic bliss with the differentness of our sexualities suppressed: no leather, no latex, no butches, no queens, no S/M, no disco, no bathhouse, no multiple partners, no multi-racial couplings, no fantasy. Hence, the 'badness' of Robert Mapplethorpe and the thundering footsteps of liberal flight from his defence in 1989.[9]

In her series of photocollages, *Paranoid Delusions*, lesbian photographer and video artist Connie Samaras spins frightening scenarios that parody the blending of fact with unfounded speculation in broadcast news reporting. Angered by government indifference to the AIDS crisis and the media's tendencies to blame the victims for their disease, Samaras gives us her paranoid version of the origin of the AIDS epidemic. Adopting an authoritative, journalistic voice, she superimposes the following lurid text over images photographed from television, the central pair of which features what appear to be clinicians conducting laboratory tests of an unspecified sort:

AIDS [is] a plot by radical right-wing Americans to make the homosexual the next scapegoat in the late 20th century . . . The Right, having a lot of money to spend, has invented, in their genetic engineering laboratories, some sort of organism that can be planted and contained in places frequented by sexually active homosexuals, like the back rooms of gay leather bars . . . Before planting this micro-organism in the gay community, the Right had to test it out first to make almost 100% sure that they could contain this virus within a specific community . . . For this experiment they chose the Haitian immigrants who had recently arrived . . . in an attempt to escape political oppression . . . Soon after the assumed success of the Haitian experiment, they tested AIDS on heroin addicts for additional data . . .

The text goes on to describe how the virus would infect the homosexual population and how public consent for the isolation (as 'humane' protection from vigilantism) and eventual elimination of homosexual populations would be secured in the face of a 'national emergency'. Five years later, certain segments of Samaras's paranoid tale ring terribly true, including the recent stepped-up physical attacks on gays and lesbians by fascist skinheads and teenage punks in the USA, as well as the continuing usefulness of AIDS for fuelling a socially reactionary domestic offensive against homosexuals, now that the apparent end of the cold war has made communism obsolete as a focus for right-wing wrath.

With the recent attacks by conservative politicians on state funding for 'obscene' and 'homoerotic' art, the state and corporate-funded art world has become a site of fear, loathing and self-censorship. But in the middle-class gay and lesbian subcultures, most notably ACT-UP and its art affiliates like Gran Fury, defiant retorts to social reactionaries, anti-porn activists and timid liberals alike continue to flourish. The success of safer-sex education and advocacy has rested on the proliferation, not the reduction, of options in sexual practice: of a much larger role for fantasy, visual and tactile rituals, the use of toys and

AIDS: IS A PLOT BY RADICAL RIGHT WING AMERICANS TO MAKE THE HOMOSEXUAL THE NEXT MAJOR SCAPEGOAT IN THE LATE 20TH CENTURY. THIS WOULD EVENTUALLY LEAD TO A GENOCIDE UNLIKE ANY OTHER IN HISTORY BE-CAUSE HOMOSEXUALITY IS NOT READILY IDENTIFIABLE THROUGH COLOR, ETHNICITY, NATIONALITY, LINEAGE, ORGANIZATIONAL MEMBERSHIP, OR RELIGIOUS AFFILIATION.

THE RIGHT, HAVING A LOT OF MONEY TO SPEND, HAS INVENTED, IN THEIR GENETIC ENGINEERING LABORATORIES, SOME SORT of MICRO-ORGANISM THAT CAN BE PLANTED AND CONTAINED IN PLACES FREQUENTED BY SEXUALLY ACTIVE HO-MOSEXUALS, LIKE, THE BACK ROOMS OF GAY LEATHER BARS.

BEFORE PLANTING THIS MICRO-ORGANISM IN THE GAY COMMUNITY, THE RIGHT HAD TO TEST IT OUT FIRST TO MAKE ALMOST 100% SURE THAT THEY COULD CONTAIN THIS VIRUS WITHIN A SPECIFIC COMMUNITY OF PEOPLE. THEY NEEDED AN EXPENDABLE & ISOLATED COMMUNITY WITHIN THE UNITED STATES IN CASE ANYTHING WENT WRONG LIKE AN UNCONTROLLED SPREADING OF THE DISEASE. FOR THIS EXPERIMENT THEY CHOSE THE HAITIAN IMMIGRANTS WHO HAD RECENTLY ARRIVED EN MASSE ON THE SHORES OF FLORIDA IN AN ATTEMPT TO ESCAPE POLITICAL OPPRESSION. THEY WERE IMPRISONED IN DETENTION CAMPS, THEY WERE EXPENDABLE AS LABORERS, THEY WERE BLACK, THEY WERE PERFECT FOR THE EXPERIMENT. SOON AFTER THE ASSUMED SUCCESS OF THE HAITIAN EXPERIMENT, THEY TESTED AIDS ON HEROIN ADDICTS FOR ADDITIONAL DATA.

THE RIGHT WING WILL CONTINUE TO ALLOW AIDS, UNCHECKED, TO REACH EPIDEMIC PROPORTIONS AMONG GAYS. EVENTUALLY, THE PUBLIC, ONCE THE MEDIA BLACKOUT ON AIDS IS LIFTED, WILL START TO PANIC. IN THE BEGINNING, THE

Paranoid Delusions: Acquired Immune Deficiency Syndrome,
1985. Photograph by Connie Samaras. In the collection of Gilbert
and Lila Silverman, Detroit. Panel 24″ × 38″.

costumes, the integration of prophylactics into sex play, role-playing, consensual head-games, and so forth. And images play a major role, images made by us primarily for our own private and subcultural consumption. For lesbians, who (as women) have historically lacked the opportunities and means to produce our own explicit sexual imagery, we have witnessed nothing short of a renaissance over the past five years!

That these images are mostly produced by white, educated, middle-class artists bespeaks the all too narrow spectrum of available venues and the limited applicability of issues like 'playing sexy and safe' for other groups, who have little leisure time and resources for the consumption and production of private fantasies, who endure more stringent communal policing by religious and ethnic customs, or to whom theoretical niceties and slick production values smack of class arrogance. Like the culture industry at large, the gay and lesbian art communities share race and class biases which run like fault-lines through our discourses and institutions and that need to be much more systematically acknowledged and addressed.

A most encouraging trend, I think, can be seen in the increasing application of theories and tactics from successful AIDS activism to issues of specific interest to women. Safer-sex education for women, the liberation of sexual fantasy for women, increased access to health care for lower income women, the opening up of drug test protocols to women and poorer patients, and advocacy for the increased accountability of the medical community and pharmaceutical industries to women, are just some issues currently being worked on by lesbian feminists who were formerly or still are involved in AIDS work.

For two decades, lesbian photographer Ann Meredith has been photographing women's communities and women's lives, mostly in the San Francisco area and, presently, in New York. Her approach to photographing women

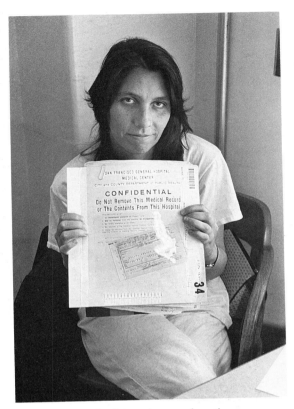

Sharon – Confidential, 1987, from the series Until that Last Breath: Women with AIDS, *by Ann Meredith.*

with AIDS, a project she began in 1987 and that has culminated in a sixty-piece show, *Until that Last Breath: Women, Children and AIDS,* can be traced to her persistent desire to document lives that have been deemed socially marginal, including incest survivors and women in prison. Many of her subjects, though not all, are poor women who contracted AIDS through intravenous drug use. Because they are women, an already sex-biased medical establishment ignores them.[10] Because they often lack health insurance, they cannot expect frontline medical care with the latest drugs or information about new treatments or drug trials. If they are Black or Latina, as 80 per cent of women with AIDS are in the USA, they are stigmatised by both whites and men within their own communities, who deny the risk of HIV infection or see it only as a 'gay disease'. When poor women with AIDS do appear in the press, they are often characterised as depraved, irresponsible mothers who have infected their babies, or as sexually promiscuous and therefore culpable. Those rare middle-class or affluent women with AIDS whose stories appear in the press are almost always 'innocent victims' of blood transfusions, the only mode of HIV infection that bears no social stigma. Meredith documents women across social strata, her subjects are united by their sex and their disease.

Meredith has circulated her work across many forums, from grassroots community spaces and in AIDS conference settings to the prestigious New Museum in New York. Her aim is quite simply 'to show' in the traditional, documentary sense – to show what is not seen nor written of, and to give some voice to those who are silenced. She exhibits very large, straight-on flash portraits of her subjects, sometimes posed alone and sometimes with partners, family and friends. Like Rosett's portraits of gay and lesbian PWAs, Meredith's photographs generally hew to the 'positive images' line of presenting afflicted individuals with dignity and strength, though unlike Rosett's, they are made primarily as art and are therefore dramatically stylised. In choosing selections of personal quotations and poetry written by the subjects to accompany the photographs, Meredith's work tends to privilege individual sentiment and the personalisation of the women's experiences with AIDS over the politics of race, class and sexuality which also inform them.

English photographer Tessa Boffin has also addressed herself to the issue of women and AIDS, but from quite another position and to quite a different end. Instead of documenting cases, Boffin has tackled the problem of convincing women, specifically lesbians, of the need to take safer sex seriously by constructing imagery that convinces from the standpoint of

pleasure rather than fear. This 'safe sex is fun' approach has been very effective among gay men, circulated through posters and educational materials published by organisations like the Terrence Higgins Trust and the Gay Men's Health Crisis. The issue of safer sex practices remains a particularly thorny subject among lesbians. This is both because of the tendency to deny the risk factors as relevant to the commerce of lesbian sex, and because of the often bitter disputes among lesbian feminists over the uses of pornography and erotic fantasy which are believed by a vocal contingent to be inherently oppressive to women. Boffin sees the AIDS epidemic as providing yet another complex ('ironic') site where discussions can be engaged 'about sexual identities, practices, fantasies and fears' as well as 'why or how we might want to adopt safe sex practices'. Far beyond their academic interest, the development and expression of lesbian sexual fantasies can be life-saving, as well as identity-affirming, enterprises.

Boffin's recent photo-tableau series, *Angelic Rebels* (1989), is a five-part fantasy narrative.[11] Initially we see a winged female figure, reminiscent of Durer's *Melancholia*, sitting in deep, gloomy contemplation. Her depression appears to have been brought on by the mainstream, tabloid press's reporting on AIDS. She is also discouraged from reading books and pamphlets on safer sex and the cultural politics of AIDS from the gay press. What is a girl to do? She identifies her plight with that of the gay man on the cover of the *Village Voice* who is fearful about loving in the climate of AIDS (though as a lesbian she is more likely to be mourning her loss of sexual liberty than lovers who have died). It is only when 'Melancholia' begins to realise that safer sex can mean the liberation of fantasy and the expansion – not the reduction – of sexual options, that she is able to 'see' the safer-sex angel and discover new heights of ecstasy. Her depression disappears and her own potential as

Angelic Rebels: Lesbians and Safer Sex, 1989, first in a series of five, by Tessa Boffin.

Angelic Rebels: Lesbians and Safer Sex, 1989, fifth in a series of five, by Tessa Boffin.

an 'angelic rebel' is realised.

From positive images to targeted, pro-active propaganda, lesbian photographers have reflected in their work over the 1980s the deep impact the AIDS epidemic and its social repercussions have had on our lives. Even for those of us whose work has not taken on AIDS as a subject directly, our voices have gained an added measure of urgency and strength. From the first days of the crisis, lesbians were in the vanguard in waging the campaign against the bigotry, ignorance and fear surrounding the epidemic, and alleviating the suffering that attended it. Perhaps because of women's socialisation as nurturers, or perhaps for more direct, angry, political reasons, lesbians took on a large share of the voluntary organising around AIDS, including the creation from scratch of networks to provide food, social services, housing and hospice facilities for PWAs.

But the politics both within and without the AIDS establishment and the blurring of lines between AIDS activism and the lesbian and gay liberation movements in recent years, have given lesbians many opportunities to pause and consider issues around their own needs as women and concerning women's health in general. Many times the question has arisen among lesbian organisers as to whether or not the men would have been there for us in equal measure had the epidemic entered our community first and devastated us with similar virulence.[12] Even to be prompted to raise such a question points to the persistence of those larger oppressions to which the gay community is not immune: sexism, racism and class prejudice. And the toll of these is being felt increasingly as the demographics of AIDS shifts in the USA from predominantly white, gay male communities to poorer communities of colour.

But even as the women's movement provided the AIDS movement with much of its theory and politics, the AIDS movement is now furnishing the women's movement with a new generation of committed lesbian (and straight) activists who are bringing their experiences, creativity and organising skills to bear on women's health issues with a new resolve and a new militance. Within three years in three major American cities, new advocacy groups for women with cancer have been started with strong lesbian leadership. [13] There can be no doubt that lesbian photographers, video-makers and artists will continue to play a vital role in these struggles, too. [14]

NOTES

[1] For example, the series *Video Against AIDS*, produced by the Video Data Bank at the School of the Art Institute of Chicago and edited by John Greyson and Bill Horrigan. Included are tapes by lesbian activists, including Amber Hollibaugh, Jean Carlomusto and Pratibha Parmar.

[2] Cindy Patton, *Sex and Germs* (Boston: South End Press, 1985).

[3] In January 1973, a relatively liberal US Supreme Court ruled (by a 7 to 2 majority) in *Roe v Wade* that a woman had a qualified right to terminate her pregnancy during the first two trimesters on grounds of her right to privacy. Despite opinion polls suggesting that the majority of the American electorate supports a woman's right to have an abortion, *Roe* is expected to be overturned by the new conservative majority on the Court.

[4] In 1986, at the height of public media hysteria about AIDS and increased bigotry against gays, an increasingly conservative Supreme Court upheld the state of Georgia's sodomy law in *Bowers v Hardwick*. The defendant, gay-rights activist Michael Hardwick, pursued the case to the high court, hoping to make it the 'test case' that would sweep away all state sodomy laws as unconstitutional. In his majority opinion, Justice Byron White wrote that the argument that gay people have a 'fundamental right' to engage in consensual sex was 'facetious'. Approximately half of the states still have sodomy laws.

Both the *Roe* and *Bowers* rulings depended upon the recognition of a right to privacy, a right not explicitly mentioned in the American constitution, but felt to be implicitly rooted in the Bill of Rights and the 14th Amendment.

[5] See Jan Zita Grover, 'Photographers and PWAs' in *Exposure*, vol. 26, no. 4, 1989, p.35; also, Michael Kimmelman, 'Bitter Harvest: AIDS and the Arts' in the *New York Times,* 19 March 1989, section 2, p.1.

[6] *The Family of Man* is still indisputably the most popular and widely-seen exhibition of photographs ever organised. Curated by Edward Steichen in 1955 for the Museum of Modern Art, *The Family of Man* was circulated worldwide by the United States Information Agency and the book continues to be a bestseller. Steichen's idea was to demonstrate through photographs the self-evident 'truth' that all of the peoples of the world form one big, human 'family' with the same aspirations, hopes, needs, joys, sorrows and social drives – investment banker and Kalahari Bushman alike. The ahistorical and blatantly pro-West ideology of *The Family of Man*, produced at the height of the cold war, was much remarked upon by critics, notably Roland Barthes in his contemporary essay 'The Great Family of Man' in *Mythologies* (New York: Hill and Wang, 1957), pp.100-3.

[7] Sage Sohier is a Boston-area documentary photographer who worked on an extensive documentation of 'couples' during the 1980s, of which her portraits of gay and lesbian couples formed one part.

[8] Robin Littauer, 'Profile: Sage Sohier' in *VIEWS*, Spring 1988, p.9.

[9] During the summer of 1989, a retrospective of the late Robert Mapplethorpe's photographs, which included explicit images of the gay leather subculture, became the focus of a right-wing political and religious attack on the National Endowment for the Arts which had funded the exhibition. Instead of rallying to Mapplethorpe's defence, Endowment administrators and many liberal critics and curators fled the field altogether, agreeing that funding Mapplethorpe had been a dreadful mistake and that steps would be taken to ensure that this would never happen again. Among the steps taken was the formulation of a 'pledge' which all grantees had to sign, promising (among other things) that they would neither produce nor distribute work that was 'homoerotic'.

[10] In 1987, the US National Institutes of Health spent only 13.5 per cent of its research budget on women's health, even though women spend more on health care than men in the USA. Every year, breast cancer claims 40,000 women even though a substantial number of deaths could be prevented with early detection. Women have been excluded systematically from all drug research trials for both AIDS and heart disease, the number one killer of women in the USA.

11 See *Ecstatic Antibodies: Resisting the AIDS Mythology*, ed. Tessa Boffin and Sunil Gupta (London: Rivers Oram Press, 1990) for the complete series of *Angelic Rebels: Lesbians and Safer Sex*. One of Boffin's earlier series about gay men, mainstream media representation and safer sex, *The Slings and Arrows of Outrageous Fortune: AIDS and the Body Politic* (1985) can be seen in *Ten.8*, no. 26, 1987, or *AIDS: The Artists' Response* (Ohio: Ohio State University, 1989).

12 See Jackie Winnow, 'Lesbians Working on AIDS: Assessing the Impact on Health Care for Women' in *OUT/LOOK*, no. 5, 1989, p.10.

13 See Mary Jo Foley, 'Cancer Organisers Push Feminist Agenda' in *New Directions for Women,* vol. 19, no. 3, 1990, p.1. The three groups are the Women's Cancer Resource Centre (Oakland, California), the Women's Community Cancer Project (Boston, Massachusetts) and the Mary-Helen Mautner Project for Lesbians with Cancer (Washington, DC).

14 Revised text of presentation for panel on Lesbian Photographers at Women's Caucus for Art National Conference, New York, 1990.

FRAMING THE QUESTIONS:

POSITIVE IMAGING AND SCARCITY IN LESBIAN PHOTOGRAPHS

Jan Zita Grover

Jan Zita Grover

I POSITIVE IMAGES

Five years ago, I wrote an essay called 'Dykes in Context' in which I argued that lesbian images read differently for lesbian and non-lesbian audiences because, among other things, of the constraints on self-identification ('this is a portrait of me as a lesbian') and distribution that precede audience readings.[1] That argument was useful, as far as it went, because it was important to challenge dismissive views from both outside and inside lesbian communities which saw lesbian photographs as merely formally conservative, 'painterly' and idealising. But in thinking about a parallel situation surrounding photographs made by Central Americans, I realised that the problem of subcultural positive imaging needed to be aired at greater length.

In 1985, I sat in the apartment of a friend who was helping put together an exhibition of photographs on Nicaragua. The exhibition was mounted in support of the Sandinista government; all those involved in the project had nothing but good intentions toward the state and people of that Central American nation. Yet as I watched, my friend rejected photograph after photograph made by Nicaraguans and Cubans in favour of photographs made by North Americans and Europeans.

Finally I asked why. A grimace, a gesture of impatience: 'They're *so sentimental*: laughing children, smiling peasants. They're *Family of Man*, salon photography. Definitely not cutting edge.'

That incident has stuck in my mind all these years, and now I know why. With the best of intentions, my friend was denying at least two important things: the aspirations of those Cuban and Nicaraguan photographers – their need (however compromised or impure it may have been) to see their own communities represented *as they wished them to be* – and the fluid nature of their meanings.

Photographs, we know, are not simply records of what has already taken place. In fact, outside of some snapshots, photographs usually function not as reflections of reality at all but as alternatives/enhancements to it: fulfilments of wishes, idealised models, what the late Raymond Williams might have termed 'subjunctive images' – photographs hurled toward the future cast ahead of us as visual guideposts to what we hope to become.

Think about the ways that photographs figure most prominently and institutionally in North American and Northern European cultures: as television programmes, magazine and newspaper illustrations; school, debut, engagement and wedding photographs, both moving and still. [2] None of these categories bears an indexical relationship to the life it purports to represent: instead, it hyperbolises, glamorises, nostalgises or sensationalises. *And always it radically simplifies.*

In the service of such motives as, for example, whetting appetites for consumption (advertisements) and reinforcing existing institutions (marriage and family photographs), photographs commonly propose the ideal as already present, as natural. In effect, they naturalise the unnatural – that realm of ideality – by giving it an illusory tangibility, a virtual presence.

It is because of this that most of us have such a stake in the terms and extent of representation; it is because of this that my friend the curator of (non)Nicaraguan photographs could fall quite easily into valorising only certain photographs as 'true', as having a useful potential. In her particular case, the 'truth' most valued was that of photographic process or mediation itself – of formal 'toughness', of television cool. The truth value of affirming the possibility of happy, laughing peasants living on their own land, of well-fed babies safe from war, seemed not as important. But both truths, I would argue, are equally subjunctive, for both tell us as much (implicitly) about *what is* as what could be. And both are equally subjective, for both tell us as much about their makers' desires as they do about the subjects within their frames.

Simon Watney, in writing about the necessity for reading photographs as more than simple records, emphasises the role of the unconscious in framing photographs:

> Psychoanalysis refuses any notion of direct, unmediated vision, since it understands seeing as a constant site of unconscious activity . . . We cannot theorise the workings or nature of *remembering* without at the same time considering the systematic mechanisms of *forgetting*. Once we begin to think of both seeing and memory as primarily defensive and self-protective operations, saturated with fantasy, then the status of photographic imagery is affected rather radically. [3]

In effect, we must learn to look at representations both for what they forget and what they remember; photographic absences ('forgetting') are equally as meaningful as photographic presences ('remembering'). Thought about in this way, ordinary photographs – advertisements, say, for beauty products – are equally important for what they 'forget' (class, colour, sickness, old age, poverty) as for what they 'remember' (youth, health, wealth, Anglo-Saxon appearance and social power). 'Romantic comedies' are significant not only for what they 'remember' (the social and economic primacy of the heterosexual couple) but for what they 'forget' (the possibility of same-sex couples, social collectives, the single person).

In the same way, countercultural or subcultural positive images propose a complex 'forgetting' of present realities – a resistance to, say, the painful realities of war, powerlessness or poverty – and 'remembering' of possible alternatives: peace, security and affluence. Thus it is naïve – or very cynical – to dismiss positive images as merely sentimental or old-fashioned. To do so is to treat them as if they proposed no arguments, embodied no aspirations, reflected no ongoing struggles.

I know this is true of the first widely circulated lesbian images, which were formally conventional portraits of lesbian couples that attested to the wish for, *willed the existence of,* enduring couplehood. In the early 1980s I looked at many lesbians' photographs of their communities constructed according to these terms and I always found them affecting at this level of yearning, of desire. Conventional portraits set up their subjects as socially respectable individuals, as a socially respectable unit, in a custom stretching back to at least the fifteenth century in Northern Europe. The lovingly crafted portraits made by so many lesbian photographers in the 1970s and 1980s attested to the growing wish for legitimation, the longing for recognition, of individuals and couples in our communities. These images of single women and couples surrounded by their cats, dogs, plants and furniture embodied the desire to stay time, to make things as perfect as one wished they could be. These photographs frequently involved a second coming-out for their subjects, for they formalised their identity as lesbian and attested to their desire to maintain the social identity embodied in the photograph – whether as couple, homeowner, biker, what-have-you.

What these photographs did *not* very often subjunctively embody was a sense of lesbians as people for whom their sexual relationships to other women were determinants of identity both within and outside their primary communities. The entire topic of identity politics is far too complex to go into here; I'll remark only that the dominant strategy in North America[4] was to downplay the sexual component in the lesbian community and instead emphasise its spiritual or emotional basis (Adrienne Rich's 'the lesbian in all of us'). There are historic reasons for this particular emphasis – for example, the homophobia of heterosexual women within the women's movement, the wish to see women defined for

once in terms *other* than sexual – that find their traces in the almost rigorously asexual lesbian portraits of the period before 1986. But what these photographs managed to 'forget' – that sexual desire is what drives a great deal of lesbian identity – resurfaced (one is tempted to say, *with a vengeance,* as in: the return of the repressed) in the second half of the 1980s.

The form in which subjunctive discourses shifted was the sudden explosion of sexually explicit lesbian imagery. This is not to say that such images were not being made *before* the mid-1980s; among the lesbian photographers whom I interviewed while writing 'Dykes in Context' (1984-6), many mentioned that tucked away amid their negatives they had some pretty hot stuff. When I asked why they hadn't exhibited or published that work, all of them told me that they didn't think their communities 'were ready' to see it. The institutions through which their images circulated were, they thought, unable to accept sexually explicit lesbian photographs. And this has unhappily proved to be the case: with few exceptions, erotic/porn lesbian photographs have been circulated through a wholly different set of channels than earlier and more 'respectable' photographs were shown. *Objectification* – lesbian feminist for 'concentrating-on-body-parts-at-the-expense-of-the-whole-woman' – and other displacements away from desire function to police the boundaries of respectable lesbianism. Thus publications like *Off Our Backs* in the USA and *Spare Rib* in Britain keep a kind of faith that is increasingly irrelevant to large numbers of lesbians, most particularly those who came of age after about 1978.

Increasingly, young lesbians are rejecting even the label *lesbian*; they are *queer*, they'll have us know, and *queer* transcends older categories of sexual and political identity. Older defectors are also donning silicon dicks, reliving the bad old days before the women's movement in masquerade – re-enacting butch/femme identities, the perils and pleasures of sexual/social pariahism. It is an invigorating time to be alive. And the photographs that explore these mutable, fantastic possibilities seem to me infinitely exciting. They are an augmentation to the existing visual arguments about what lesbians are and can be, just as Nicaraguans' photographs of laughing children and well-fed peasants are. No one has the right to censure these evocations of what is yet to be – lesbian sexuality as present, hot and inclusive.[5] These images, so frequently scorned as *pornographic* or *obscene*, are much more complicated than such dismissals suggest. They are before anything else idealising: they attempt to fix desire as iconically as formal portraits fix identity. Where scarcity existed, they propose plenitude: tattooed women, non-thin women, women of colour, physically disabled women, butch women, femme women. And this, I would argue, can only advance *everyone's* agendas – from the delighted inventors of lesbian porn to the women who cancel subscriptions to *OUT/LOOK* and threaten in print to burn *On Our Backs*.

II THE PROBLEM OF SCARCITY

What are the usual effects of any form of scarcity? People hoard; people attribute immense value and power to whatever commodity has become or is designated as scarce. For example, diamonds are not actually scarce gemstones; it is the artificial scarcity created by the De Beers cartel that gives them their enormous metaphoric and material value.

In a similar way, subcultures that are consistently *un*-represented, *under*-represented or *mis*-represented[6] deal out of a scarcity of images that does not accurately reflect either their sense of current realities or their aspirations for future ones. I can think of no other explanation for the extraordinary passion – most of it, unfortunately, splenetic and censorious – that meets any but the blandest representations of lesbians or, for that matter, gay men, blacks and other socially marginalised peoples.

So few representations, so many expectations: how can any image possibly satisfy the yearning that it is born into? If a sexually explicit lesbian image depicts desire in the terms of a soft-focus greeting card, a significant portion of those among whom it circulates deride its sentimentality and sexual evasion: they want something to reflect *their* reality. If another photograph fixes desire through signs of otherness – for example, leather and sex roles – it will be decried by women who associate desire with romantic merging.

So few representations, so many expectations: the burdens of scarcity. Look at images of social and sexual identity for heterosexual women in, say, the movies. Does Jane X feel 'threatened' or 'oppressed' by the heroine of *Nine And A Half Weeks* if she is instead drawn to the heroine of a romantic comedy? Must the existence of Pauline Reage's *O* be obliterated because of its threat to women who prefer *Pride and Prejudice*? Does a giddy, drunken, flirtatious white woman in public leave her more sober white sisters feeling compromised, complicit, guilty? The likelihood is that she does not – there are so many available models *and examples* of public behaviour of white women that one embarrassing woman does not seem to imply shameful identity in others superficially like her.

In the case of a woefully under-, un- or mis-represented subculture, however, the unseemly beahviour of even one member – or one representation – carries a far greater significance, a much heavier burden. Here, there are few or no examples to provide counter-arguments for the centrality of this particular identity or behaviour. As a result, subcultures are more likely to actively police members' behaviour and representations than are dominant cultures. When was the last time you heard a lesbian (or a black woman) described as 'a disgrace to her community'?

Details from Drawing the Line, *Kiss & Tell, 1990. Photos: Isa Massu*

When was the last time you heard a white person described as 'a credit to his/her race'?

III

I'd like in the light of the above comments to briefly discuss some sexually explicit lesbian images that were exhibited in San Francisco last summer. Kiss & Tell, a three-woman art collective from Vancouver, British Columbia, produced a wonderfully ingenious exhibition, *Drawing the Line*, that made the individual mechanisms of 'remembering/forgetting' and the collective consequences of subcultural scarcity stunningly clear.

Drawing the Line consists of a suite of sexually explicit photographs. The images depict a variety of sexual desires and practices ranging from hugging and soft kissing through

whipping, bondage and voyeurism. The actors in all the photographs are two of Kiss & Tell's members, Persimmon and Lizard, while the third member, Susan, took all of them. The images ranged round the walls in an order running from the commonest expressions of affection to those that most viewers would regard as extreme. Kiss & Tell's wall labels invited viewers to consider where they would 'draw the line' on what was erotic/permissible/pornographic. But unlike most gallery shows, which prevent viewers' reactions from becoming part of the exhibition's extended argument, *Drawing the Line* invited spectators to write their reactions to the photographs and to the question of *drawing the line*, right on the walls. (Black pentels were supplied for this purpose.) But only

Women were invited to respond in this highly public manner; men were instead invited to write their comments in 'The Men's Book'.[7]

As a casebook example of the intersecting roles played by unconscious viewing mechanisms and scarcity of representation, *Drawing the Line* makes several things a bit clearer. First of all, the comments scribbled on the walls were frequently more projective than descriptive. For example, viewers frequently overlooked the fact that *all* the photographs framed the same two models. Instead, they complained that the couple in a given photograph were less attractive, less 'hot' than the couple in a previous one. Or they objected to the 'loveless' interaction of one couple.

Such comments suggest that the site of interpretation was not so much the photographs' contents than the viewers' own mechanisms of 'forgetting' or 'remembering'

catalysed by the photographs. Viewers who objected to the enacted representations of sado-masochistic sex were reacting *not* to *SM* but to a depiction of it designed to provoke response. They responded as if they were gazing through a keyhole and deriving guilty pleasure from it, reacting in rage toward other viewers' enthusiasm.

Watching lesbians cancel each other's work – including the framed photographs, which several times were scrawled across with big black pens – is not a pretty sight. Clearly it does not arise out of a wish to protect anyone else, to initiate a debate, to frame an argument. It arises out of complex individual resistances transmuted into social behaviours designed to assuage one's own dis-ease by projecting that dis-ease onto other viewers' experiences, which must then be monitored and censored. Instead of understanding these photographs as gestures toward wider possibilities, other futures, censors interpret them literally, naïvely, as if they were direct reflections of an already-existing world.

The second thing that becomes clear from looking at *Drawing the Line* is that the stakes are terribly high because of the relative paucity of lesbian imagery, never mind lesbian sexual imagery. Although Kiss & Tell chose to limit its models for the series to the same two women in order to deflect debate from questions of the models' individual desirability (body type, age, colour, facial features, and so on), this decision was lost on many viewers – they either missed it entirely or rejected it. I believe this was a naïve hope on their part, given the burdens imposed by scarcity of representation. It was hardly likely that women of colour, non-thin women, women whose sexual valence was tall blondes or tiny Asians or muscular Latinas would be appeased by Kiss & Tell's decision to avoid addressing the part played by the specificity of desire, the paucity of their own presence, in one of the few projects to address lesbian desire and sexual practice so openly.

Were there thousands of sexually explicit

lesbian images circulating unimpeded throughout our communities, such objections would not be voiced. But there are not, and this is precisely why lesbian feminists who would limit production and circulation even further are so far off-base. We need more, not fewer, sexual representations to choose from: a greater variety of women to enact them, a wider range of practices to be enacted.[8]

L'homme Français qui posait pour son amie lesbienne avec son soutien gorge et les portes-jartelles de sa petite amie. Photo: Isa Massu

IV

But the current debates around lesbian porn, lesbian sexual and social representation may well become moot before long. A new generation of women whose primary sexual commitment is to members of their own sex is already rejecting the terms in which the debates have historically been couched. As

queers (not *lesbians*), they claim affinity with men, transvestites, bisexuals, transsexuals – an entire panoply of self-defined sexual communities. They mean to go beyond our impoverished archives to create representations far more inclusive, far more transcendent, than my generation's. (Yes, I know, you're thinking: *they'll learn. They're young.* Thank god: *there lies possibility.*) They're making photographs like this one below. And they're only beginning.

NOTES
[1] J.Z. Grover, 'Dykes in Context' in *The Contest of Meaning* (Cambridge, Mass: MIT Press, 1990).

[2] I localise because these are the only cultures I pretend to know anything about; I suspect that photographs function similarly in other places but cannot make a claim to know that.

[3] Simon Watney, 'Introduction' in *The Image of the Body* (Cambridge: Cambridge Darkroom, 1988), n.p.

[4] With the exception of Quebec, where French feminist theory held sway during the 1970s and early 1980s in a way that it would not in Anglophone Canada and the USA until later.

[5] I don't know if this apocryphal tale is common in Britain as it is in the USA, but it is nonetheless telling: 'If you put a penny in a jar for each time a lesbian couple has sex in the first year of their relationship and then *withdraw* a penny for each time they have sex in subsequent years together, you will never get to the bottom of the pennies.' *QED*.

[6] I am indebted to Douglas Crimp for this particularly pithy phrasing of the problem.

[7] An all-too-short selection of Kiss & Tell's project appears in the Fall 1990 issue of *OUT/LOOK*.

[8] In the Winter 1991 issue of *OUT/LOOK*, Julia Creet argues that it is gay male sexuality, not straight male sexuality, that provides the terms of new debates and practices within lesbian sexual communities.

PORTRAITS

Mikki Ferrill

These photos are reflections of one of society's differences, without diversion society would lack colour. We must approach life with an open mind so that we may broaden our understanding. I'd like to thank the people in the photographs for their courageous stance to be different, and for giving society a glance at those differences.

Gay Ball, Chicago.

'Dykes on Bikes', Gay Pride Parade, San Francisco.

'Dykes on Bikes', Gay Pride Parade, San Francisco.

Hallowe'en, Castro Street, San Francisco.

Castro Street, San Francisco.

JAMES DEAN
THE ALMOST-PERFECT LESBIAN HERMAPHRODITE

Sue Golding

There's nothing much deader than a dead motion
                                    picture
                                    actor
                                    and yet . . .

john dos passos, *Midcentury*

This is a personal piece. Not so much in the sense of being a dramatic confession with its need for absolving some guilty, hidden truth. There is not a shred of truth-as-such in this piece. Nor is there any guilt, although there is a small secret I'd like to share.

This is a piece about a particular kind of erotic sensibility that those of us who wear it and feel it and know it, will now, finally, have a chance to name. For this is about the kind of sexual imaginary specific to the '80s – a sexuality that emerges from a peculiar mixture of pre-pubescent tom-boyism, the celebration of the female genitalia, lost innocence, perversity and dirt. It's a piece about lesbian hermaphrodites and the playful existence of our fictionalised sexuality.

I know you've seen the type: no tits, no

James Dean with his camera, 1954. Photograph by Roy Schatt ©
Roy Schatt, Peter Rose Gallery.

cock, oozing with a kind of vulnerable 'masculinity' and sheathed in a '50s style black leather motorcycle jacket. Or to put it slightly differently, it's James Dean, with a clit.

But before we expose any more of this hermaphroditic body (and the kind of lesbianism to which she may subscribe), there are three possible points of confusion which must be cleared away. First, we are not speaking here of 'androgyny'. That is, we are not speaking of that kind of being who can blend and balance so completely the male/female antagonism that she creates a pleasure aesthetic out of the erotic mutiny of her genitals. We are not speaking of a kind of erotic sensibility, very much a product of the '60s, that for a variety of reasons (all, I'm sure, quite interesting but beyond the scope of this essay) heralded in an entire sexual aesthetic around an 'absence' or 'lack' or – at best –

blurred 'sameness', even 'perfect [w]holeness', of the sexual organs themselves.

Neither are we speaking about, in the second place, a kind of eroticism that took on the name, more generally in the 1970s, of 'gender-fuck' fashions. That is, we are not speaking of the kind of sexual aesthetic born out of an acknowledged irony of the ways in which society enforces gender-specific clothing depending on the kind of sexual organ sitting between one's legs. We are not trying to describe, however interesting that aesthetic might be, the kind of woman who inverts and doubles her body image by donning, let's say, a suit and tie, a pert little dildo and neatly placed moustache, all in the name of maintaining an erotic irony of the female genitalia, in drag. In speaking of hermaphrodism, we are not attempting to describe that kind of pleasure aesthetic derived through an eroticisation of a double imagery sarcastically counterposed in one body.

Finally, in what could be taken as an odd sort of disclaimer, it must be emphasised that the kind of hermaphrodism spoken about here (and one could go further and say all kinds of hermaphrodism, but that, again, is another story) is not meant to be taken in the specifically 'biological' sense. We do not for a minute want to suggest that the '60s and '70s somehow ushered in an amazing phenomenon in delivery rooms everywhere, of little girl-infants with internal 'male' organs (or vice versa), who suddenly upon reaching puberty seemed to descend on the rest of the population with the kind of fatal foreboding of a Future Shock. There is no sense of 'discovery', no revelation being uncovered about some excessive amount of mutated sexual organs leaping into the erotic focus of the '80s.

We are not speaking, in other words, of a kind of 'true' hermaphrodism, medically verifiable using the latest in genetic engineering. Our concerns are not in the slightest way connected to some formulaic equation of the X and Y chromosome, scientifically tested in relation to the size and shape of the breast and clitoris (the usual body parts under scrutiny by the medical experts), in order to deduce – or so they claim – how much and to what extent the human being involved can be given the sexed status of 'male' or 'female' (and hence be expected to reflect a variety of aesthetically evocative roles and behaviours specific to that 'sex').

This may be very interesting for those truth-seekers of the human anatomy, but it has nothing to do with understanding the erotic reality of a female hermaphrodite, lesbian or otherwise. And it has even less to do with our clitorised James Dean.

Luckily for us we have at least 188 years of recorded insights, important gains in feminism and a few good films, novels, paintings and sex toys (videos included) which have often broken that biology = destiny 'truth'. But we have something else, too, not available until recently that, by way of a small detour, I'll try to explain in some detail.

Let's begin by considering a bright piece of medical wisdom drawn from the subdued lips of Dr Moreton Stille MD, and his lawyer friend, Francis Wharton. In their 1855 *Treatise* on, among other things, female herma-phrodites, they take as a given the usual claim that what it means to be 'woman', 'feminine' and 'normal' can be summed up and equated to each other and – more to the point – can find their anatomical expression in the female body itself. A real woman, a feminine woman, ie one who is 'normal', is one who necessarily manages to have a high voice, a heterosexual and submissive orientation (at the time considered both interchangeable and a directly physical attribute) and, needless to say, large breasts. Most importantly, however, it was imperative that she have a small (shall we say 'petite') clitoris. The size of the elbow, knee and navel, on the other hand, were singularly unimportant for the assignment of a sex.

If by chance or by design you happened to exhibit any other opposing combination of attributes described above, then, depending on the degree to which your body parts differed, you would be 'in essence' an hermaphrodite, pure and simple. So smug were they in their scientific reasoning (and why not? it was the common sense aesthetic of the period) that they would sort out the 'problem' of hermaphroditism quite routinely by spewing forth a logic based on definition:

Section 409 (2.) *Female hermaphrodites*: By far the greater number of these [they observe] owe doubts concerning their sex to an unusual size of their clitoris. Commonly associated with their circumstance are an unfeminine appearance, more or less a beard, a rough and masculine voice and manner . . . [etc]. [For] the usual size of the clitoris in the adult female is about half an inch in length, but Remer mentions having seen a clitoris an inch long in a girl of 7 years of age and Home, one of two inches long and thick as a thumb . . .

Woe be it to any woman so possessed of these fine attributes. For unlike the god, Hermaphrodite, who was revered *because of* these mutations, seen as flesh and blood she could only draw a malignant repulsion to her entire being, itself eroticised only at the level of mythology. And if unwilling to 'give up' her genitalia, if unwilling to stop being 'sexual' in the midst of these variegated organs and attributes, this creature of the 1850s would immediately be seen as a sexual subversive. And indeed, she was one, given the norms of society, outside of which she unglamorously fell.

So clearly was she considered to be a transgressor in the worst sense (that is in the sexual, dirty sense) that it very quickly became self-evident to the good doctor and his lawyer friend that the reverse must indeed be true as well: that female sexual subversives must, *ipso facto*, be hermaphrodites. For what else could account for that kind of 'abnormal' sexual activity but that it was born from a raging conflict of the two physical and opposing essences awkwardly (and irrepressively) functioning in one body. What could possibly account for that kind of aggressiveness except to say that somewhere lurking in the body of that rebel was the presence – in whole or in part – of a man.

They found proof of their theory in the following case study, meticulously undertaken and summarised by Robert Merry, Surgeon (1840), and included in their section on 'Female Hermaphrodites':

A woman, 25 years of age, on account of her notorious commerce with both sexes, was placed under strict police supervision. Resorting to masturbation, her health became so much impaired that she died in the course of sixteen

months. The external genitals were found to have their natural conformation, with the exception of the clitoris, which was three and a half inches long and three inches in circumference, and imperforate, except at the base. The uterus and one ovary were rudimentary, and the general conformation of the breasts was masculine, although, owing to the occurrence of a trifling periodical discharge, she was considered to be a woman. It was proved that this person had been guilty of the most astonishing and unnatural excesses with young people of both sexes.

Feared, trapped, swept from public view and spliced open under the private auspices of those experts on truth, our female hermaphrodite of yesteryear dies an empty, pathetic little death. Ignobly, her body is killed off by the brutal ignorance of a society which works hard to display – while she feverishly reaches out to maintain – her *manhood* in all its sordid and mutated glory. Remarkably enough, she does not die in vain.

Through the twists and belches and belly-aches of a century moving out of an industrial milieu and into the fractured glitz of a technological age, emerges her modern counterpart, but with a bit of a difference. What emerges is the 'virile girl', the butch baby, full of attitude but not of scorn, lots of street smarts and a bit of muscle. This new hermaphrodite embodies forever the image of the destructive adolescent dramatically and in one being, teeming with a creative, raw energy and beckoning with the possibility of a new era. She's the Peter Pan who reaches puberty and survives – her boyhood and her cunt intact, and ready. Most of all, she's public.

But she's public in quite a different sense to meaning simply 'out of the closet'. For she is the orphan of a people's imaginary; a peculiar

A self-portrait - there's something about you (girl?) - make me sweat

And he stabbed out his cigarette in the dashboard ashtray as I dug my hands into his sweaty crotch + pulled out his cock I began to lick the side + top of his cock like I knew he wanted bending my head way over + sucking I wished I could swallow him up then the car was completely lit by headlights behind us + a flashlight probing the front seat shit he dove for the bag of dope + the bottle as I fumbled with my fly - you - outta the car - okay okay officer - ID - AGE - shit shaking sticky hands pulling the wallet out of my jacket - 15 - you gotta come downtown with us, kid

Anna Marie Smith 05-86

offspring of the avant-garde art world, the butch '50s 'diesel dyke', and that kind of feminism which knew above all that sexual difference was ever only a *political* and not biological category. She is public in the most profound sense of the term: a composite copy of a mass invention, a replica of our own societal icons, which are themselves never anything other than a public fiction. She is James Dean over and over again: James Dean with his arrogant hair; James Dean with his tight black denims; James Dean with the bitter brat look; James Dean with the morbid leather boots; James Dean against the whole boring suburban middle class; James Dean, deader than a door nail, wedged into anti-hero.

Ironically, this infinite copying makes her an original invention of the '80s. And she becomes the quintessential embodiment of an erotic impossibility; a fiction as 'real' as the specific body parts of her hermaphroditic predecessor. Only this time, her 'truth', the clues to her sexual transgression, will never be found in the physical attributes of her body *per se*, but only in their 'look' – only in the defiant aesthetic of the erotic masculine shot through with the voluptuousness of the female sexual organs. For she is the split woman, the '80s hermaphrodite, uniquely the site specific reflection of the virile promise, in all its sexual perversity and imagination.

But more than that: she's the celebration of the female genitalia. Respectfully, knowingly, she's the proud owner of a vaginal hole and carbide clit, refusing once and for all to see her genitals as a 'bleeding wound' of castrated cock. She's the sexual love of being woman. And as such, this hermaphrodite becomes a signature for lesbianism itself.

Not surprisingly that makes her, at one and the same time, a slightly more dangerous creature. Indeed, it makes her repulsive. For the emphasis on sexualness and the perverse iconography it produces makes her, of necessity, a defiler of the prudish world, be that world filled with lesbians or straights. In the eyes of the prudish world, the female hermaphrodite can only be the pornographic filth in the age of AIDS, the frankenstein without a cause.

And because she is this erotic mutant, because she is this transgressor who excessively, self-consciously refuses to give up sex, she comes closest to the nether world to which her predecessor had been subjected: the world of ignorance and hate, the world of 'scientific' observation, the world of isolation and extinction all in the name of Truth.

One would like to think, despite the odds, that the female hermaphrodite of the present might somehow survive this kind of warfare. And indeed, there is the minute chance that she might. For unlike her ancestor, the reasons which bring this hermaphrodite close to the putrid edge may be precisely the same ones that, in the end, give her the advantage. Because she is the composite series of an infinite erotic fiction, a fractured playfulness of social icons copied over and again. And there, she'll find her strength in numbers. [1]

NOTES
[1] This article also appears in the collaborative project *Sight Specific: Lesbians and Representation*, ed. L. Fernie (Toronto, 1987) and *On Our Backs* (Winter, 1988) for which republication is gratefully acknowledged.

Dalston, London, 1981. Photograph by Jill Posener.

DIRTY GIRLS' GUIDE TO LONDON

Jill Posener

LESBIAN SEX IN PUBLIC PLACES; Writing slogans on the wall; Abseiling through the House of Lords; ACT-UP shouting down the US Health Minister at an AIDS conference in San Francisco; All these are on a continuum; If we don't take public spaces nobody will hear us. The state isn't in any mood to help our cause. In 1990, President Bush said, 'AIDS breaks my heart, but putting money into it isn't going to help.' Rap group 2 Live Crew charged, tried and acquitted on obscenity charges in Florida. A gallery in Cincinnati, Ohio, charged, tried and acquitted for showing Mapplethorpe's photographs. The law telling us what to look at, what to hear. The juries still able to think for themselves. Section 28 is still firmly in place. LESBIAN SEX IN PUBLIC PLACES.

Dirty Girls in London, 1988.

UNTITLED WORK

Jude Johnston

Black and white photomurals with text, each 48" × 55", 1987.

WHEN I SEE HER IN THE STREET/OFFICE/BAR WE RECOGNIZE OURSELVES AS SIMILAR.

WHEN I ASK HER ABOUT HERSELF WE FIND WE HAVE DIFFERENT BACKGROUNDS.

WHEN WE SEE FEW REFLECTIONS AROUND US WE ARE GLAD WE HAVE OUR NETWORKS.

WHEN WE TALK POLITICS BUT DISAGREE WE STILL FEEL EMPOWERED.

WHEN I AM WET FROM WANTING HER WE UNDERSTAND WHAT I MEAN.

WHEN I KISS HER ON THE SUBWAY WE GET ASTONISHED LOOKS FROM OTHERS.

WHEN SHE SAYS SHE WANTS TO MAKE LOVE WITH ME I AM OVERWHELMED WITH DESIRE.

WHEN I PUT MY HAND INSIDE HER CUNT WE DISCUSS OUR SEXUAL DIFFERENCES.

WHEN I SUCK ON HER NIPPLES WE FEEL INCREDIBLY CONNECTED.

WHEN I REALIZED I AM LESBIAN WE DISCOVERED EACH OTHER.

DENY: IMAGINE: ATTACK

Ingrid Pollard

DENY.

oh no, not my daughter, she's a career women

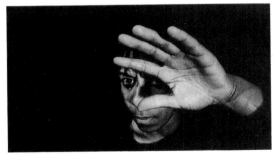

confidant... secretary.... constant companion.... friend....

IMAGINE

attire when practicable...   butch...

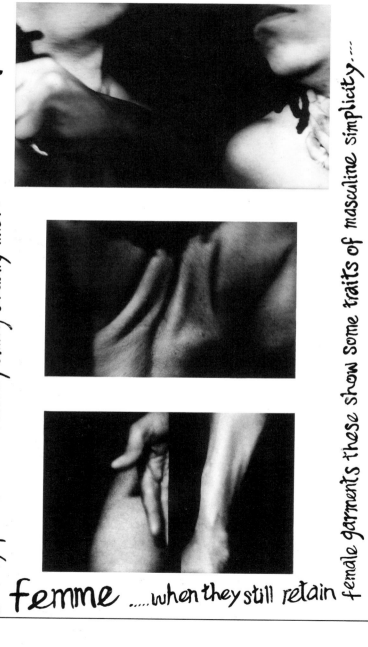

...a very pronounced tendency among sexually inverted women to adopt male

female garments these show some traits of masculine simplicity....

femme .....when they still retain

WHAT IT MEANS TO BE COLOURED ME[1]

Jackie Goldsby

I

The perfect moment was missed. In the wake of Senator Jesse Helms's (re)action against Robert Mapplethorpe's federally funded exhibition – the artist boycotts, the congressional debates, the newspaper editorials – the public furor over the S/M images displaced what would have been an equally charged discussion about Mapplethorpe's sexual *oeuvre*: the late photographer's (re)presentation of Black homoeroticism. For all of the theorising about censorship, the meaning of Mapplethorpe's racial aesthetic remained unarticulated in the analysis and protest – despite the fact that *Man in a Polyester Suit* probably bothered Senator Helms as much as the self-portrait of a leather-clad Mapplethorpe mooning his camera with a whip clenched between the cheeks of his ass:

> But *Man in a Polyester Suit* bothers *me*. Mapplethorpe cuts the model off just below mid-torso in a frame so still that we don't know if we're viewing a live subject or a mannequin. Striking a catalogue-type pose, the model/mannequin is clothed in a freshly cheap three-piece suit whose co-ordinated symmetry is disrupted by an unzipped – or burst-open – seam, out of which hangs an uncut penis. Dark, thick, arching, bow bent but not broken by so much more life, by so much more sex than can possibly be restrained by the false trappings of commodified civilisation. Rousseau's noble savage revisited.

Man in a Polyester Suit's reduction of Black men to their all-important cocks (a commodified construction in itself) eclipses the power of Mapplethorpe's Black nudes – the four views of Ajitto or *Thomas in Circle*, for example – where form, line, proportion, and gesture are dissociated from whiteness and located in blackness, thus subverting traditional ideas of classicism. Because the polyester itself invokes issues of class, however, the photo is finally about privilege: it's not about Ralph Lauren's

Darrel Ellis, Self Portrait after Photograph by Robert Mapplethorpe, *1986.*

pseudo-aristocratic Polo-land of blond-gentried wealth. Scaling down the ladder of 'success' is precisely the camera's focus; if you don't have money, you do have sex. The satire is in the objectification. But for whose pleasure?

In his *Self-Portrait after Photography by Robert Mapplethorpe*, Darrel Ellis deliberately places his lower torso out of the line of sight, behind and below the dizzying, entrapping height of the pedestal. His elbows rest on the circular surface, a post of flesh – his own flesh – against which he rests his face. The shadow cast by the back of his hand counterposes a gentle edge to his profile, accentuating his slim countenance. His lips pursed, his eyes searching, contemplating, looking directly at the viewer. Looking directly at me. Engagement: an erection of subjectivity:

After *Self-Portrait* I cannot look at Mapplethorpe's images without

thinking of Ellis and other Black men. This visual disjunction and its political implications deepen my ambivalence about Mapplethorpe's aesthetic politics. Was *Self-Portrait* drawn after Ellis posed for Mapplethorpe? Was Ellis one of the photographer's subjects? The ambiguity is the point: does it really matter?

II

John Frohnmayer, chair of the National Endowment for the Arts, wanted to cut funding for New York's AIDS-inspired show *Witnesses: Against Our Vanishing*, where Ellis's portrait was exhibited. 'The nature of the show had changed from an artistic focus to a political focus,' Frohnmayer asserted. Read: the catalogue notes openly criticised the implications of the Helms amendment. Frohnmayer's *faux pas* sharpened the irony of A Day Without Art to an even finer point.

This mobilising of the arts establishment and the gay press to participate in this nationwide display of anti-anti-representation struck me as tremendous. But the event stopped short of moving me to . . . what: tears? rage? because there is a kind of art I could learn to live without:

CITY IN SOUTH SAYS POSTER IS RACIST
Shreveport, La., Tourist Unit Vows to Destroy Copies
SHREVEPORT, La. Dec 28 (AP) — A poster that depicts blacks as roaches being sprayed by a white hand and as suspects running away from a white judge bore the logo of the local tourist bureau and was sold to businesses in the Shreveport area this fall.
The *New York Times* 28 December 1989

That we rally against the censorship levied at Mapplethorpe only to remain silent on the racial dimension of his work makes this news report all the more chilling to me because it reveals the different codes by which racism operates in American culture at large and in gay cul ture in particular. Where one wreaks literal, physical violence against Black bodies (witness Howard Beach, Bensonhurst, and the string of bombings in the South), the other symbolically erases a Black presence: the critical silence about Mapplethorpe's Black subjects is not a simple matter of omission, nor is it just an 'oversight'. It suggests how, in the gay community, racism is increasingly perceived as an old story, an ever-present constant in American politics that has become expendable in the face of the new narrative of the AIDS epidemic (Who has time to worry about racism when we're all dying?)

No doubt about it, AIDS is our collective nemesis, and to that extent the crisis has prompted us to be more vigilant about defining our culture and protecting ourselves, of taking care of 'our own'. Openly gay and lesbian editors at major publishing houses are bolstering the efforts begun by independent publishers to sign on gay and lesbian writers. Academics are making careers out of interpreting 'homoeroticism' and so contributing to 'the canon debate' currently booming throughout academia. And, though the impact is sometimes hard to discern, the guerrilla information networks and direct-action protests of AIDS activists are making a dent in the way American health policy is formulated and executed. This consolidation of the gay community into institutional forms bespeaks who we are and how we see ourselves at this critical time. In short, it constitutes a discourse, one that ultimately centres on the theoretical project of (re)articulating identity and identity politics: who do we mean, after all, by 'our own'?

III

I, for one, am not sure that I have the answer to that question. It's a query that haunts my writing this essay: where do I locate myself in the 'we's and 'us'es that I've invoked so far, when I don't find that these pluralities fully embrace my Black lesbian self? How can I, when both the lesbian and the gay male communities figure race in such disparate ways? Dykes politicise it, gay men eroticise it, either perception effectively neutralising any middle ground on which I can stand and say my piece.

Lesbians of colour did up the ante when, in 1981, the publication of *This Bridge Called My Back* insisted that white (lesbian) feminists must set racism at the top of their political agenda(s). And, for all its half-steps and near-misses, the critique of patriarchal power relations advanced by lesbian feminism in particular, is admirably ambitious, aiming for nothing less than to battle against all the -isms that accord privilege to difference – (hetero)sexism, racism, classism, ageism, ableism, sizeism . . .

That the list could go on signals how circumscribed lesbian politics can be even as it attempts to make broad connections between and analyse forms of oppression. Ironically, as lesbians attempt to dismantle the institutionalised illogic that assigns unequal meanings to neutral facts of identity such as colour, gender, and size, we mystify those facts even more. It becomes difficult to talk about identity in any context other than oppression. Instead, we turn to platitudes: lesbians are so busy 'honouring' diversity that we reify it in as problematic a way as gay men do when they sexualise it. Earning political halos becomes its own kind of fetish in the recovery process from patriarchal rule, a spoil of war that comes from toeing politically correct lines, even when those lines are nappy-edged with contradictions:

> I am in love with a white woman and have been partners with her for four years. We have carefully examined our motives for taking up with each other and can safely pronounce to any and all who ask that our attraction is 'healthy' and that neither of us, me in

particular, is succumbing to internalised racism. We say this, even to ourselves, even though we know differently: where, in the context of lesbian political discourse on race, can we acknowledge that our knowingly crossing boundaries of race and class *is* part of our desire for each other?

That I am involved with a white woman is not at odds with my self-perception, my self-identification, nor my self-love as a Black lesbian. Yet within lesbian racial politics that is a contentious stand to take. White lesbians would have me search for long-buried 'issues' underlying my attraction and resolve them in therapy. Lesbians of colour would argue that my relationship is just a 'stage', a weakness I'll outgrow when I'm ready to 'come home' and accept the love of Black women. Both presumptions are dangerously stifling. They seriously undercut the authority of lesbian-feminist racial politics by insisting on essentialist codes of being that deny individual selfhood.

Gay men spare themselves such angst by seemingly ignoring such questions altogether:

I'm White! You Black?

Are you like me: well-endowed, very masculine, physically fit, over 5'9", over 150 lbs, and avoid drugs? Would you like to screw my lights out? Send me a photo (the nuder the better), and I'll send one of me. Then you put it inside me and we can do one of those happy-ever-after things. Please write . . .

Just Sex, No Entanglements

Would like someone to play with on a regular basis. Straight, gay, bi. Prefer tall, thin white guys; however open to the rest of God's children as well. Long hair is a plus. Me: Black male, 6'1", 170 lbs. What turns you on? Respond with letter and recent photo. Reply FG Box SW90.

When I read ads like these, I'm tempted to trust what my mama told me before she passed: Don't lay your hopes for freedom with a white boy – they've got too much to gain from the way things are to change anything for real. Though eroticising difference is a nose-thumbing gesture of sorts against racial ideologies of power – when a white man specifies he wants to 'service' Black cock, he is, in that moment, relinquishing the privileged status the culture ascribes to him as 'top' – that reversal depends on accepting racial hierarchies as legitimate truth. Difference must be enforced, not transformed, and the privilege accorded it reinscribed if the sex is to keep its charge.

I discovered this ad in a local newspaper (and in the last issue of *OUT/LOOK*). Not in the Personals section but up

The San Francisco Bay Times, February 1990.

front in the 'legitimate' zone of the news. The headline and photo are smartly juxtaposed so as to invoke double readings: is this service aimed at thoughtful Black gay men who are 'tired of "GWM seeks GWM" ads'? Or is it intended for white men who are bored by homogeneous homosexuality? The clue is in the hard hat: like *Man in a Polyester Suit*, a class-specific reference tips the scale of power back to the viewer. In this context, appealing to 'interracialists', the surveyor is revealed to be white. The racial/sexual pecking order is confirmed once again. [2]

I would wager that it's not unconcern that accounts for the comparable absence of an anti-racism movement among (white) gay men – though at times it seems that way to me. Rather, an economy of desire (as represented by these ads) is invested in maintaining status quo racial politics; coming matters as much as overcoming the power dynamics that fix gay men of colour into a peculiar status of (in)visibility, one that restricts them to being conspicuously consumed by the imaginings of gay male sexual culture.

The gay male community's relative silence on this issue speaks volumes and takes a very deliberate toll on the community's social structure and relations, both within and outside its own ranks. But I want to disrupt my own discussion here, because I can't continue to speak as one who is 'within the ranks'. I don't want to appropriate the right of gay men of colour to speak about their marginality in their own language any more than I have, because I do believe that the brothers have a rap the rest of us need to hear. That we've only heard or read snatches of such dialogues can be attributed in part to the tight reins held by the gay print media that have resisted and restricted the free flow of ideas on the subject of racism in the gay male community, proving once again that ignorance isn't innocent; it's

organised. [3]

Standing outside this male world, I find myself both in league with it – based on the fact of my queerness – and opposed to it – because of this kind of censorship through denial and exclusion. The ways in which white gay men can still play by and into racial rules as they've been written mirror the gender rank they can pull on me as woman/lesbian lesbian/woman, and distance me even farther from the idealised 'we' I'm trying to relate to. So I make my own categories: 'okay' white boys and 'ofay' white boys, names that distinguish exceptions from the rule that measures political trust: who *is* the white gay man who would catch my back if *I* were to fall? Not the ofay.

And yet, if I'm honest, I must admit that I envy the (gay) male sexual prerogative to render differences of all sorts – hairy chests and smooth skin, swimmers' builds and chubby bellies, tight buns and bulging sacs, as well as race – into mere categories of pleasure. I find it difficult to acknowledge what the sage, James Baldwin, knew in another time: that it's unreasonable to think that those who've been without power can deny their attraction to it. So I confess: I want the gender privilege that allows men the 'freedom' to flaunt their access to sexual culture in ways that my pseudo-Catholic self can only imagine.

It's the terms of that liberty I want to reconsider, though. Switching identities from objectified to objectifier is not the political freedom I'm seeking. In and of itself, my skin colour means nothing. American political culture heaps its psychic insecurities onto me and mine so as to oppose us as 'Other' to whiteness, as difference personified, feared, repressed, and, (so) oppressed. But yo: there's more to life than objectification. There is subjectivity in 'race': *I* can speak first, out of the primacy of my existence; I can speak first, out of the rich is-ness of my Blackness: *I* think, therefore I is:

I'm at a dance with over a hundred Black

dykes out by the ocean. I can hear the waves roaring onto shore, but inside it's thick with heat and the windowpanes are panting for fresh air. SHE'S BAD SHE'S BAD SHE'S BAD BUT ALL I KNOW IS THAT I WANT HER WANT HER WANT HER UMPH. Keith Sweatt is singin' 'bout our heart's desire – I WANT HER – that New Jack Swing swinging low sweet chariot comin' for to carry me home, and so we all take up the chorus and give up the funk, shoutin' for all the Marin Headlands to hear, on the downbeat: I WANT HER.

'Racism', on the other side, wouldn't let me tell this story to you. 'Racism', on the other side, would make me doubt the truth of my memory and persuade me to hide this scene, to keep this experience secret so it doesn't get co-opted and belong, suddenly, to the public domain. 'Racism', on the other side – that violent ideology which pegs difference into hierarchies of power and privilege – would let stereotypes pre-empt narrative possibility so that subjective truths remain unvoiced:

> A white South African friend and I debated Spike Lee's *Do the Right Thing*. He felt that the skimply clad dancing machine in the opening sequence just fed into the image of the oversexed/lewd wench white men secretly fantasise about. I saw the movie three times, mainly to watch Rosie Perez shake it/robocop it/snake it/Pee-wee Herman it/boogaloo it to Public Enemy's 'Fight the Power' because Black folk do have a way of grinding into a beat that is sexy and, given the history of our sexuality in American culture, is political as well: because when your language has been marginalised, you learn to speak in different tongues.

As the gay community counters its marginalisation by institutionalising itself, I'm concerned about the erasure of *race* from gay political culture; that is, I worry that the subjective voice of people of colour is being excluded from the crosstalk of culture and politics that's regenerating the gay community. It's no small matter that entire fields of knowledge are being constructed and political machines established that are once again inscribing the absence of people of colour. In the growing 'canon' of AIDS literature I want to read memoirs written by gay men and lesbians of colour – published by powerhouse presses – that bear witness to the power and meaning of our lives (albeit through death). In the classroom I want to see queer academics of colour step up to the lectern and recover our place in our respective intellectual histories, teaching the texts and constructing the critical paradigms that make up our traditions. In the hospital corridors I want Reaganesque funding politics to stop, so that *all* who are 'truly needy' get the attention they deserve.

IV

These are the issues that present themselves to me as I move in the world. I have to make sense of headlines like these two – reconcile and address them *both* with the resources at my disposal:

> LAG IN APPROVING LOW AZT DOSES IS ASSAILED
> AIDS PATIENTS ARE SUFFERING NEEDLESSLY, THEIR ADVOCATES SAY.
> *New York Times*, 27 December 1989

> WE'RE TALKING ABOUT THE LOSS OF GENERATIONS.
> In New York, with the highest incidence of AIDS in the country, 84 percent of women with AIDS are black or Hispanic, as are 90 percent of the children with AIDS. Among Hispanic and black residents, both men and women, between the ages of 25 and 44, AIDS is the leading cause of death, as it is for white men.
> *New York Times*, 27 December 1987

Far from being a burden, my 'double consciousness' as a lesbian of colour powers my insight and interpretations of politics and culture; even more than bilingualism, it informs the very questions I ask. Which is why getting air time or print space in the gay press isn't just about letting the Black dyke have her say. It's not about force-feeding the minimum required/politically correct quota of coloured input (four doses of guilt from the major historically oppressed groups: Blacks, Latinos, Asians, and Native Americans). Rather, it's about insisting on intellectual integrity. It's about deconstructing the unfounded authority of white experience as Universal Truth and Model for Knowledge:

> Of all the showings scheduled at last year's Lesbian/Gay Film Festival, the one for which my girlfriend and I purchased tickets in advance was the lecture 'All-Girl Action: A History of Lesbian Erotica', curated by Susie Bright, editor of *On Our Backs*. Smart girls we were, because the show sold out. Fifteen hundred lesbians packed the Castro Theatre and watched porn for nearly two hours. But it only took one film clip, a two-minute snippet from a Russ Meyer sex spectacle, to alienate me from the pro-porn agenda Bright had, up until that point, persuaded me to accept:
>
> The opening shot showed the blond-haired Eve-type wedged in the forked trunk of a tree. Her Black fuck-buddy's long, overly long tongue flicks and darts across Eve's precious torso (is this a re-vision of the Fall from the Garden? Black dyke as evil serpent?). Then the Black woman straps on a larger-than-life white dildo and proceeds to ram Eve to a fascistic orgasm – the scene concluded with a tight frame of Eve's feet, rhythmically striking out and up to the roar of mass cheers (I can't

> remember now: did the noise come from the soundtrack, or were bloodred anger and a blues-based sadness ringing in my ears?). The allusion to Hitler is complete when the camera cuts to two men finishing a blow job: the top pulls his partner's head out of his crotch to reveal none other than a Führer look-alike smirking in post-fellatio glee.

While Bright was thrilled by the thrusting potential of the sex toy (the dildo or the dyke?), that film clip hardly excited me. Bright's reading of it was no more than a dismissal of porn's racial politics: stereotyped images exist, but at least it shows you (who?) images of inter- and interracial sex. This analysis, though, failed to explain the alienation I experienced watching that scene: as Bright's lecture presented it, lesbian eroticism – its icons, its narratives, its ideologies – is white.

It isn't that I expect Bright to understand Black (homo)sexuality so well that she could ask the questions that matter to me. (For starters: How has Black sexuality been historically constructed so that its representation in porn is *never* not racist, if the presumed gaze is either male and/or white? What modes of narrative and production would upend that power dynamic?) It's that her analysis gets the stage, publicity, uncritical reception, and institutional nod of a film festival. *And that no one seems to mind that she's promoting a theory with a flawed premise, because no one has yet articulated that these limits exist or has looked at what lies beyond.*

V

An analysis of *race*, along with a commitment to eradicate *racism*, must remain on the forefront of gay theory and political activism. To argue otherwise is not only intellectually naïve but politically dangerous. Such a stance decontextualises the epidemics – poverty, homelessness, and crack cocaine, to name three – facing politically marginalised groups as a whole. For those of us whose community allegiances and identities originate from more than one source, splitting our affiliations just won't do. More important, the federal government's response to the AIDS crisis will not budge one progressive, life-affirming inch as long as gay identity is perceived as 'criminal' and therefore undeserving of affirmation. The homophobia encoded in such an equation has its roots in racist ideology, which, along with sexism, is American culture's most cogent articulation of the theory of 'the Other'. Gay politics must advance anti-racism within its agenda, because homophobia is another manifestation of the same warped thinking that produces racism. As long as we allow any language and practice of oppression to remain in circulation, we can always expect to hear 'faggot' or 'dyke' hurled at us in words and violent deeds and watch indifference accumulate enough venom and momentum to become public policy.

Another reason why an anti-racism analysis must be part and parcel of gay critical theory and political activism is that if racism provides the language and epistemology for gay oppression, resistance to it is also the model for gay liberation – or so we all like to claim in our speeches. I don't know how many times I've heard gay politicos acknowledge that the Civil-Rights Movement inspired gay liberation: Stonewall was our Selma, drag queens our Martin Luther King. Indeed, what gay civil rights do exist often come from broad (re)interpretations of court decisions and ordinances that began as racial conflicts. If that's the case, by turning away from an anti-racist programme, the gay movement would be ripping off Black politics the same way the dominant culture ripped off (among other treasures) Black music. And, as Cameo says, you can't talk out of both sides of yo' neck.

VI
But folk are talking. Black lesbians and gays are tying up the conference lines, jamming on the word processors, and mixing it up in the editing rooms, producing some live cultures that deserve more than clinical petri dish examinations. For the third year running, the National Black Lesbian and Gay Leadership Forum is sponsoring its national conference. The National Coalition of Black Lesbians and Gays is starting its eleventh year of publishing *Black/Out*. Black poets and writers are self-publishing or inking their contracts with the lesbian of colour-owned Kitchen Table Press. A promising regional press is being birthed in San Francisco (the lesbian-produced *Ache*) and in Los Angeles (the multigendered *BLK*). And in 1989 two important, daring films were made by Black gay filmmakers: Isaac Julien's re-vision of Black gay life during the Harlem Renaissance, *Looking for Langston*, and Marlon Riggs's brilliant autobiographical musing about contemporary Black gay identity, *Tongues Untied*.

The closing of the gates to the gay cultural canon stands to replace the worn-out offense of slamming the bar door on lesbians and gay men of colour. That's why it's time lesbians and gay men of colour took up cultural criticism, so *we* can interrogate and articulate what these films and other primary texts mean. We need to become critical text-readers, not only to extend the vision of the gay community or to rebut the homophobia of the Black cultural establishment (the gay community should have denounced the Langston Hughes estate's yanking of Isaac Julien's film out of circulation as widely as it did the National Endowment for the Arts clamping down on Mapplethorpe's restrospective) *but to affirm our presence as producers of cultural texts in need of public discussion.*

The post-Iran Contragate/poststructuralist cultural message that's trickled down to me is that some of 'the master's tools' are just implements used in specific ways to rationalise specific power relations. But there's nothing inherently 'white' about the genre of criticism or theory – the high-flown language, the constant references to European sources, the seeming disengagement with the social world. It's that the coding white people bring to those conventions is valued and valorised over and above the ways of telling and seeing by 'Others'. And, given the ways in which I believe the lesbian and gay community problematises race, I don't want to leave it solely to white lesbian and gay historians and literary and film critics to (re)define the meaning of race in the lives of lesbians and gays of colour. The critical voice is as self-reflective as the poetic voice and as crucial to the establishment of a legacy. Leaving a paradigm of understanding will be as treasured as the poetry, prose, song, dance, music, and film that certainly will live beyond us, because with it not only will future generations find themselves reflected in the mirror of understanding that theory provides, but they will be able to see the larger forces that converged to make these things – that made us – possible.

VII

Not a day passes during which I don't muse on the irony of the age we live in: that in the wake of death, in the pools of absence caused by AIDS, gay life insists on defying the odds stacked against it and is in a state of rebirth; that rather than give in to this terror, gay culture will settle for nothing less than both being remembered and advancing the state of knowledge itself. But this wasn't a simple matter of choice; the historical moment demanded this activism. What we say and to whom and how we say it – discourse – has become a political issue and turf on which decisions are made. Dig it: the notion of 'the underclass' is a partisan symbol used to legitimise the elite's disgust with the poor no less than the term accurately describes the political status of the disenfranchised in

American society. Don't believe the hype that 'the canon debate' is full of hot air: whether Langston Hughes or Audre Lorde or Walt Whitman or Edmund White makes it to class syllabi will greatly influence how others see us and how we see ourselves. As long as the politics of Mapplethorpe's racial aesthetics remains uninterrogated by Black gay men, the meaning of his work will never be complete. Whether gay politics and culture continue to exclude people of colour from their organisations and analyses will depend on our response. We know that when it comes to signifyin', testifyin', and throwin' the dozens, no one can talk our talk. Snap! [4]

NOTES

[1] I adapted this title from Zora Neale Hurston's 1928 essay 'How It Feels to be Colored Me'. Check it out. It's both humbling and disturbing to know Hurston struggled with similar problems about voice, address and identity (dis)placement so long ago.

[2] See p. 246 for Thom Bean's response as Publisher/Editor, *QI*, San Francisco, included at his insistence.

[3] Editor's note: Before the Helm's controversy over Mapplethorpe's work, Black, gay men in Britain had started to analyse the photographer's racial aesthetic in the pages of the 'alternative' photographic press. For different views see: Kobena Mercer and Isaac Julien, 'True Confessions' in *Ten.8*, no. 22; Sunil Gupta, 'Desire and Black Men' in *Ten.8*, no. 22; and Kobena Mercer, 'Imaging the Black Man's Sex' in *Photography/Politics: Two*, ed. P. Holland, J. Spence and S. Watney (London: Comedia Publishing Group, 1986).

[4] Reprinted with permission of *OUT/LOOK*, the national lesbian and gay quarterly, Issue 9, Summer 1990.

ACKNOWLEDGEMENT
My writing happens in revision. The support, criticism and suggestions of Deirdre Rettenmaier and the *OUT/LOOK* editors mattered a great deal in that process. Thanks to you all.

PORTRAITS

Tee Corinne

Yantra # 7 from Yantras of Womanlove *(1982).*

Yantra # 22 from Yantras of Womanlove *(1982).*

A Woman's Touch # 7.

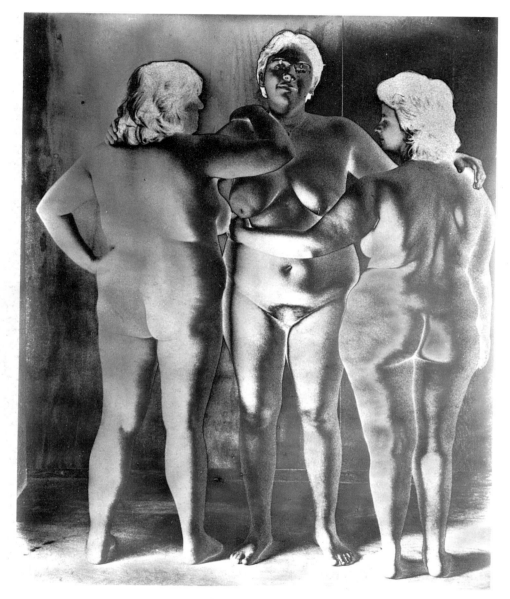

The Three Graces.

Isis in the Woods.

Corinne's 'body work' rests on a seemingly stable, universalising base – 'flowers as symbols of women's genitals', flowers as 'labial forms in nature' standing for that which is everywhere yet repressed . . .

When Corinne has produced photographs explicitly depicting women having sex with each other, she has abstracted sex acts through solarization, flipped negatives, negative images. This deliberate obscuring arises out of her concern for 'afford(ing) my models some measure of privacy' rather than prurience.

Unlike . . . Vanessa Williams, the former Miss America who posed for 'lesbian action' photos subsequently sold to *Playboy* – whose identity resides in her professed status *as an actor*, Corinne's subjects are acting out their personal life, which is paradoxically more in need of protection than the public behaviour of models.

Here again, the social difficulties that would follow upon identification as a lesbian have moulded the photographer's decisions to a considerable degree, resulting in a body of work on sexuality that cannot be understood in terms familiar to art/academic analysis – that in fact looks coy and sentimental by those institutions' standards: work that displaces sexual feelings onto acceptable symbolic replacements so as to 'afford some measure of privacy' and work that elaborate 'images complex enough that people would want to stay with them for a long time, puzzle them out . . .' These heavily manipulated images function not only as protection for the individual model's identity, but also as a correlative for the status of the public lesbian: present yet invisible, out yet hidden, provocative yet in need of protection.

Jan Zita Grover, 'Dykes in Context' in *Ten:8*, no. 30, 1988, pp.42-4.

BUTCH/FEM PICNIC

Morgan Gwenwald

CERTAIN PARTS OF CENTRAL PARK ARE ALMOST DESERTED.

*ONE WEEKDAY MORNING, WHILE EVERYONE ELSE
WENT TO WORK, LIZ AND CHRIS DIDN'T.*

*LIZ FORGOT THE THERMOS, AND CHRIS DIDN'T
THINK THEY NEEDED A TABLECLOTH.*

EVERYTHING TASTES SO MUCH BETTER OUTSIDE.

These photographs originally appeared in *On Our Backs*, vol. 1, issue 3, Winter 1985.

UNMEDIATED LUST?

THE IMPROBABLE SPACE OF LESBIAN DESIRES

Cindy Patton

In 1983, I reviewed two photographic projects for Boston's *Gay Community News*: the Robert Mapplethorpe photographs of bodybuilder Lisa Lyon; and *The Theater Project,* a visual ethnography of a local porn cinema by Christian Walker.[1] Gay male photographer Mapplethorpe's photos played with ostensibly straight Lyon's body – she is photographed nude flexing on a rock, in classic 1950s male-physique magazine style, and vamping in 1950s porn postures. She is shot in a wedding dress and in black leather, in a fashion model series and during a workout at the gym.

Walker's photographs represent months spent in a porn palace in Boston's Combat Zone ('redlight' district), an area of town being slowly mowed down to make way for larger buildings and more lucrative businesses. Walker wanted to document the life of this once elegant theatre, a seedy porn cinema and male cruising space since the late 1960s. Although (or perhaps because) the theatre was not part of 'politically correct' or even proudly 'gay' culture, Walker believed the space

constituted an important and subversive form of male (homo)erotic life existing on the margins of political consciousness, a kind of liminal space from which a common sensibility might emerge, or in which 'gay culture' might find refuge in times of fewer public possibilities. This theatre was not one of the 'all-male revue' cinemas which enabled purveyors of vice to capitalise on the increasing social possibility/visibility of gay men following gay liberation. It was a 'straight' theatre where men enacted sex in a protective domain of male desires constructed as heterosexual by the showing of 'heterosexual', that is 'girlie' or male/female, fuck films, or at any rate, oblivious to organised (male) homoeroticism.

SKIN DEEP

The unsettling Orientalism[2] of Mapplethorpe's cross-race, male-male photographs which play on differences in skin texture and tone, have no precise analogue in the photographs of Lyon. Lyon must counterpose her own masculinity and femininity, sometimes in adjacent compositions, sometimes through gender-fuck within a composition (as in the wedding dress/flexing photograph). Her female skin is made soft, hard, textured through comparison with fabric or through application of graphite or mud. The sheer breadth and incoherence of *Lady* suggests that Mapplethorpe lacked generic references for a female version of his classically stylised (male) homoerotic compositions. Mapplethorpe worked to reveal the facets of Lyon's quirky personality, but he also aspired to a transcendent statement on the body, on gender. In this sense, his work, however haunting, was quite traditional. He *interpreted* Lyon rather than working with her to speak in a less generic way about her erotic 'reality'. Especially when he renders her in gay male codes, however transgressive this transposition of gender/sexuality, Lyon, as the embodiment of infinitely mutable femaleness, is entirely explained in terms of male desire. That enigma, Woman, is reduced to a set of ideograms which each reference male desire. Not only can Lyon be classically feminine and daintily sadistic for a presumptive heterosexual male, but she can be Fashion or Toy Boy for a (male) homoerotic gaze. There is no space left for a female appropriation of Lyon, no point of view for a lesbian gaze. And yet some of the images in the Mapplethorpe series became enormously popular within lesbian culture, and lost their references to (heterosexual) bodybuilding and gay male photographic cultures. The postcard versions of Lyon flexing nude against a harsh rock landscape said power, strong woman, eroticism to a generation of lesbians. However, the representations which ambiguate gender and the ideographically 'heterosexual' and (male) homosexual S/M photos, did *not* become artifacts of lesbian culture: in 1983 butch-femme and S/M were only beginning to be reconstructed as lost erotic styles.

Mapplethorpe's homosexual status and his sophisticated use of classic (male) homoerotic (van Gloeden-like)[3] and gay/sado-masochistic countercultural codes subverted the strict sexuality/gender division presupposed in theories of looking. He nevertheless produced iconographic lesbian imagery which allowed the viewer to disregard the sexual positioning of the photographer. In stark contrast, the erotic photography emerging from within the lesbian community insisted that *lesbians* must interpret lesbian experience, and often that *only* lesbians could properly read off the lesbian erotics of such photographs. For example, Tee Corinne used avant-garde and documentary conventions to work out of and 'present' lesbian erotic experience.[4] This argument was blatant (though insufficiently theorised)[5] in the interdict that a whole range of cultural artifacts produced by/for lesbians which were not to be sold to men. According to this logic – not necessarily held by particular photographers but palpable in the practices of women's bookstores which labelled such items, placed them in a separate area or refused to allow men to purchase them – men would read in or read over and therefore 'rape' the feminist intentions of the photographee, writer or photographer.

SPACIALISED EROTICS

Walker's *Theater Project* represented the coherences and order of male (homo)sexual culture by apparently documenting a 'real' place and transposing it into a future or imaginary space, which was 'unreal' at least for those who have traditionally been excluded from these bastions of male sexual expression. Here, ordinary men were photographed against the architectural order of a space they had taken over for themselves. Where Lyon had been posed against a range of backgrounds designed to problematise traditional associations between gender and skin, muscle, fabric, Walker's men and transsexuals were in an environment of their own making. They had colonised the formerly elegant cinema house with their male desires and ritual migrations. Walker contextualised male (homo-erotic) desires: he humanised male bodies by showing their movement *in* rather than their surface relation *to* the cinema interior. Unlike classic portraiture which would pick up the lines of the body in the composition of the objects or set, Walker never allows the camera to view a pipe or railing or the line of a toilet stall as an extension of a penis or continuation of the plane of a thigh. Here was a desire interpolated into a space: a production by a man familiar with the practices of desire in this world which is at least partially his own.

Again, I was struck by the reeling dislocation of lesbian desire. Where were the *lesbian* erotic spaces which might be ethnographically reproduced to show the choreography of lesbian desire? Material and historical conditions, certainly, meant that we had no porn cinemas, although the traditional pre-feminist bars might be an exotic locale of unpolitically corrected lesbian desire. But could we be ethnographers/voyeurs of ourselves? Even if we produced works ourselves, could we escape the objectifying effects ('voyeurism') many theorists believed were inherent in photography? Certainly, radical feminists like Andrea Dworkin would argue that any mediation of sexuality is an objectification, and thus anti-woman, a step onto the slippery slope of producing the violent pornographies which are disturbing to many female readers and viewers.[6]

CREATING SPACE: THE EMERGENCE OF LESBIAN SEX MAGAZINES

It was during this time (1983-4ish) and in the context of these representational practices that lesbian sex magazines appeared in the USA. Each had its own approach to representing lesbian sexuality which was particularly well defined in *Bad Attitude*, *On Our Backs*, and 'S/Mzine' *Outrageous Women*. Although all three were created in direct response to the stated interests of lesbians to see what the terrain of mediated lesbian sexual desire might look like/be, their specific conceptions and production values show serious differences in ideas about the nature of lesbian desires. *Bad Attitude* grew out of the experience of lesbians working on Boston's always quirky leftist and gender-mixed *Gay Community News*: the early material was 'found' work that had been produced in the absence of a place to publish. *On Our Backs* emerged from a San Francisco sex shop with a large lesbian clientele and represents a commercial, lesbian controlled, response to a perceived market demand. The Boston women's S/M group Urania, which had just been chucked out of the Cambridge Women's Centre, produced *Outrageous Women* as its public forum. Perhaps the purest expression of lesbian micro-community produced and consumed sexual media, *Outrageous Women* featured home-made photographs produced by women who were themselves practitioners of the activities in the photographs. Distinctions between documentary, instructional and erotic material break down in these unstylised, unself-conscious sexual texts. Indeed, whether these 'home-made' ('by/for') photographs, which are characteristic of most of the non-commercial 'porn' I have seen, are *about* sex or *are* sex is impossible to decide. *Outrageous Women* exemplified the trend for direct, authentic, self-expression in photography, while *On Our Backs* quickly produced style guidelines for photographers whilst establishing a photospread in each issue which covertly promoted a *look* distinguished from the more experimental approaches to lesbian erotic aesthetics (or anti-aesthetics). *Bad Attitude*'s visual coherence changed over time, but never attained the stylisation of *On Our Backs*, at least until the editorial board turned over at Issue 7 (in 1986): in the first six issues there were no narrative photospreads, photographers were never asked to illustrate a particular story and generally photos stood on their own, often with little or incoherent relation to adjacent articles. Its 'punkish' design style and anxiety about leaving much white space gave *Bad Attitude* a look closer to gay left newspapers than to pornography.

These magazines doubly constituted a political space of lesbian desires. In their very mode of production – lesbian-'owned' and produced – and mode of circulation – in sealed, unmarked envelopes and at feminist and gay bookstores – the magazines sought to extend the narrow margin of lesbian-community mediated communication.[7] In the age of desktop publishing and improved offset printing, moderate production-value periodicals in small print runs (*Bad Attitude*'s was typically about 1,200 copies) were economically viable, and decreased mail censorship enabled the construction of an 'imagined community' by sharing ideas and erotic sensibilities through participation in magazine production and consumption.[8] In the context of a love that had only just dared to speak its name, the magazines simply in their existence constituted a space for straightforwardly articulating formerly inaudible or dissimulating lesbian desires. However, this space not only resisted institutionalisation (except perhaps in San Francisco, where the magazine's imaginary community overlapped with the face-to-face communities of women attending lesbian strip shows or comparing commodities at the sex shop), but was foreclosed from becoming a 'safe house' of lesbian desires.

SECRET AGENTS/DANGEROUS DESIRES
I borrow the phrase 'safe house' from B. Ruby Rich, with whom I had the following conversation at the 'How Do I Look?' gay and lesbian media conference in New York in October 1989.[9] After confessing that I had chickened out during a lecture on safe sex pornography and simply eliminated a clip of lesbians having safe sex, B. Ruby Rich said, 'I'm interested in that terror, why does that happen even to those of us who have been so involved in these debates? We need a safe house for

lesbian pornography.' I like the idea of 'safe house' with its double connotation: protecting spies or foreign agents who had been underground operatives and who now risk harm because their 'cover' has been blown and, in the rubric of the battered women's movement, houses of ordinary women who are willing to take in their sisters who are in imminent danger.[10] The notion of multiple and hidden identities embedded in the 'safe house' of popular culture spy epics played off against the protection of women's bodies, provides an important complement to Benedict Anderson's idea of 'imagined communities'. The safe house is the home of distressed bodies and the centre of networks which are 'imagined' not only in being only transiently face to face, but also because they are prevented from existing in face to face forms precisely because of their marginality, their foreignness to the hegemonic 'imagined community' of nationalist (hetero)sexuality.

The homoerotics of the porn cinema is protected precisely because it is men, and (in the case of non-'gay' cinemas) men who assert heterosexuality, despite their male-male erotics and practices. It is a source of humour in gay male culture that so many 'straight' men have 'sex' 'with' other men at the porn cinema. However, there is an important gap in the definition of what constitutes 'sex'. In hegemonic culture, penile-vaginal intercourse is considered 'sex', and in true Freudian form, everything else (from actual homosexuality to voyeurism and 'lingering over the touch') constitutes perversion. So it should be no surprise that jerking off in front of or 'lingering over the touch' of other men, even being fellated by them, is not understood as homosexuality by these 'straight' men, especially when an authenticating heterosexual porn film is the image ostensibly producing their desires. Thus, in the calculus of mainstream culture, the porn cinema remains structurally heterosexual: the act of publicly seeking sex and the ritual precation inscribes *masculinity*, not the anxious *effeminacy* which defines male homosexuality within the same dominant culture. To go to a porn cinema and seek sex is an act so blatantly masculine that it is logically impossible to consider any male-male acts engaged in there as 'homosexual'. It seems to me that the thrill gay men get from seducing straight men at the cinema is based in this anxious contradiction within American masculinity which denies effeminacy (homosexuality) *in the very act* of publicly having sex with another man.

IN THE MARGINS OF DESIRE

I can think of no similar space of contradiction existing within lesbian erotic practice or imagination; in fact, almost the reverse seems to occur. As films like John Sayles's *Lianna* or the more opulently erotic *Desert Hearts* or even the lesbian porn 'Oral Annie' series suggest, having sex with another woman constitutes entry into the 'hidden world' of lesbianism. In this sense, revelation of lesbian desire seems paradoxically to always make the lesbian bodies vanish to this secret world.

The possibility of even an imagined lesbian safe house was destroyed in part because some feminist bookstores refused, with a flurry of accusatory rhetoric, to carry the new lesbian magazines. They were deemed no different than the mainstream, heterosexual porn targeted by the anti-porn movement. Other feminist bookstores, uncomfortable with their first instinct to censor, quietly stocked the magazines under the counter so the curious lesbian had to proclaim her unreformed lesbian desire in order to acquire the magazines. Gay men were more welcoming of this heretical newcomer to the homoerotic landscape, however in their anxiety about the inexplicability of female sexuality, they often appropriated lesbian sex magazines to defend themselves against feminist anti-porn women and elided the important differences between lesbian sex magazines (all 'owned' by lesbians) and glossy gay male porn (with few exceptions,

owned by straight publishing houses – there is, in fact, a corollary set of non-commercial gay male, grassroots sex magazines with production values, modes of circulation, the quirkiness of the lesbian magazines).

Both gay men and anti-porn feminists missed the point that the lesbian sex magazines were a quirky, tentative move toward mapping the terrain, limits and margins of a sexuality always discursively disappearing. The photographs in particular attempted to spacialise lesbian sexuality, to demonstrate what might be in the imaginary of lesbians who were constantly told that their sex wasn't real. If women's orgasms were hidden, mysterious, made readable only through the display of a penis or through stylised facial expressions (which look the same in advertising and in porn), then lesbian pleasure was completely impossible to visualise.[11] There was no *place* of lesbian desire, no women-only venues of practice, no visual code of women's bodies in pleasure not already colonised by heterosexuality.

The anti-porn analysis of pornography assumes the existence of a 'free' sexuality, transcendant or at least unmediated. But surely, sexuality is always socially constructed[12] as such, always mediated. In the context of the loss of 'originals', the recognition of the inescapability of intertextuality in systems of interpretation and the commodification of aesthetic pleasure (and its poor cousin, *sexual* pleasure) apparently characteristic of postmodernity, the lack of lesbian spaces (other than futuristic Utopias) within (or from) which to stake claims for an essential lesbian subjectivity suggests that lesbian sexuality is already textually constructed,[13] and indeed, a postmodern lesbian politic might make its stand *in* a textual reconstruction that made no claims about a relation to an 'authentic' or 'original' or 'properly lesbian' essentiality. Such work would create conditions in which viewers could work on, rather than 'consume', photographs; viewing would be an active production rather than an evaluation of fidelity to a hypothesised 'real lesbian'.

DESIRE AS FOREIGN AGENT: LESBIAN SEXUALITY IN DISGUISE

Mainstream culture, with its greater ability to produce circulate and promote standard interpretations and interpreting practices, is able to colonise non-dominant sexualities by purporting to describe what they are about. The power of the hegemonic culture to discursively narrow the space of sexual self-definition is not to be underestimated. Indeed, this is what Foucault was trying to suggest: far from sexual repression, from the Victorians to the present, we have witnessed an incessant and increasingly pitched cacophony of speech about sexuality. But to the extent that a hegemonic culture secures the intepretive logics, marginal sexualities (and all but a few sexualities are marginal under the vast and insistently gender-role conformist dominant discourse) can have very little to say for themselves.

The solution, at least if one adopts a strategy derived from the Foucaultian critique, is not to stabilise this tiny discursive space by solidifying a transcendent identity. Rather, we should subvert the lack of centre in the dominant discourse by putting down our tents right there. This is what gay men have been doing when they have sex with straight men in the porno cinema. Lesbians do not yet have the discursive ability to conquer heterosexuality on the 'feminine' side, as female desire is already discursively disappearing. Seducing heterosexual women merely increases the number of lesbians (which might be a desirable but independent project), but does nothing to perform the 'difference' (the homoness) in female desire required to constitute it as lesbian (rather than as simply independent, narcissistic or masturbatory categories which could also use some creative recoupment). However, subverting the democratic brotherhood of gay

male sexuality by appropriating their images of fuckability in black leather suggests that lesbians have already been where homo-masculinity is seeking to be.

For the last few years the lesbian sex magazines have been quite openly playing with the (gay) boys. At first, there was a tinge of envy in these images, but once dressed for the occasion, we discovered that we had already been over this turf. (The marvellous revival of butch-femme erotics also reminded us that we knew how to turn masculinity on its head, and that we did not have to be afraid of these powerful transgressions.) Having conquered masculinity as secret agents of lesbian desire, we must now deconstruct any female desire that insists that it must be constructed against masculinity. We must create images for Monique Wittig's polemic assertion that lesbians are not women: perhaps lesbians in black leather, foreign agents operating under the cloak of pseudo-masculinity, are engaged in gender sabotage. Working through the existing discursive spaces of masculine presence and feminine absence (though not *lack* as lesbians' reclaiming and possession of dildos shows), change the unconscious interpretive erotics so that even the most recalcitrant heterosexual male cannot help but be disturbed by his exclusion from lesbian produced representations. The 'don't let men read it' ethos acknowledges that we have not yet produced images that defy colonisation. To make lesbian desire visible and safe (that is, not appropriable within the heterosexual masculine/male/top: feminine/female/bottom logic), it must be visible as *lesbian* desire within the hegemonic discourse. Anything less is another disappearing act.

The image of 'women in control' (women desiring) must first be separated from the visual encoding of heterosexual desire. Lesbians first tried to accomplish this by producing 'authentic' presentations of lesbian eroticism: perhaps the black leather brigade will finish the work by pulling the plug on the heterosexual-desire-machine. Lesbian desire, in order to be made visible, must evade the heterosexual male desire to appropriate lesbians as women (or as boys). A first step may be to lure into the open the heterosexual male desire to be appropriated, not by women ('male masochism') or by men (civilisation?), but to being 'taken' (in?) by the unpleasant lesbians in black leather who are so utterly aesthetically incomprehensible ('ugly') to them. There must be a way of encoding this absence of desire – not the absence of desire *for* men, as men have misunderstood lesbian desire, not the conflation of power with desire, as radical feminists have misunderstood S/M, but the absence of desires mapped onto genders, the absence of desire for gender as power. Once freed from the bonds of gender, transgressive desires (and what could be more transgressive than bodies that slip out of heterosexuality?) may linger on many objects, engage in many reclamation projects.

It should be possible for countercultural pornographies, like other countercultural media, to traverse and disrupt hegemonic gender and sexual codes. We do not, it seems to me, want to produce lesbian desire as 'impenetrable' to hegemonic interpretation, as 'invisible' except to the few who recognise the codes. Rather, we want to produce images of lesbian desire that undo and de-centre gender, rip and tear at the foundations of hegemonic heterosexuality. To some extent we can't 'think outside' the cultural constructions of the moment, but this is not to suggest that a pure lesbian desire somehow transcends or fully disrupts hegemonic heterosexuality. Indeed, it is in the anxious, noisy space of the construction of heterosexuality that the margin for lesbian desire is reduced to a small and receding dot. Gay men subverted the space of heterosexuality in the porno cinema by inscribing male-male sex within masculinity. Paradoxically, macho dykes in leather have undone the phallus with their collections of dildos. Lesbian erotic imagery must now subvert feminity by . . .

That remains to be seen. Some of the images in this volume attempt to rework the erotics of feminity. But we cannot judge these images by evaluating the degree to which they escape colonisation by the 'male gaze', rather by the degree to which they disrupt the poles of gender on which heterosexuality now teeters. They are part of an ongoing attempt not simply to articulate a lived experience in a documentary fashion, set in a moment, but to articulate the ways in which lesbian desire always and insistently subverts dominant sexuality. Lesbians are not simply women who love women, but women whose daily sexual practice is a resistance to the cacophony of heterosexual anxiety. The lesbian erotic images constitute not a static safe house of lesbian desire, but the roving bivouac of an advanced team of sexual guerrillas plotting discursive strategies for a next assault on heterosexuality.

NOTES

1 Robert Mapplethorpe, *Lady: Lisa Lyon*, text by Bruce Chatwin (New York: Viking Press, 1983). The photos of *The Theater Project* show were published in 1985 in Christian Walker, *The Theater Project* (Nexus Press, 608 Ralph McGill Blvd. NE, Atlanta, Georgia, USA).

2 See both Susan Sontag, *On Photography* (New York: Dell, 1978) and Edward Said, *Orientalism* (New York: Pantheon, 1978) for different approaches to the construction of the visual Other. See also Homi Bhabha, 'The Other Question: The Stereotype and Colonial Discourse', in *Screen*, vol. 26, no. 6, 1983.

3 Wilhelm von Gloeden was an early, turn-of-the-century photographer noted for his idealised portraits of young men in classical Greek and Roman settings. There is an excellent review of his work in relation to later gay male iconography in Bruce Russell, 'Von Gloeden: A Reappraisal' in *Studies in Visual Communication*, vol. 9, no. 2, Spring 1983, pp. 60-4, plates pp. 72-80.

4 There was little concept within lesbian cultural practice ('production' or 'consumption') at the time that artifacts were a representation: despite feminist psychoanalytic film theory, most grassroots photographers in American Second Wave feminism

were working to 'uncover' the lost and hidden voices of women/women's desire. I think it is fair to say that the lesbian photography of the late 1970s and well into the 1980s was viewed as empowering lesbian erotic reality by 'making visible/present' lesbian experience. Joan E. Biren (JEB), in her slideshow of lesbian images which toured the USA extensively, argued that there were indeed visual cues which marked photos as 'by lesbians'. This cathection of visual artifacts was for the most part theorised outside the concurrent debates about representation in the academy and constituted the obverse of the claim that mass culture presentations of sexuality caused violence against women. For JEB's statement on her theoretical relationship to her subjects, see her 'Lesbian Photography – Seeing Through Our Own Eyes' in *Studies in Visual Communication*, vol. 9, no. 2, Spring 1983, pp. 81-6, plates pp. 87-96.

5 Feminist psychoanalytic representation theory at the time was beginning to question whether 'the gaze' *was* always male, the object female; however, the conceptual innovations resulting from this reassessment had not trickled down into popular critical practice. This debate begins with Laura Mulvey's innovation in spectator theory in her 1975 'Visual Pleasures and Narrative Cinema' in *Screen*, vol. 16, no. 3, where much of the ensuring debate about gender and the gaze occurred.

6 See Andrea Dworkin, *Pornography* (London: Women's Press, 1981).

7 Andrea Dworkin and Catherine McKinnon, in lectures, persistently question 'who is behind' the emergent lesbian sex magazines, suggesting that mainstream pornography producers are somehow related. *Bad Attitude*, *Outrageous Women*, the short-lived *Cathexis* and *Power Exchange* were all clearly low-budget, grassroots, volunteer-produced publications which contained no or little advertising and survived on subscriptions, bookstore sales and occasional donations. *On Our Backs* is more upscale and contains advertising, but anyone who has published countercultural periodicals can easily calculate that no huge financial interests are involved in its publication. The truly grassroots, subscription-based publications had no capital or assets, thus, the idea that they were 'owned' is a nominal, political statement, rather than a statement about commercialness.

8 I am extending the argument proposed in Benedict Anderson's *Imagined Community* (London: Verso, 1983). He examines the creation of national and supranational 'community' identifications through the rise of national languages and systems of communication. Likewise, the lesbian sexual media create a space for the exploration of lesbian sexual desires at the margin of both feminist (and sexually self-censoring) and gay male (sometimes misogynist) discourse.

9 The proceedings of the conference are forthcoming from the Bay Press, Seattle, Washington, USA.

10 The 'Safehouse' movement in the USA, at its peak in the late 1970s and early 1980s, involved neighbourhood organising to train women in crisis intervention and support. Women who were part of the network put a back-lit green symbol of a house in their window to indicate that theirs was a safe place for a woman in danger.

11 For a longer discussion of the representation of female and male orgasm and the difficulties this creates for lesbian/gay representation see Cindy Patton, 'The Cum Shot – Three Takes on Lesbian and Gay Sexuality' in *OUT/LOOK*, Fall 1988.

12 This is the weight of a generation of lesbian/gay studies in a range of social scientical and historical projects, see, for a summary of this data and argument, Jeffrey Weeks, *Sexuality* (London: Tavistock, 1986); Pat Caplan, ed., *The Cultural Construction of Sexuality* (London: Tavistock, 1987); Ann Ferguson, *Blood at the Root* (London and New York: Pandora Press, 1989).

13 Dr Vickie Mays at the University of California found that 88 percent of young lesbians said they had learned about lesbianism from the media. By contrast, 96 percent of the young men said they learned about gay sexuality from having sex with other men. Paper presented at the 1987 Lesbian and Gay Health Conference in Los Angeles.

BIOGRAPHICAL NOTES

Deborah Bright is an artist and writer who teaches at the Rhode Island School of Design. Her writings on photography and cultural politics have appeared in *Views*, *Exposure* and *Afterimage*. Her photographic work has been exhibited widely, and a catalogue of her work, *Deborah Bright: Textual Landscapes*, was published by the State University of New York, Binghamton (1988). She was the recipient of the David and Reva Logan Award for new critical writing on photography in 1989.

Kaucyila Brooke teaches at the University of California at San Diego. Before doing graduate work at the University of Arizona, she lived in Eugene, Oregon, for seven years where she worked in a shelter for battered women and co-ordinated women's programming for public access radio. She recently co-produced *Dry Kisses Only* with Jane Cottis which is a videotape about lesbian subplot in classic cinema.

Cathy Cade is 48, a white lesbian photographer teaching photography at two high schools and travelling with shows titled *The Subject is Lesbians* and *Lesbian Moms*. She is working on a postcard series from Lesbian and Gay Freedom Day Parades and a book on lesbian mothering. She lives in Oakland, California, with her two sons.

Tee Corinne was born in the USA in 1943. She holds a MFA degree in art from Pratt Institute (1968). Her images have been published in the US women's movement press since 1974. She co-facilitated the Feminist Photography Ovulars (1979-81) and co-founded *The Blatant Image, A Magazine of Feminist Photography* (1981). Her book of solarized erotic images, *Yantras of Womanlove*, was published by Naiad Press in 1982. She is the author of *Dreams of the Woman Who Loved Sex* and of *Lovers*, and has edited a book of lesbian erotic fiction, *Intricate Passions*.

Jacqui Duckworth initially studied sculpture, and subsequently film-making, at the Royal College of Art, London. Her films, which include *Home-Made Melodrama* and *An Invitation to Marilyn C.*, have been shown at the National Film Theatre and on the independent film circuit. She idolises dogs but was turned down by Battersea Dogs Home as an unsuitable dog-owner. She is currently seeking a suitable dog through the personal ads of the gay press.

Mikki Ferrill is a photojournalist whose work has appeared in a wide number of US and international journals and newspapers. She has exhibited all over the USA; her *Black Cowboy* exhibit was part of the *Transatlantic Dialogues* exhibition which toured both in the USA and the UK. She was curator for the Black Esthetics Art and Photo Exhibit at the Museum of Science and Industry, Chicago, and for the Malcolm X College Black History Week Photo Exhibit. She lives in Berkeley, California.

Sara Furse works as a picture researcher at Magnum Photos, London. Previously she was a freelance photographer and assistant to Eve Arnold. She has worked as cinema programmer/publicist at the Side Gallery, Newcastle, and has exhibited at the Spectre Gallery in Newcastle (where she organised the *Women Live* group show in 1982) and at Camerwork, London. She was a prizewinner in the South Bank Picture Show in 1988. Her published work includes illustrations for a book on cervical cancer and an article on Vietnam for women travellers. She has travelled throughout the world.

Martha Gever is the editor of *The Independent Film and Video Monthly* and has written articles on media for a number of publications, including *Afterimage*, *Art in America*, *The Nation*, *October* and *Screen*. She is co-editor of *Out There: Marginalization and Contemporary Cultures*, published by MIT Press and The New Museum.

Sue Golding, a lesbian hermaphrodite, focuses her intellectual work on theories of radical democracy and popular movements. A long-time feminist and gay activist, her writings for the alternative press concentrate on the wondrous pleasures of sexual perversities and the questions that may arise for a more progressive and compassionate society.

Jackie Goldsby is a scholar and culture critic studying for a PhD in American Studies at Yale University. She is a contributing editor to *OUT/LOOK*, the US national lesbian and gay quarterly.

Della Grace, sometimes known as Della Disgrace, has been photographing lesbian lifestyles for the past ten years in her quest to discover and create erotic lesbian imagery. Her work has been published in *Time Out*, *City Limits*, *Square Peg*, *Rouge*, and Gay Men's Press will publish a book of her photographs in Spring 1991.

Jan Zita Grover is a writer and critic. She was the executive editor of *OUT/LOOK*.

Morgan Gwenwald has been creating images of lesbian erotica for over a decade. She is interested in exploring and recording the diversity of lesbian sexuality. Morgan earned her BFA in 1975 and has been widely published in the lesbian and women's press in the USA. In the face of the rising censorship movement she is more committed than ever to getting her work published and onto gallery walls. She also works extensively as a photographer for the Lesbian

Herstory Archives and the Lesbian and Gay Community Services Centre of NYC.

Jude Johnston has produced photo, text, graphic and multi-material installations that have dealt with language, lesbians, media, class and notions of community. She has been an Editor (*Fuse* magazine), Board member (A Space, Women's Art Resource Centre, Toronto Women's Bookstore) and is currently employed as an abortion counsellor in Toronto, Canada.

Mumtaz Karimjee is a self-taught photographer. She was born in 1950 in Bombay, India, and has since lived, studied and worked in Tanzania, Britain, Germany and China. Issues of representation form a central theme to her work. She is now based in London.

Jackie Kay is at the forefront of Black women's writing in Britain. She has had two theatre plays produced: *Chiaroscuro* (Theatre of Black Women) and *Twice Over* (Gay Sweatshop). She co-edited a volume of international women's writing, *Charting The Journey*. She acted as Consultant Director on a *Bandung File* feature on cross-racial adoption. She reads widely from her work, both at home and abroad. Her poems have appeared in many anthologies, including: *Beautiful Barbarians*, *Dancing The Tightrope* and *A Dangerous Knowing*. She is currently writer-in-residence at Hammersmith and Fulham in London.

Nina Levitt is a Canadian photographic artist and arts administrator. She has been an exhibiting artist since 1981 and has been a recipient of numerous government grants for the production of explicitly lesbian works. Since 1986, she has produced photographic works which address notions of femininity and lesbian sexuality. She is a 'mistress' of appropriation, preferring to deconstruct existing representations in order to critique images and text of lesbians in popular culture.

Nathalie Magnan is a graduate student at the University of California, Santa Cruz, in the History of Consciousness programme. She writes about issues of gender, class, race and sexuality as represented in independent video. She has also produced several videotapes with Paper Tiger Television.

Rosy Martin was born in 1946 in London. She qualified, practised and taught as a chemist, then as an industrial designer. She is currently working at Women's Design Service. Since 1988, in collaboration with Jo Spence, she has originated and developed the new photographic practice 'phototherapy'. Exhibitions of this work have been used in a range of contexts, from community centres to international galleries. She has run workshops, lectured and written articles on phototherapy, self-image and identity.

Mandy Merck lectures, writes and makes TV programmes. She has edited the media studies quarterly, *Screen*, and the Channel 4 lesbian and gay series, *Out on Tuesday*. A collection of her essays is forthcoming from Virago.

Ann Meredith has worked for twenty-one years documenting women's culture. She has photographed and recorded oral histories of women ageing, lesbian women and their concomitant canine companions (their dogs), women in blue-collar work, women dying, women at the United Nations Conference on the Decade of Women in Nairobi, Kenya, in July 1985, and now the 'Hidden Population' of the AIDS epidemic – women with AIDS, ARC and who are HIV Positive. Meredith is now working on documenting women in prison and a new series on cowgirls.

Lynette Molnar is an artist and activist and received both her BFA and MA in photography at Ohio State University. Her recent professional experience includes being Guest Associate Curator for the Wexner Centre for the Visual Arts and the University Gallery of Fine Art at Ohio State University. She has also been, since 1985, a lecturer with the Department of Photography and Cinema at Ohio State. She has participated in numerous exhibitions throughout the USA. Her solo exhibition, *Film in the Cities*, is forthcoming at St Paul, Minnesota.

Cindy Patton is a writer, activist and critic, who teaches in Amherst, Massachusetts.

Ingrid Pollard was born in the winter of 1953 and has lived in numerous locations all over London since she was 4. She is currently working as a freelance photographer and burgeoning film-maker. She knows no national or cultural boundaries in her search for the perfect fifty-word biography.

Jill Posener was born in London in 1953, raised in Berlin, and lives in San Francisco. She has published two books on political graffiti, *Spray It Loud* (1982) and *Louder Than Words* (1986). She transformed from vehement anti-porn protester to fierce anti-censorship campaigner in the turbulent late 1980s.

Jane Rosett is a freelance photographer and works as Director of Publications for the People With AIDS Coalition in New York City of which she is a founding Board member. She is also a founding and active board member of NYC's Community Research Initiative which conducts community-based clinical trials on promising AIDS drugs. Rosett has received numerous awards to continue her AIDS-related photography. She was recently awarded a grant from the New York State Council on the Arts (NYSCA) to continue her photographic work entitled *Living With AIDS*. She has also received photojournalism awards from the International Gay and Lesbian Press Association as well as the Human Rights Campaign Fund.

Sonja Ruehl lives in London and makes her living teaching economics in higher education. She has written on issues of sexuality and gender and contributed to establishing a Women's Studies course at the Open University, where she previously worked.

Connie Samaras grew up in Albuquerque, New Mexico. She came out the year after the Stonewall riots with a woman who was obsessed with both role-playing and disregarding rules, and followed her current lover to Ann Arbor, Michigan, during the mid-seventies where she discovered both tornadoes and another politically lively and diverse lesbian and feminist community. She lives in Los Angeles where she's a visiting lecturer in photography at UCLA and where she's discovered both earthquakes and politically-motivated lesbian and gay graduate students.

Hinda Schuman is a photojournalist currently living,

with Susan Toler, in Philadelphia and hoping for a full-time contract with health insurance. She has exhibited locally in the USA and at Camerawork Gallery in London. Her work has also appeared in *Ten.8*. She is working at present on a series about professional boxers. She is attracted to photography both for its story-telling and its investigative potential.

Anna Marie Smith is a doctoral student in the Ideology and Discourse Analysis Programme at the University of Essex. Her thesis research is on 'post-modern' social and political theory, and British New Right discourse on race, nation and sexuality. She is also a member of Feminists Against Censorship.

Linda Thornburg is currently writer-director for a feature film based on May Sarton's novel, *Mrs Stevens Hears the Mermaids Singing*. She has written and directed documentary film, television and a play about two women who live in a bed, *Leap of Faith*. Her early work documents women's history and music: *Odetta*, *Oh Dear*, *Alive!*

Elizabeth Wilson is the author of several books, including *Adorned in Dreams*, *Hallucinations* and *The Spynx in the City*. She lives in London.

BIBLIOGRAPHY

Historical Perspectives
Brassai, 'Sodom and Gomorrah' in *The Secret Paris of the Thirties* (London: Thames & Hudson, 1976).

Emmanuel Cooper, *The Sexual Perspective: Homosexuality and Art in the Last 100 Years in the West* (London and New York: Pandora, 1986).

Michel Foucault, *The History of Sexuality* (London: Penguin, 1984).

Jewelle Gomez, 'Showing Our Faces: A Century of Black Women Photographed' in *Ten.8*, no. 24.

David Green, 'On Foucault: Disciplinary Power and Photography' in *Camerawork*, no. 32, Summer 1985.

Jan Zita Grover, 'Dykes in Context: Some Problems in Minority Representation' in *The Context of Meaning: Critical Histories of Photography* (Cambridge, Mass; MIT Press, 1990).

Roberta McGrath, 'Medical Police' in *Ten.8*, no. 14, 1984.

Ann Novotny, *Alice's World: The Life and Photography of an American Original, Alice Austen, 1866-1952* (Boston: Chatham Press, 1976).

Screen, 'Deconstructing "Difference"', Winter 1987.

Staging the Self: Self-Portrait Photography 1840s-1980s (London: National Portrait Gallery, 1986) features Alice Austen's work.

Pretended Family Albums
Cathy Cade, *A Lesbian Photo Album: the Lives of Seven Lesbian Feminists* (Oakland: Waterwoman Books, 1987).

Jo Spence, *Putting Myself in the Picture: A Political, Personal and Photographic Autobiography* (London: Camden Press, 1986).

Judith Williamson, 'Family, Education and Photography' in *Ten.8*, no. 14, 1984.

Subverting the Stereotype
Tessa Boffin and Sunil Gupta, eds, *Ecstatic Antibodies: Resisting the AIDS Mythology* (London: Rivers Oram Press, 1990).

Judith Butler, *Feminism and the Subversion of Identity* (London and New York: Routledge, 1990).

Richard Dyer, 'Seen to be Believed: Some Problems in the Representation of Gay People as Typical' in *Studies in Visual Communication*, vol. 9, no. 2, Spring 1983.

Signs of Erotica
Kate Ellis, Beth Jaker, Nan D. Hunter, Barbara O'Dair, Abby Tallner, eds, *Caught Looking: Feminism, Pornography and Censorship* (Seattle: Real Comet Press, 1988). Reviews by: Rosalind Brunt, *Ten.8* no. 31, 1988; Lorraine Kenny, 'Rated X' in *Afterimage*, vol. 15, no. 5, December 1987.

On Our Backs, 526 Castro Street, San Francisco, CA 94114, USA.

Quim, BM 2182, London WC1N 3XX.

Carole S. Vance, ed., *Pleasure and Danger: Exploring Female Sexuality* (London and New York: Pandora Press, 1989).

Simon Watney, 'The Homosexual Body: Resources and a Note on Theory' in *Public* 3 (Canada: Carnal Knowledge, 1990).

Censorship
USA

Varda Burstyn, ed., *Women against Censorship* (Toronto: Douglas & McIntyre, 1985).

Gail Chester and Julienne Dickey, eds., *Feminism and Censorship: The Current Debate* (London: Prism Press, 1988).

Lisa Duggan, 'Sex Panics' in *Democracy: A Project by Group Material*, ed. Brian Wallis (Seattle: Bay Press, 1990).

Allan Sekula, 'The Weight of Commerce' in *Ten.8*, no. 35, 1989.

Ann Snitow, Christine Stansell, Sharon Thompson, *Desire: The Politics of Sexuality* (London: Virago, 1984).

Carole S. Vance, 'The War on Culture' in *Art in America*, vol. 77, no. 9, September 1989.

Great Britain

Feminists Against Censorship, 'Do You Really Want More Censorship?' (38 Mount Pleasant, London WC1X 0AP).

Simon Watney, *Policing Desire: Pornography, AIDS and the Media* (London: Comedia/Methuen, 1987).

Simon Watney, 'Pseudologia Fantastica' in *Artforum International* XXVIII, no. 10, Summer 1990.

Contemporary Representations
Feminist Review, no. 34, Spring 1990, 'Perverse Politics: Lesbian Issues'.

Lynne Fernie et al., eds., *Sight Specific: Lesbians and Representation* (Toronto: A Space, 1988).

Diana Fuss, *Essentially Speaking: Feminism, Nature & Difference* (London and New York: Routledge, 1989).

Jackie Stacey, 'Desperately Seeking Difference' in *The Female Gaze: Women as Viewers of Popular Culture*, eds., Lorraine Gamman and Margaret Marshmont (London: Women's Press, 1988).

Jan Zita Grover, 'Dykes in Context' in *Ten.8*, no. 30, 1988, discusses the work of American lesbian photographers.

Square Peg, 'the journal for contemporary perverts' quarterly, B.M. Square Peg, London WC1N 3XX.

Sunil Gupta, 'Homosexualities Part One: USA' in *Ten.8*, no. 31, 1988, features work by Kaucyila Brooke, Doug Ischar and Hinda Schuman.

Sunil Gupta and Pratibha Parmar, 'Homosexualities Part Two: UK' in *Ten.8*, no. 32, 1989, features work by Emily Andersen, Tessa Boffin, Jean Fraser, Sunil

Gupta, Mumtaz Karimjee, Brenda Price and Bob
   Workman.
Ten.8, 'Body Politics' issue, no. 25, 1987, features the
   work of Emily Andersen, Diana Blok, Sunil Gupta,
   Rosy Martin and Susan Trangmar.

Letter from Thom Bean, Publisher/Editor, *QI*, in response to Jackie Goldsby's article, first published in *OUT/LOOK*, issue 9, Summer 1990.

I was in agreement with Jackie Goldsby's article until I got to her irritating little foray into gay men's figuration of sex and race. I felt obliged to defend my ad; to defend male sexuality.

Then it occurred to me – one of the few perks that comes with being gay is the freedom to define one's sexuality through interaction with one's own sex! I'm not real interested in having women define my sexuality for me.

Women don't have a monopoly on grappling with the political ramifications of sex. My definitions come from male bonding. I presume Goldsby's come from female bonding. Though we share something in common, I question how productive it is for Goldsby to critique the homoeroticism of men. By definition, lesbians and gays process sexuality differently. Goldsby's intellectual understanding of male attraction is different from feeling it. I dare say there are some things she will never feel.

Goldsby insinuates my ad panders to the prurient interests of white men because my Black model has a hard hat! The flaw in her logic is the presumption that men view hard hats as class-specific. Hard hats don't reveal the socio-economic class of the wearer. In the *QI* ad, the hard hat may be more closely associated with 'butchness' than class.

Goldsby implied my ad should not have been 'upfront in the legitimate zone of the news.' Why not? I'm not peddling guns, snake oil, or sex. I'm advocating the networking of a seldom recognised group, interracialists. Our gay press needs to make us feel more wonderful about sex again. If not in our press, where?

I resent the comparison of my ad to Robert Mapplethorpe's *Man in a Polyester Suit*. My model is an unexploited, whole person, fully clothed, presentable, and overwhelmingly appealing to men of all races at whom *QI* is aimed. *QI* is a safe place for men to share their politics, their sexuality, and a functional dialogue. We must find our own answers. Just as Goldsby said: 'The brothers have something to say.' And we will say it ourselves, thank you.

Thom Bean
Publisher/Editor, *QI*
San Francisco, California

INDEX